Issues in Americanisation and Culture

Issues in Americanisation and Culture

Edited by
Neil Campbell, Jude Davies and George McKay

EDINBURGH UNIVERSITY PRESS

© Editorial organisation Neil Campbell, Jude Davies and George McKay, 2004.
Copyright in the individual contributions is retained by the authors.

Edinburgh University Press Ltd
22 George Square, Edinburgh

Typeset in Sabon and Gill Sans by
Pioneer Associates, Perthshire, and
printed and bound in Great Britain by
Antony Rowe Ltd, Chippenham, Wilts

A CIP record for this book is available from the British Library

ISBN 0 7486 1942 9 (hardback)
ISBN 0 7486 1943 7 (paperback)

The right of Neil Campbell, Jude Davies and George McKay
to be identified as authors of this work has been asserted in
accordance with the Copyright, Designs and Patents Act 1988.

Contents

Contents

Cultural Geographies

Popular Music

Literary Narratives

Mass Media

Visual and Material Culture

Illustrations

Acknowledgements

This collection originates from the Americanisation and the Teaching of American Studies (AMATAS) project run from the University of Central Lancashire 2000–4, and involving a consortium with the University of Derby and University College Winchester. This was a Fund for the Development of Teaching and Learning project, and as such relied on contributions from many people – apart from the contributors to the book – and organisations which I as Project Director want to acknowledge here.

For their work at UCLan, we owe thanks to Megan Taylor, Daniel Lamont, Patrick McGhee, Fiona Bayntun-Roberts, Eithne Quinn, Mike Paris, Bernard Quinn; Mike Milne-Picken, Sue Ellwood and colleagues in the Bids Support Office; Jacquie O'Hanlon and colleagues in the departmental office. Thanks too to Derek Drummond for technical advice. At the National Co-ordination Team, thanks to Alison Holmes and Nick Allen. At the LTSN Subject Centres, thanks to Alison Dickens, Siobhan Holland, Dick Ellis. Thanks to Phil Davies and our many friends and colleagues in the British Association for American Studies. For project advice, support, energy, friendly criticism, thanks to Deborah Madsen, Steve Mills, Scott Lucas, Stephen Shapiro, Peter Rawlings, Alasdair Kean. At Edinburgh University Press, it's always a pleasure to work with Nicky Carr, and thanks to Douglas McNaughton and to the book proposal's anonymous readers too.

And Professor Kate Fullbrook of the University of the West of England: you were a great transatlantic friend, and we miss you, Kate.

Acknowledgements

On a solely personal note, love and thanks as always to Emma, Ailsa and Dora.
GM

With thanks and love to Jane, as always.
NC

Many thanks to the participants of the many events over the past decade whose international perspectives on America and Americanisation were as stimulating as the atmosphere was warm. I would like to express my appreciation to the organisers of the following conferences – British Association for American Studies 1992–2004, the European Association for American Studies 2000, 2002, and 2004, the Nordic Association for American Studies 1999, and the Netherlands Association for American Studies 2003. Conference organisers rarely receive adequate thanks or resources especially in Europe, yet such events remain crucial to the stimulation of new knowledges.

Heartfelt thanks and greetings to the lucky band that made up the Salzburg Seminar ASC 30 'The Foreign Politics of American Popular Culture', in 2002, and especially Lou Erenberg, Elaine Tyler May, Lary May, Rheinhold Wagnleitner, and Marty Gecek.

I also thank University College Winchester for helping to fund work on this book, and providing colleagues among the best one could wish for.

And with love as ever to Carol.
JD

Issues in Americanisation and Culture

Neil Campbell, Jude Davies and George McKay

An American imaginary?

Ian Jack opens the collection *What We Think of America* (2002) with a question that has been asked in many different ways in recent years:

> America shapes the way non-Americans live and think. Before the Cold War ended, that had been true of half the world for several decades . . . Now, with the possible exceptions of North Korea and Burma, it is true of all of it . . . What do we think of when we think of America? Fear, resentment, envy, anger, wonder, hope? (Granta 2002: 11)

These statements might be used to frame many of the issues examined in this collection of essays, for they register the complex and changing nature of how America is viewed in a world dramatically reconfigured by the end of the Cold War, the events of 11 September 2001 and the subsequent 'war on terror'. Revealed in these questions are ongoing concerns about the USA's role in the world as global superpower and as cultural dominant spreading its multiple influences outward, and receiving in return direct, ambivalent and even contradictory responses. In the flurry of extraordinary exchanges on the subject of America since September 11th, what has been revealed more than any single position is the range of divergent views, from inside and outside, on the issue of Americanisation, from the Paris newspaper *Le Monde*'s headline 'We are all American' ('*Nous sommes tous américains*') to Gore Vidal's and Noam Chomsky's forthright critiques of US foreign policy.

Yet such is the complexity of Americanisation[1] that many of the commonsense assumptions concerning a newly globalised America are open to question. In what ways can it make sense to lump together 'non-Americans', as if Pakistanis, Palestinians, Congolese, Indians, Israelis and Iraqis – everyone outside the USA, with the possible exception of North Korea and Burma – share some common condition? Jack goes on to imply that during the Cold War America meant nothing to those in the Soviet bloc. This might surprise alike those for whom anti-American feeling was allied to the positive self-image of the communist bloc, and those who found in some elements of American culture the promise of some kind of freedom, as in Václav Havel's account of the influence of the New York group the Velvet Underground on Czech dissidents (see the section on 'Freedom' below and Reed 1992: 151–2). Moreover, Jack's assumption that during the Cold War the world was somehow divided into two halves, presumably the East and the West, tends to ignore those vast regions in the South, Asia, and elsewhere for which the term 'third world' was and remains a highly problematic catch-all. To pose the question in this way then is to assume – wrongly – that the perspective from western Europe can comfortably stand for the many different experiences of Americanisation around the globe. It would be unfair to blame this on Jack himself. It is not a simple matter of unthinking Eurocentrism, but rather a product of the long history whereby for many Europeans America functions as a 'constitutive other' of their own nation and continent. The distinction between the 'Old World' and the 'New World' predates Columbus's landfall in 1492, let alone the subsequent colonisations and later emergence of independent nations in the Americas. It is a truism that 'America' was imagined by Europeans before it was 'discovered' (see Kroes 1993: 313), but this has often been forgotten by recent generations of western Europeans locked into a binary opposition between their own indigenous culture and the American other which either menaces or promises to transform it.

Like Jack, we would argue that due to its global reach achieved post-Cold War, and signalled apocalyptically by 9/11, the nature of America's influence has qualitatively changed – and Jack carefully distances himself from earlier postwar European traditions of anti- and pro-Americanism exactly by posing Americanisation as an open question for an international, ethnically diverse 'us'. Rather than generalising out from Britain and western Europe, we think it is important to investigate the specifics of their cultural relationship with America. Paradoxically enough, a sense of the power and prestige of America as the other can be used to bestow importance upon western Europe as a more acceptable (because less imperialist, more 'liberal' in the European sense) alternative. Versions of this strategy played a significant role in nation-building in many parts of western Europe during the Cold War. Thus welfare democracies like the Netherlands, Sweden, Norway, Denmark and Finland developed various forms of a self-conscious 'middle way' (i.e. between American capitalism and Soviet communism) – the Dutch consensus pattern or *poldermodel* itself came to be cited by both Bill Clinton and Tony Blair as inspiration for their 'middle ways'. In a somewhat different version, cultural and political anti-Americanism is manifested in French legislation that mandates minimum amounts of French music, television and film for national dissemination. The end of the Cold War has not dislodged this ideology as much as might have been expected.

This book therefore is offered from a perspective that sees globalisation as a new phase in the cultural as well as economic power of America, but argues that Americanisation can only be understood fully by reference to the local, social and national contexts outside the USA. After two scene-setting essays which analyse the contemporary moment of America's globalisation from American and British perspectives, our main but not exclusive focus is on Britain. Grouped by their subject matter, individual chapters offer case studies in the history of transatlantic cultural flows and resistances, charting how several generations have responded to American culture as providing positive inspiration or baleful influence. Obviously there are historical, political, cultural and linguistic factors that make Britain a special case, so we are not suggesting that British examples should be regarded as typical even of western Europe. Rather, we focus on showing how Britain's relationship with America and things American is always shadowed by (and indeed casts into shadow) Britain's internal diversity and its relationship with other nations and entities: the Commonwealth, Europe, and the regions and nations of the rest of the world. We hope to demonstrate how the working out of this relationship has helped to mould the specifics of British national identity over the last fifty years. Yet in the questions posed by this basic condition, whereby notions of Americanisation constitute ways of dealing with, or failing to deal with, worldliness, Britain is no different from anywhere else.

It is necessary then, but not enough, to acknowledge America and Britain, and America and Europe, as pairs of constitutive others. The point is also to think about what is excluded by these binaries. Many of the case studies that follow analyse examples of how notions of Americanisation have worked to shape people's understanding of the divisions within Britain and historical changes in the nation – in terms of politics, class conflict, gender, 'race', cultural values, and generation. But in doing so, they suggest the limitations of a purely national perspective, and start to map out international affiliations and disaffiliations, cultural calls and responses that make sense primarily in terms of identities other than the national. In terms of academic positioning, this tension could be worked out in several ways, and naturally our contributors research and teach in a variety of disciplines, including cultural studies, popular culture, literature, and film. The book as a whole is designed as a contribution to current debates over the internationalisation of American Studies (see Radway 1999; Wagnleitner and Tyler May 2000; Pease and Wiegman 2002), which is reflected in developments such as the International American Studies Association (founded in 2001) and the *Journal of Comparative American Studies* (which commenced publication in 2003). Such debates have been prompted from a variety of sources in addition to the recent historical development of American-led globalisation – a reaction against the assumption that any nation can be understood in isolation, issues raised by US military and political intervention in South and Central America, south-east Asia and the Middle East, the hemispheric economic hegemony of the USA signalled by the NAFTA agreement, and most importantly for us the work of a group of critics primarily interested in 'race' who have discerned cross-national cultural flows and forms of identity. This latter work, epitomised by Paul Gilroy's hugely influential *The Black Atlantic* (1993), questions the very notion of using the nation-state as a category of enquiry, in ways that put at stake the terminology and definition of 'American' Studies itself. Our focus on Americanisation is an indirect response to this challenge since the term and the processes it calls up are intimately involved in tensions between the local, the national and the international. As is demonstrated time and again, American culture is rarely exported intact – whether as a resource or a threat for non-Americans, it has been reinterpreted, recast and transformed – yet it is never completely free from the economic, political and military power of the USA. The rest of this introduction provides an overview of how these tensions have been approached from various critical and theoretical perspectives, and

4

suggests how such debates can be moved on. In doing so, it aims to put the specific case studies to follow in global and critical contexts.

An imaginary America?

Backtracking a little, we first want to examine the varied, dialogic reactions to America that have long been a staple of debates about the power of Americanisation before being brought to a new focus by recent events. European commentaries on America, for example, illustrate ways in which both Europe and America have defined themselves in relation to the other, through emulation, assimilation, resistance and opposition. One of the most extreme and (in)famous examples of this is the postmodern theorist Jean Baudrillard's book of theoretical reflections and 'traveller's tales from the land of hyperreality' (Baudrillard 1988: inside cover) first published in French as *Amérique*. Baudrillard well conveys a European sense of displacement at the strangeness yet ubiquitousness of America as a place whose landscape and urban space are already mythic. For Baudrillard the USA is only New York, Los Angeles, and the Western deserts and highways, but is also transcendent, dreamed of all over the world. These are extreme synecdoches that define the USA's dominance through specific and limited iconographies: 'I was here in my imagination long before I actually came here,' he writes (ibid.: 72). Hence Baudrillard ignores clear signifiers of regionalism, just as many Europeans do in their consumption of American popular culture. Few, for example, enter a Kentucky Fried Chicken or Break for the Border restaurant in Europe with any awareness of their regional signification (see Campbell 2003), while the Confederate flag is reproduced endlessly as a vague and polymorphous sign of rebellion.

'Astral America' (the title of a chapter in *America*) signals the collapse of the local and regional into universals, a process symptomatic of America as, in Baudrillard's view, the place where distinctions between myth and reality break down. Baudrillard highlights an unsuspected aspect of this relationship, in that while Europeans are in some sense at the mercy of the power of America, this gives them a privileged insight not shared by Americans themselves. Put another way, America's symbolic, iconic status derives its power from its reception and 'use' by others: 'America is the original version of modernity. We are the dubbed or subtitled version' (Baudrillard 1988: 76). Rather than trying to resolve or mediate this hall-of-mirrors effect, Baudrillard jacks up its contradictions. 'For me there is no truth of America,' he writes, adding less than a page later, 'It may be that the truth of America can only be seen by a European, since he alone will discover here the perfect simulacrum – that of the immanence and material transcription of all values' (ibid.: 27, 28).

Like the average European tourist for whom certain iconic American landscapes are simultaneously typically American and universal, Baudrillard presents America not only incredibly partially but also with extreme hyperbole. For him the USA is

> a world completely rotten with wealth, power, senility, indifference, puritanism and mental hygiene, poverty and waste, technological futility and aimless violence, and yet I cannot help but feel it has about it something of the dawning of the universe. Perhaps because the entire world continues to dream of New York, even as New York dominates and exploits it. (ibid.: 23)

Through its extravagance, Baudrillard's style enables us to see the European love/hate relationship with America in terms of specific cultural forms. The power of American culture is double edged, since its global domination is dependent on its being codified and deterritorialised, so that it is dreamt like Baudrillard's 'dream' of New York, not specified as the South or the South-west borderlands. 'America exported never equals America at home' (McKay 1997: 13) since the discourses that construct its international imaginary are predicated on 'mythical power' (Baudrillard 1988: 116) and fragmented images. Moreover the fact that non-Americans, and especially Europeans themselves, participate in these discourses continually undermines the rigid separation between America and its others, even as non-Americans strain to define themselves as such.

Baudrillard's hyperbole constitutes an interesting response to this state of affairs. Where a more cautious approach would seek to mediate these contradictions by reference to one's own delimited status as a French citizen, as an ambassador, so to speak, rather than a tourist, Baudrillard pushes the position of the tourist to its extreme. In doing so, he implies that European attitudes to America cannot expunge from themselves an element of tourism, however much they (we) try to become ambassadors. We might conclude in turn that the real threat to the European posed by America is less that of imperial subjugation than of displacement – of becoming a tourist at home. Highly suggestive as this is, Baudrillard's detached touristic, spectatorial self-positioning in *America* sometimes borders on the offensive exercise of white racial privilege, as when he describes the spectacular ethnic neighbourhoods of New York and the 'natural make-up' that, he thinks, pigmentation confers on black skin (ibid.: 15–16, 18–19; see Davies 2003: 218–21; Mahoney 1997: 184). Here and elsewhere Baudrillard registers without fully facing up to his own implication within cross-national hierarchies of 'race' and economic privilege.

We will return later to the ways in which notions of Americanisation are interwoven with such cross-national hierarchies, even as they often camouflage them. Having stated this major reservation, we now want to look at some positive readings of the fragmented discourse described in *America*. Out of these fragments Europeans have often constructed a complex metanarrative weaving between individualism, freedom and self-fulfilment at one extreme, and at the other extreme violence, expendability and oppression. As Wim Wenders, the German film maker, once put it, 'AMERICA,/ always means two things: / a country, geographically, the USA, / and a concept of this country, its ideal' (Wenders 1986: 142). The mobility of this 'concept' or 'ideal' and its availability for resignification outside the USA is demonstrated by the contrast between Baudrillard's view of America and that framed by Gilles Deleuze and Félix Guattari, who are generally regarded as belonging to the same general milieu of French post-structuralism. In the wake of the 2001 attacks on the World Trade Center, the symbolic heart of New York and America, Baudrillard extended his earlier descriptions of America as a totalising, inescapable system. For him the terrorism was an act of '*ressentiment*', 'the impulse to reject any system growing all the stronger as it approaches perfection or omnipotence', and the attacks were a retaliation against an American 'system' that 'by seizing all the cards for itself . . . forced the Other to change the rules' (Baudrillard 2002: 7, 9).

On the contrary, for Deleuze and Guattari, America and its artists has represented an endless and dynamic process of uprooting, of 'deterritorialization' and rupture: 'In them everything is departure, becoming, passage, leap, daemon, relationship with the outside. They create a new Earth' (Deleuze and Parnet 1987: 30, 36). This is in marked contrast to a tradition-based French culture obsessed with real estate, land ownership as a source of wealth, power, and status and less concerned with 'becoming' (Mathy 1993: 188). Deleuze and Guattari celebrate American artists and their 'flight', knowing 'how to leave, to scramble the codes, to cause flows to circulate, to traverse the desert of the body without organs. They overcome a limit, they shatter a wall, the capitalist barrier. And of course they fail to complete the process, they never cease failing to do so' (Deleuze and Guattari 1996: 132–3). Their imagined America – usually identified with the West and westward movement – is neither fixed by its roots which 'plot a point and fix an order', nor an end product in the form of a totalised national imaginary, but is 'rhizomatic', growing outward, not down, in complex, multiple ways, both 'nomadic' and mobile (ibid.: 5).

These outside formations of an American imaginary remain powerful and have many sources, but one central factor has been the spread of its mass culture through Hollywood, literature, the music industry and television, which initially contributed to an 'Americanisation' process at home that 'translated' immigrants from many different nations into Americans in the US through rituals of nation-building, including powerful mythic foci, like the frontier and democratisation, as well as other cultural and economic factors like consumerism. From the outside, the elements of exclusion and marginalisation associated with these rituals were always less visible than their apparent inclusiveness. This imaginary of America as the refuge of 'poor huddled masses', a device of Americanisation both at home and abroad, has further defined (and redefined) the duality of Europe and the USA, as Richard Pells spells out in his two sets of binary oppositions comparing the old world with the new, as seen from each continent's perspective. Thus, conventionally Americans see 'American innocence, hope, optimism, freedom, opportunity, and modernity versus European decadence, decay, pessimism, social and ideological conflict, war', whereas Europeans reverse the polarity, so that 'America is seen as irredeemably avaricious, materialistic, frantic, violent, culturally sterile, standardised, vulgar, without spirit or soul – in vivid contrast to a refined, mature, sophisticated, socially conscious and responsible European civilisation' (Pells 1993: 69). Dick Hebdige further dramatises relations between America and Europe as constituting a 'taste war',

> between the Old and the New Worlds, between an America which, as Leslie Fiedler puts it, 'has had to be invented as well as discovered' and a Europe with its long literary and aesthetic traditions, its complex codings of class and status – between that is, two continents and a history, between two symbolic blocs: 'Europe' and 'America'. (Hebdige 1988: 120)

There is another, less narcissistic, way of reading the duality of

Europe and America, one which seeks to widen the view out from the western imperial consensus of these continents. Rob Kroes identifies 'Americanisation' as a word which 'normally serves in a discourse of rejection to point to the variety of processes through which America exerts its *dismal influence* on European cultures', adding that this view 'reduces the complex processes of cultural influence . . . to the stark binary form' (Kroes 1993, 303; emphasis added). Any model of Americanisation must move beyond the simple binaries of Europe and America, old and new, self and other to offer a more complex version of what Kroes terms, rather than Americanisation, 'cultural globalization' (ibid.). The point here is that we move from a self-regarding and self-maintaining binary model, in which America and Europe both fear and protect each other's past or present imperial and cultural authority, to a larger one which seeks to locate discourses of Americanisation and related ones of imperial cultural power in a global context. As we have already seen, to do this fully requires a truly global knowledge which few possess. One way to start though is by assessing how useful the term 'Americanisation' is as a label for global economic trends.

With this is mind, Peter Taylor suggests that 'Americanisation is the name given to a process of emulation and adaptation under the condition of consumer modernity' (Taylor 1999a: 6) and therefore that it is best understood by reference to the growth of mass production, mass consumption and mass mediation, processes intimately bound up with this increasing 'footprint' of America in the last century. However, as he points out, this has not guaranteed the USA's continued key position in the world system since there has been something of a shift from what Taylor terms 'capacious Americanisation' in the 1970s towards what he calls 'the demise phase' of 'resonant Americanisation', whereby American culture is ubiquitous but has, in many respects, lost its hegemonic legitimacy. Taylor reminds us of the presence of America – its 'resonance' and influence – but claims this is not at the expense of other cultures who adapt and hybridise it locally through the complex contacts of accommodation, emulation, resistance and fear. Hence 'none of these Americanisations . . . eliminate the cultural distinctiveness of the countries caught up in the process. Rather a hybrid culture is produced in which American influences are clear but where national cultures remain intact' (ibid.: 7 – this theory is discussed in more detail in Chapter 11).

Here the 'dual gaze' that framed Baudrillard's and Deleuze and Guattari's approaches has taken on a different twist, with Americanisation's presence revised in the light of new globalising forces and no longer seen as 'a simple diffusion and imposition', but more likely to be a co-existing aspect of a 'hybrid' cultural formation (ibid.: 10).

Elsewhere Taylor maps the trajectory of Americanisation onto globalisation:

> McDonaldization, Disnification, Cocacolarization, the Levi generation and so on have come to be interpreted as much as symptoms of globalization as Americanisation *per se*. The obvious explanation of this is that a transformation of Americanisation into globalization has occurred, signifying the ultimate success of the former. (Taylor 1999b: 123)

Being too obvious an explanation, Taylor immediately undercuts it: 'It is better to see Americanisation and globalization as opposites reflecting very different times. Globalization as threat is a sign that the American Century as hegemonic cycle is coming to its end' (ibid.: 124). What Taylor is identifying here is a sense that, when once (perhaps at the peak of the Cold War) the global penetration of American business went hand in hand with the global dissemination of American culture and ideology, since the 1980s the gap between the two has been ever widening. The reasons for this are manifold, but we can point to ideological resistance abroad and the fracturing of the ideology of consensus at home, which is often somewhat pejoratively associated with notions of multiculturalism. Everyday if somewhat banal examples of this range from the marketing disaster of the early 1990s whereby advertising for 'new Coke' was tailored specifically to different generational and ethnic groups, rather than to the population as a unity as it had been previously, to the shifts in McDonald's international policy in 2003–4. After sustaining its first ever financial loss in the previous year, McDonald's deliberately downplayed its Americanness, publicising its adoption of local and national culinary traditions in markets such as Greece and France, while an advertising campaign shown in Britain proudly announced that, 'sorry, America', the latest burger offered to British consumers was not available in the USA.

Taylor characterises traits of Americanisation as 'universal optimism' and 'mammoth self-confidence', while globalisation is perceived pessimistically as a threat. He regards this primarily as a social change that could be understood in simple terms as a loss of overt ideological content. What has remained constant or accelerated is the global spread of patterns of economic exploitation, production and consumption that are contingently American due to the historical accident of their national origin. What has recently been lost is the ideological promise of transformation, futurity or modernity that such patterns had carried with them, coded as American. Again this could be seen as a specifically western European and especially British view. Once, Britain and western Europe might have felt themselves at the receiving end of American cultural imperialism. Now, following the isolationism of US foreign policy since Ronald Reagan's presidency, and the increased importance to the US of economic relations with Central and South America, the Pacific rim, China, the Middle East, and the former Soviet bloc, 'we' are faced with something worse – American indifference. The flashpoint of the 2003 invasion of Iraq illustrates some results of this situation. The issue of unilateral intervention in Iraq without United Nations support did indeed split the European Union basically on pro- or anti-American lines. From the American side, Secretary of State Donald Rumsfeld distinguished between 'old Europe' (France and Germany), which he dismissed as stuck in its own imperialist past, and 'new Europe', central and eastern European states that were economically and ideologically friendly to the USA (see Anonymous 2003a; Anonymous 2003b.)

Rumsfeld's distinction draws upon a long-standing ideological form associated with Americanisation, its association with the new, which has played a crucial role in mediating between the actuality and the ideal (recalling Wenders's phrase) of America. His hectoring tone may simply reflect a personal impatience, but it may also reflect a need to compensate for the waning of this important ideological connection between America and modernity.

Modernities

> The Twentieth century has become the American century.
> Gertrude Stein (1935: 490)

From the vantage point of the twenty-first century, this is not quite the clarion call to modernity it may once have been, but nonetheless the American modernist writer Stein's famous maxim testifies to the conviction that America encompasses, embodies even, the modern, the new. 'Americanisation and modernization are frequently conflated, especially by Europeans,' argues a European Americanist group in Holland (NIAS 1993: 322); as Paul Smith argues, 'a conveyed sense of the utter modernity of American life and praxis, a modernity aided and abetted by the vast array of technological means of both production and consumption' (Smith 2003: n.p.). This can be taken back to an earlier founding moment of modernity, pre-twentieth century, whereby modernism and postmodernism alike are read within the context of Black social and cultural experience. In 1988, the African American novelist Toni Morrison articulated that 'modern life begins with slavery. From a woman's point of view, in terms of confronting the problems of where the world is now, black women had to deal with "postmodern" problems in the nineteenth century and earlier... certain kinds of dissolution, the loss of and the need to reconstruct certain kinds of stability' (quoted in West 1992: 213; ellipses original). Cornel West has viewed postmodernism itself as a phenomenon 'in which political contestation is central. Even if we look at it principally as a form of Americanisation of the world, it is clear that within the US there are various forms of ideological and political conflict going on' (West 1992: 217).

In the early twentieth century not only did immigrants travel to America on steamboats and liners, but the appeal of America was advertised by shipping companies through poster images of huge ultra-modern ships. (Modernity is the destination, modernity the means of travel.) Such an iconography was not necessarily shared by Americans themselves. For example, in his 1930s WPA-funded murals of New York harbour in the rotunda of the US Customs House, Reginald Marsh painted the large ships in terms of a smoky, effortful modernity in which the human labour of dockhands, pilots, sailors, journalists and others was crucial. Later in the century, the design styles of stream-lining on cars, trains and planes – and vacuum cleaners, cigarette lighters – came to signify modernity and America. As David Gartman has pointed out in his history of automobile design, by the 1950s such design styles offered a specifically American resolution of the contra-dictions in capitalist labour relations: 'Both sexes, particularly among the working class, wanted a beautiful, effortless automobile that insulated consumption from all the ugly reminders of drudgerous work, at home and at the factory' (Gartman 1994: 167). As early as the 1940s, Gartman shows, aeronautic design cues were used on cars 'to lend mundane sheet metal the allure of technological progress, military supe-riority, and escape' (ibid.: 161). When the jet age was itself superseded by the space age, cars were updated, modernised again by copying rocket parts. (In science fiction, America is almost as important a location as outer space itself; America is a topos that represents the future itself. A slogan from the 1939 New York World's Fair: 'Tomorrow – Now!')

Sometimes within the US, in movies such as *The Day the Earth Stood Still* (dir. Robert Wise, 1953) and *Them!* (dir. Gordon Douglas, 1954), but more frequently in Europe, this science fiction future was rendered in dystopian terms: 'America as a warning (America's present will be Britain's [Europe's] future) becomes a standard trope in the rhetoric of Americanisation' (Webster 1988: 180). Either way, technology and the cultural imagery of technology have largely come to dominate the iconography of modernity and to frame that dominant modernity as American.

Modernity, in the form of the poet Ezra Pound's call from the *Cantos* for the continuing revival of literature, 'MAKE IT NEW', has often been read as a seductive grand narrative of the American cultural project too. In ways that encompass popular and high culture, America comes to be seen as the new and as the source of the new. Thus the English novelist D. H. Lawrence wrote in 1924 that 'all this Americanising and mechanising has been for the purpose of overthrowing the past' (Lawrence 1965: 21). A rhetoric of newness can be identified that threads through America's images and reinventions of itself, from de Crèvecoeur's 'American, this new man' of the eighteenth century right up to the Age of Aquarius in the 1960s and the New Age of the 1990s. If Americanisation is then fundamentally simply another word for change, what difference does it make that the new, the modern, is conceptualised as American?

For Richard Pells, the post-World War II 'European lament' about the irresistible rise of American modernity 'masked a generational conflict, the parental fear of losing control over children and adolescents' as well as 'a general discomfort with the technological advance, urban sophistication, and physical mobility' (Pells 1993: 69). This 'conflict' around ideas of the youthful presence of things American, new and modern and their incipient threat to older ways can be clearly seen in Richard Hoggart's *The Uses of Literacy* when he describes the pulp fiction-reading British 'juke-box boys' whose 'clothes, . . . hair-styles . . . facial expressions all indicate [they] are living . . . in a myth-world compounded of a few simple elements which they take to be those of American life' (Hoggart 1962: 247–8). Here the youths with 'an American slouch', listening to the 'mechanical record-player', playing records that 'almost all are American', with their 'hollow-cosmos effect', 'great precision and competence', sitting on 'tubular chairs' and staring 'as desperately as Humphrey Bogart', surrounded by 'modernistic knick-knacks . . . [and] glaring showiness', are part of 'an aesthetic breakdown' detached from 'a balanced and civilized [British 'old world' tradition]' (ibid.: 248).

Here, Americanisation is inextricably bound up with discourses of youth, newness, and modernity signifying danger as well as promise and once again underlining the complex 'exchanges' surrounding this concept and its uses. Hoggart's negativity contrasts with the vitality that groups such as the Beatles and Rolling Stones actually derived from a largely *African*-American 'myth-world', which led in turn to shifts in the racial composition of American popular music when re-exported (see Chapter 7). It seems as though it is not so much cultural change or transformation that is at issue with Americanisation, but something more subtle or complex, cultural appropriation and reinscription perhaps.

Theories and definitions of popular culture, and the ideological assumptions inscribed within those theories, need then to be considered within the context of Americanisation, since the worldwide presence of American culture, via global developments in capital and technology, is a dominant and relatively new phenomenon. A reductive mass cultural analysis might suggest cultural imperialism at work, whereas a popular cultural analysis would be as concerned with ways in which the consumption and reinscription of American popular culture might function positively or even as liberation. How people 'use' or 'reinscribe' America differently suggests less of the 'hypodermic' notion of Americanisation by which that culture is 'injected' (or imposed) into their lives, but rather a more creative process in which consumption and production are interwoven (see de Certeau 1988). That is, consumers of 'America' are also engaged in a production of new meanings as they use, manipulate and resist its cultural processes and objects. As Michel de Certeau convincingly argues, the image of a consumer 'grazing on the ration of simulacra the system distributes' (de Certeau 1988: 166), perpetuated in texts from Eco (1986) and Baudrillard (1988) to Ritzer (1996) and encapsulated in the concept of McDisneyisation (see Rojek and Urry 1997), is a reductionist vision that defines the consumer as a 'receptacle' 'similar to what it receives . . . passive, "informed", processed, marked, and [with] no historical role', when in reality they can be more inventive, '*travel*[ling] through . . . texts' with 'detours, drifts . . . produc[ing] by the travelling eye, imaginary or meditative flights' (de Certeau 1988: 167, 170). For de Certeau, 'readers [and consumers] are travellers; they move across lands belonging to someone else, like nomads poaching their way across fields they did not write . . . not *here* or *there*, one or the other, but neither one nor the other, simultaneously inside and outside, dissolving both by mixing them together . . . ' (ibid.: 174). In this poetic vision, de Certeau provides a more dialogical and nuanced way of seeing Americanisation that is an alternative to cultural-imperialist versions which define it as a one-way process of imposition and threat. It is therefore an attractive vision, but one which needs to be contextualised with respect to the power relations which exist both between and within national boundaries.

Empire

American influence overseas has often been defined as cultural imperialism, where imperialism is taken to mean a capitalist operation normally referring to the acquisition and control of extrinsic territories by a nation-state through economic and if necessary military means – African lands by European countries in the nineteenth century, east European states by the Soviet Union in the twentieth, for instance. The term has been more widely used since to include economic dependency rather than overt control, and domination by cultural influence.[2] Viewed through the frame of imperialism, culture takes on the role of transmitting positive images of America in order to ideologically position foreigners to be sympathetic to the United States. This could be more or less accidental, in that American popular culture has inscribed within it either overtly or covertly ideological assumptions which foreign consumers internalise consciously or unconsciously. It is also subject to state intervention through the co-opting of culture for political or social purposes overseas, as when, during the Cold War, the US government sent out 'goodwill ambassadors' such as jazz performer Louis Armstrong (see Von Eschen 2000). These different gradations of active involvement, and their complicated relationship to internal power relations (as in this example the validation of jazz as a Black cultural form within America as part of an imperialist project to influence others abroad) demand a sophisticated approach to the notion of cultural imperialism. John Tomlinson's book *Cultural Imperialism* rehearses some of the complexities:

Take the obvious example of the arch-imperialist, the United States. Granted, the States are not as united in cultural terms as

15

they advertise themselves: the famous 'melting pot' has not formed a homogeneous nation out of the world's huddled masses. This does not prevent us from identifying 'the American way' as a hegemonic culture (or at least one aspiring to hegemony) within the contested terrain of United States culture. It is clear that, for example, black, Hispanic or American Indian cultures are in real senses dominated by a mainstream white American culture. It is reasonable to think of this 'hegemonic' culture, this dominant 'version' of America, as that exported by corporate capitalism, such that this will appear to other nationalities as American culture pure and simple. The slogan, 'Yankees go home' recognises no subtleties of cultural variation in the Yankees. What it recognises are the bearers of cultural practices which are dominant at home and abroad: dollar power and its manifestation in cultural goods; Madonna and McDonald's. (Tomlinson 1991: 75)

We emphasised earlier how the version of America experienced by overseas consumers is partial, a misrepresentation. Tomlinson places this partial version of America in the context of a nationalistic project of self-representation. Thus he identifies 'a hegemonic American national culture as experienced from the outside . . . [defined by] certain symbolic materials: denim, celluloid (at one time, chromium), and symbolic forms and dimensions: high-rise buildings, multi-lane highways, shopping malls (at one time, "streamlining")' (ibid.: 75). So where earlier we noted that the mythic nature of 'America' meant that its identity was open to negotiation and resignification, Tomlinson reminds us that such negotiation and resignification takes place in the context of actual differences in power – it is a struggle over meaning. There is therefore a need to distinguish between a real and a mythical (in Roland Barthes's sense of the word) America: 'such aspects of *perceived* American culture may be distinguished from a more complex "reality" in which the symbolic images exist in a contested or contradictory form, or at least alongside other "versions" of American culture' (ibid.: 75; emphasis original). Myth-making in America then, as elsewhere, is a struggle to assert some meanings over others, which covers its tracks all the better to make some meanings seem 'natural' or self-evident. For Barthes myth is precisely a strategy for concealing power, for masking ideology at work in popular culture. Barthes's groundbreaking analysis of popular-cultural texts in *Mythologies* laid bare the 'mystification which transforms petit-bourgeois culture into a *universal* nature' (Barthes 1973: 9; emphasis added); what is at stake here is to lay bare the mystification which transforms American popular culture into an apparently universal narrative.

For a Welsh-born critic like Edward Relph, for example, America's imperial authority was transforming material landscapes in the form of homogeneity:

Placelessness does comprise look-alike landscapes that result from improved communications and increased mobility and imitation, behind these lies a deep-seated attitude that attends to the common and average characteristics of man and of place. This 'inauthentic attitude of placelessness' is now widespread – to a very considerable degree we neither experience nor create places with more than a superficial and casual involvement. (Relph 1976: 79–80)

Relph recognised early on the growing influence of American consumer practices and saw them, to some extent like Hoggart, as a threat to diversity and tradition formed from the 'result[s] of "disneyfication", "museumisation" and "futurisation" . . . [leading to] the destruction of the local and regional landscape . . . and its replacement by conventional tourist architecture and synthetic landscapes and pseudo-places' (ibid.: 93). As such, Relph's position might be seen as implicitly bringing to bear Barthes's critical attitude to myth on the 'astral America' that, as we have seen, Jean Baudrillard presents as intractable.

Relph's anxiety that 'perhaps' 'uniformity and placelessness are inevitable consequences of the American form of democracy' (ibid.: 115) anticipates more recent concerns about the spread of American economic practices in general and 'McDonaldisation' in particular. Just such a transformation is what is claimed, indeed lauded, by the headline of a 1996 newspaper advertisement for trainee managers by the McDonald's fast-food chain in Britain. In large letters the advert informs the reader that 'the price of a Big Mac is used by *The Economist* as an index for comparing the relative value of world currencies'. McDonald's is appealing to business graduates in a language they should understand, that of finance, and by association with a magazine like *The Economist*, it is claiming a universal importance which supersedes that of any local context, even to the extent of proudly erasing national financial systems. As the triumph of capital in popular culture it presents itself as a replacement currency – where once there were conch shells for trading, and then francs and deutschmarks, now it seems there are Big Macs. Even if we are aware of the differences in names and accompanying relishes between burgers in America and

Europe, if only from having viewed Quentin Tarantino's film *Pulp Fiction*, this advert presents the globalisation of America as a success story to be celebrated, to aspire to be a part of. The rise of fast-food outlets in America in the years following World War Two is evidenced by the McDonald's, Burger King and Pizza Hut chains, and has given rise to a particular theory of social organisation and practice termed McDonaldisation by George Ritzer (Ritzer 1996). Ritzer has argued that McDonald's, like Disney, represents the perfection of 'theming' in America, operating through four main strategies: efficiency, predictability, calculability and control to create a totally rationalised environment. This is not just to do with how burgers are ordered, prepared, served and consumed, but also defines how people consume and behave in everyday life. McDonaldisation replaces risk with familiarity, so that people expect a levelled-out service, without surprises and with certainty (see Ritzer 1996; Ritzer 1998). This 'ruling rationality' is everything in Ritzer's reworking of Max Weber's arguments (see Gottdiener 2001: 51). We mentioned earlier that McDonald's had recently begun to offer adapted regional and national foods in selected European markets. Hence this 'ruling rationality' can operate both to export American practices, and to incorporate other national customs. The implications of Ritzer's argument have been much discussed and debated, with Ritzer himself reflecting upon his own 'thesis' in a second book in 1998, where he states that 'McDonaldization as a form of Americanisation, does represent something unique . . . it brings together in one package a threat to both European business and cultural practices . . . McDonaldization involves both a revolutionary set of business practices and a revolution in one absolutely key element of culture – the way in which people eat' (see Smart 1999; Ritzer 1998: 74; and Chapter 1 of this collection).

At the opposite extreme to Ritzer's warnings, some critics have expanded the notion of popular culture to negate fears about Americanisation. Thus Simon During writes that 'Disneyland, Teenage Ninja Turtles, Michael Jackson, Arnold Schwarzenegger, and even Bart Simpson, like Coke, McDonald's, and Sony Walkmans, belong to the global popular' (During 1993: 22). John Tomlinson would prefer to keep these processes apart: for him, there are two ways of reading cultural imperialism. First is the familiar 'discourse conducted around the binary opposition of "us and them" . . . the discourse of Americanisation and so on'. Second is the idea of 'the broader discourse of cultural imperialism as *the spread of the culture of modernity itself*. This is a discourse of historical change, of "development", of a global movement towards, among other things, an everyday life governed by the habitual routing of commodity capitalism' (Tomlinson 1991: 90, emphasis original).[3] While in some respects Tomlinson offers an attractive way of rethinking the imbrication of Americanisation with globalisation, During's point suggests the two are so intertwined that they cannot be distinguished from one another so easily. Similarly, there is a fundamental problem with a call to culture such as that offered by Richard Pells's analysis of Americanisation, in which his aim is to lay 'the foundations for a genuinely international culture in the future' (Pells 1993: 68) through dialogues between American culture, whose international character Pells emphasises, and indigenous European cultures. The notion of a series of two-way dialogues between America and its others reproduces the binary models discussed and rejected above, and what Pells envisages is not truly dialogical because America is conceived of as already hosting an international culture. As generations of debate over multiculturalism within and outside the US attest, there is no innocent model for the bringing together of difference, and this applies to nations as well as to groups within nations. The point is reinforced by the ideological discourses of the 'New World Order' evident in much US political rhetoric since Ronald Reagan's presidency, whereby the US takes on the mantle of world leadership in part by virtue of its self-image as the paradigmatically post-ethnic nation. This discourse, which could crudely be termed the appropriation of multiculturalism in the service of the imperial nation, is one of the key inheritances of the 'Reaganite revolution', and can be discerned across a wide political spectrum. One of its most striking formulations was made by Madeleine Albright, Secretary of State in Bill Clinton's White House, when in 1998 she justified the use of cruise missiles against Iraq on the grounds that the US was the 'indispensable nation'; it was reactivated by George W. Bush in 2003 (see Crockatt 2003; Davies 2003; and for a filmic example, Roland Emmerich's *Independence Day* (1994)).

Yet in debates about cultural imperialism, whose empire are we really talking about? There is a reverse angle to the above readings of the discourse of Americanisation as strands of American cultural imperialism, which suggests that Americanisation is much more a product of a concern with *European* authority and cultural hegemony. More specifically, it is concerned with the absence or at least attenuation of European cultural authority. From this perspective Americanisation is less an expression of American cultural empire than a sign of, say, Britain's sense of loss of empire in the same period. Duncan Webster notes that 'the discourse of Americanisation is shadowed and generated by an unquestioned ideology of Englishness' (Webster 1988: 195). David Forgacs has suggested that 'Americanisation is, in part at least, a symptom of *anxieties* about one's own national identity' (Forgacs 1993: 158, emphasis added). From this perspective Americanisation is generated by a questioning, a crisis, in the ideology of (in our case) Britishness. It is perhaps more a signifier of one's own culture's place in the world than of American culture's. In effect, we project our own fears and weaknesses, and our cultural nostalgia, onto America, and by doing so we construct it as the root of our problem. We preserve our (invented) past by lamenting its passing, and by blaming America for the change. In this reading, the idea of America as icon of modernity, of the new, discussed in the previous section emphasises not the energy, confidence and vitality of American popular culture but the retrogressive, even terminal, state of decline of the European (see this discussed in relation to the 1950s in Chapter 6). If America has a culture industry, Europe has only a heritage industry. Webster identifies this characteristic as one of long standing. 'America-as-threat goes back to the mid-nineteenth century and the reason that Americanisation is "absorbed" into the Culture and Society tradition [of Victorian and later cultural criticism] is because that is where the term came from' (Webster 1988: 183). Similarly, Dick Hebdige uncovers a common set of 'ideologically charged connotational codes' that is understood and agreed on by an extraordinary range of groups and individuals from the 1930s to the 1950s. This gives some sense of the loaded nature of class and cultural antagonism towards American popular culture in Britain at the time:

> Groups and individuals as apparently unrelated as the British Modern Design establishment, BBC staff members, *Picture Post* and music paper journalists, critical sociologists, 'independent' cultural critics like [George] Orwell and [Richard] Hoggart, a Frankfurt-trained Marxist like [Herbert] Marcuse, even an obsessive isolationist like Evelyn Waugh, all had access to these codes. (Hebdige 1988: 71)

Not only had they access, but all those named by Hebdige here sought to maintain the ideological charge of 'America-as-threat', a charge whose purpose was – from left and right critics, from high- and low-culture institutions alike – to preserve Anglo-European cultural authority. To recap and sum up, when we talk of cultural imperialism, of empires of culture, sometimes we also need to be asking: 'Whose empire?'

Contact zones

As indicated above there are many ways to add the required nuance and detail to notions of cultural imperialism, with many theorists drawing on the ideas of Michel de Certeau to question its perceived one-way process of subordination since the 'colonized' can 'make', 'use' and 'subvert' the colonizers' culture, becoming 'other within the very colonization that outwardly assimilated them; their use of the dominant social order deflected its power, which they lacked the power to challenge; they escaped it without leaving it' (de Certeau 1988: xiii). Putting individuals in a wider context, anthropologists have spoken of 'the wider global world of intercultural import-export' (Clifford 1997: 23) as a way of understanding how different exchanges take place between groups and cultures within what has become commonly referred to as a 'contact zone'. Our contention here is that a productive rethinking of Americanisation within an increasingly globalised world ought to consider the 'exchanges' and dialogues within the contact zones of global 'trade' – in every sense of the word. The concept of 'contact zone' is best defined by Mary-Louise Pratt as 'where disparate cultures meet, clash and grapple with each other, often in highly asymmetrical relations of domination and subordination – like colonialism, slavery, or their aftermaths', and through these 'ongoing relations' there emerges a 'co-presence of subjects previously separated by geographic and historical disjunctures [such as the UK/Europe/USA] . . . whose trajectories now intersect', with the possibility of productive dialogical, hybridised encounters (Pratt 1995: 6–7, 4). Thinking beyond the colonial encounter, the concept of 'contact zones' may be applied to the different ways in which America interacts with others in a complex 'interplay of economic and cultural dynamics, involving confrontation, contestation and negotiation' under the shifting conditions of 'resonant Americanisation' (Robins 2003: 245).

A further advantage of this kind of thinking is that it enables us to get a critical purchase on the production of nations as unified cultures – consciousness of which is often erased by the binaries of America/non-America – and to understand other forms of identity not encompassed by national boundaries. Thus Paul Gilroy productively rethinks how essential, racial 'roots' can be dialogised by the acceptance of 'routes', and the hybrid quality of encounter. His work on the 'Black Atlantic' is based upon an interrogation of 'essences' and 'absolutist discourses' and an interest in 'the space between them' as a means of questioning the fixed and 'overintegrated conceptions of culture' that promulgate nationalistic and essentialist notions of identity (Gilroy 1993: 1–2). These ideas can also be helpfully applied to debates over Americanisation to suggest the shifting sense of complex cultural 'relations' of exchange as multiple and hybrid – as 'stereophonic, bilingual, or bifocal cultural forms' (ibid.: 3). Gilroy employs the concept of diaspora, that is, migratory movement or dispersal, as a 'valuable idea [that] . . . points towards a more refined and more worldly sense of culture than the characteristic notions of soil, landscape and rootedness' that are often used to fix national identity in very specific, bounded concepts of place (in Woodward 1997: 328). Diaspora, as applied especially to the experience of Black people moving between Africa, America and Europe, initially forcibly by European slavers, reassesses this thinking about place and identity as essential and absolute, and 'problematizes the cultural and historical mechanics of belonging' by disrupting the mythic, explanatory 'links between place, location and consciousness' (ibid.). Diaspora can also challenge primordial concepts of identity rooted in some idealised, essential past where the race was formed, or of simple imposed formations under imperial conditions, for under diaspora, identity is constructed as dynamic, inter-linked and fluid. There is no authentic 'home-place' in which one's roots are planted, for identity is formed by the 'routes' it travels (cultural and political exchanges, tourism, imagination, mediation, etc.) and the contacts it makes in that process, as much as by any settlement that might take place. Cultural identity has to be seen as 'spatial' and not locked into a version of 'tradition' imagined as 'a one-way transmission belt; an umbilical cord, which connects us to our culture of origin' (Hall in Massey and Jess 1995: 207). The breaking of these old boundaries is often interpreted as a threat, as a loss of identity and nationhood, but taking a lead from postcolonial critics such as Gilroy, Stuart Hall and Kobena Mercer may suggest a different appreciation of transnational, hybrid or travelling cultures and identities that thrive on the acceptance of difference and exchange.

The traditional view of imperial contact sees the original culture as diluted the further it moves away from its 'roots' and its origins, hence Britain or Europe is always under threat through the presence of a strong American 'empire'. Conversely, however, one might see this collision as dynamic and productive, with identity 'travelling' and encountering along its complex 'routes' of diasporisation, with 'identities . . . constantly producing and reproducing themselves anew, through transformation and difference' (in Rutherford 1990: 235). James Clifford has developed these ideas to emphasise the importance of 'travel' – of 'routes' as well as 'roots' – so 'that specific dynamics of dwelling / travelling be understood comparatively' (Clifford 1997: 24). Travel brings people and places together in contact, questioning culture as simply 'a rooted body that grows, lives, dies, and so on', but seeing instead 'disputed historicities, sites of displacement, interference, and interaction' (ibid.: 25) where negotiations take place between groups. Clifford's work is concerned precisely with dialogically 'tangled cultural experiences' (ibid.: 2) related to the experience of these frontiers of cultural collision as contact zones of 'intersecting histories – discrepant detours and returns' (ibid.: 30). His definition of 'diaspora' is particularly apposite:

> Diaspora . . . involves dwelling, maintaining communities . . . [and] articulates, or bends together, both roots and routes to construct . . . alternate public spheres, forms of community consciousness and solidarity that maintain identifications outside the national time/space in order to live inside, with a difference. (ibid.: 251)

Clifford's new geography explores the possibility of hybrid landscapes as 'sites of collision' where, echoing de Certeau, 'American culture is not monolithic and homogenous' but is 'used and enjoyed' in many complex and unexpected ways, ways that include resistance and opposition (Webster 1989: 72).

As Homi Bhabha has argued, there is a 'need to think beyond narratives of originary and initial subjectivities and to focus on those moments or processes that are produced in the articulation of cultural differences', since it is in these 'in-between spaces' that 'new signs of identity, and innovative sites of collaboration' are initiated (Bhabha 1994: 1–2). Within this approach to a rethinking of Americanisation there is an active amendment and supplementation taking place, whereby cultures are not betrayed by mixing and dialogue (see Gilroy 2000: 106), but are potentially enlarged and expanded by the 'routes' of cultural contact and inter-relations. Indeed these forces may indicate, as some have suggested, the wider effects of globalisation diminishing or altering the centrality of the USA and replacing the perceived homogenisation of culture with something different – 'a new basis for thinking about the relation between cultural convergence and cultural difference' (Robins 2003: 245).

However, just as in the preceding section, a major reservation must be made about the uses we have suggested for these insights from postcolonial criticism. Critics such as Gilroy, Hall, Mercer and Bhabha are deeply suspicious about constructions of the nation for several reasons – nations enforce racial, ethnic and other hierarchies in the name of national unity, and impose the very boundaries that diasporic thinking is designed to circumvent. It would do them a disservice therefore to appropriate their work as a means solely of revitalising national identities, however diverse and mobile. Gilroy's ideal form of social solidarity, for example, derives from what he calls 'postcolonial cosmopolitanism'. There is a call here to go beyond the nation, and beyond the binary of America/non-America. The point of the *Black Atlantic* is that it is Black, and insists that the relationship between America, Europe and Africa must be understood together. Some of the chapters that follow therefore focus explicitly on the fracturing of the America/Europe binary by specific forms of difference such as race (Chapters 3, 4, 8 and 14) and gender (Chapter 13). All of them should be read with this caution.

Anti-Americanism

September 11th, 2001, has made it difficult to explore versions of anti-Americanism: the enormous impact of that event obstructed and even made apparently insignificant earlier or other manifestations of anti-Americanism. At the same time it had the effect of making all anti-Americanisms appear heinous, treacherous: the political rhetoric of 'those who are not with us are against us' allowed little room for criticism of or active opposition to US foreign policy, or even of criticism of American export culture. In fact, of course, 9/11 is one of those moments (others may be the strategic anti-Americanism of the nineteenth-century Abolitionist movement in Britain, or the sustained protest around the world against the neo-imperial military project of the US's war in Vietnam through the 1960s, for instance) that make an understanding of versions of anti-Americanism the more timely and essential.

Is anti-Americanism primarily emotive, generated by envy, snobbery or fear of the (frequently – perhaps only ever? – self-proclaimed) 'greatest nation on earth'? Here anti-Americanism goes with the territory of being a, now debatably the, global superpower. For others it is even a form of contemporary racism (made more worrying by virtue of its apparent acceptability). The idea of 'America-as-threat' – whether in the straightforward sense of militarily, or culturally, through 'Disneyfication' or 'Coca-Colonisation', or even environmentally, as the US is identified as the world's prime polluter – does elicit periodically negative responses from within other cultures round the world.

Is this understandable, even valid? Fredric Jameson has viewed exported American culture as being wedded to military and industrial concerns, while Noam Chomsky has extensively and critically explored the direction of US foreign policy according to the interests of US capital and corporations (see also Scott-Smith and Krabbendam 2003). These two American commentators illustrate that anti-Americanism is not the preserve of non-Americans, that there is a lengthy tradition of critiquing global power, even when exerted by US interests, and that distinctions do need to be articulated between different kinds and usages of anti-Americanisms. A second awkward form of internal or domestic anti-Americanism, from the other end of the political spectrum, is the far-right Patriot or militia movement, which frequently argues that it is anti the American government, but, pro-American in its claims to defend the 'original' ideals and constitution of the country. An index of this antithesis is the ambivalence of the term 'new world order'. Employed earlier to denote the notion of US hegemony attendant on the end of the Cold War, for the far-right patriots it denotes the surreptitious takeover of the US government by international capital or worldwide conspiracies.

It is therefore crucial to be aware of the different contexts for external expressions of anti-Americanism, depending on the political or historical relationship between the US and for example, the Caribbean, Central or South America, the Cold War Eastern bloc, Western Europe, al-Qaeda. The anti-Americanism expressed by many people in Chile during the early 1970s, at a time when their democratically elected (Marxist) government was destabilised and a military dictatorship put in its place with the aid of the covert action of the US Central Intelligence Agency, may be evident and explicable. Anti-American propaganda in communist regimes during the Cold War was one politico-cultural activity in the struggle for the protection and extension of spheres of influence. At the same time, an overfunctionalist view of anti-Americanism should be avoided: many Cubans have forcefully criticised the US economic blockade of their country, while at the same time they use Cuba's unofficial second currency of the US dollar; while Russian leaders during the Cold War criticised the decadence of American culture and capital, young Russian intellectuals and artists formed a subculture known as the *Shtatniki* (after *Shtaty* – the States), wearing American suits and listening to jazz music. The contradictions and compromises within anti-Americanism require attention.

Cultural anti-Americanism lies in expressions of resistance towards or resentment of the development of mass media and the dominant export cultures of the US. The European twentieth century, for instance, was punctuated by regular moral panics around the latest craze emanating from America, which would generally also involve youth pleasure and autonomy and a generational disruption. European elders railed against the symptoms of what they perceived as a nervous, vacuous, immature export culture, whether in the form of hot jazz, comic books, juvenile delinquency, rock and roll, LSD, burger bars, video nasties, or crack cocaine. Though each alone may appear a relatively minor novelty, and some are demonstrably more dangerous than others, reactions to them formed a current of distrust of the US and its pop cultural pleasures from significant sectors of European society. There was a concomitant sense of European traditions being threatened, cheapened, 'dumbed down' by such Americana, and the strength and longevity of the antagonistic experience of the US by such sectors should not be underestimated.

As we noted at the close of the section on 'Empire', manifestations of anti-Americanism can signify varying degrees of crisis or uncertainty in the (cultural, national, political or religious) identity of its proponents. From this perspective anti-Americanism is less reflective of the United States and its political, economic or cultural force, but is instead a symptom of an identity in transition, not emergent but residual, even terminal. For example, strands of British anti-Americanism through the twentieth century are explicable as consequences of Britain's loss of hegemonic status as a world power. Evident from the 1930s to the 1950s was an ideologically loaded range of cultural organisations and leaders united only in the articulation of 'America-as-threat'. The purpose of this charge was – from British cultural critics of the political left and right, from high- and low-culture institutions alike – to preserve Anglo-European cultural authority. The frequently proclaimed (by British politicians, at least) 'special relationship' with the United States is thus often more fraught and ambivalent than political leaders would care to utter. French manifestations of anti-Americanism have been identified as symptoms of cultural anxiety in France, as its key signifiers of national identity are perceived to be under threat from US cultural imperialism: the production and consumption of French cuisine and wine are seen by traditionalists to be threatened by US fast food and fizzy drinks, or by US-originating genetically manipulated agriculture, while the French film and music industries enjoy legislative protection against non-domestic (essentially American) products. Examples such as these from Britain and France indicate that anti-Americanism says as much about its proponents and their construction of identity as it does about American hegemony.

How far do the events of 9/11 problematise or confirm the survival of anti-Americanism as a socio-political (as well as cultural, specifically media-centred) phenomenon? On the one hand, it would appear that, even in a globalised world, postnationalism has its limits, since the single nation-state of the USA was targeted; on the other, al-Qaeda itself appears to be or have been a significantly postnational organisation, with members from a number of countries, west and east. Others have identified in the attack on the United States an outdated, residual analysis on the part of al-Qaeda, evidence of a retrogressive understanding based on national boundaries, patriarchy, rigid social hierarchies, and religious fundamentalism. Retrogressive or otherwise, there remains for the world's only superpower a powerful contemporary manifestation of the extent to which it can be criticised, opposed, even hated. It would appear that globalisation has not yet entirely removed the need for an identifiable national enemy (nor has globalisation quite fully yet become the new enemy), and the US is so grand in its achievements, energy and ambition that each can still find in it some version of the enemy he or she wants.

To an extent, resistance to Americanisation has recently been linked with the 'anti-globalisation movement' as it is often termed, a name rejected by its organisers, who prefer 'Civil Society Movement', 'Global Justice Movement' or 'Anti-Capitalist Movement' (see News From Nowhere 2003). The strategy of 'culture jamming' for example aims to 'alter the way we live and think . . . change the way information flows, the way institutions wield power, the way TV stations are run, the way food, fashion, automobile, sports, music and culture industries set their agendas' and ultimately to change the way 'meaning is produced in our society' (Lasn 1999: xi). The idea is to 'jam' the messages of 'a barren American monoculture' and interfere with its one-directional set of meanings by introducing a critical multiplication of images to counter and to unsettle the 'official' and the authorised practices of corporate, multinational organisations poisoning our physical and

'mental environment' (ibid.: xiv). This 'dialogic' intervention is directed against American corporations who have hi-jacked and 'branded'
the familiar landscapes of everyday life, destroying a sense of 'country',
its people-produced 'culture', its 'free, authentic life', its 'promise of
belonging', 'communities, traditions . . . whole histories' (ibid.: xii–xiv).
Culture jammers 'have given up on the American dream' and are looking for another new beginning that involves a waking up from the
spectacle the dream has become (ibid.: 112).

Naomi Klein's *No Logo* (2000) contextualises the territory that Kalle
Lasn explores through his *Culture Jam*, arguing for a great awakening
to the 'secrets of the global logo web' and to the transnational corporations that determine production and consumption throughout the
world (Klein 2000: xviii). Klein describes and interrogates the cultural
landscapes of advertising and brand creation in a number of interesting
ways that should be examined as the persistence of certain myths of
America, now extended, as Lasn argues, into a global marketplace. 'A
good jam', writes Klein, 'is an x-ray of the subconscious of a campaign,
uncovering not an opposite meaning but the deeper truth hiding beneath
the layers of advertising euphemism' (ibid.: 281). For example, in discussing Tommy Hilfiger branding she writes of the advertisement's

> tangle of Cape Cod multiculturalism: scrubbed black faces loung-
> ing with their wind-swept white brothers and sisters in that great
> country club in the sky, and always against the backdrop of a
> billowing American flag. 'By respecting one another we can reach
> all cultures and communities', the company says. 'We promote the
> concept of living the American dream' . . . (ibid.: 76)

To 'read' this advert in Europe adds to the audacity of its claims, but
confirms the immense authority of its images which have become
internationalised – taking the brand America and exporting its values
and myths to the world. 'Fewer interests control ever more of the
landscape,' Klein writes (ibid.: 130), leading to an increasingly reduced
set of choices despite the constant appeal to vast consumer variety –
creating a 'double world: carnival on the surface, consolidation under-
neath, where it counts' (ibid.: 130). Klein's language is all about the
'assault' on the cultural landscape by a pervasive, invasive new iconography of corporate geography which she often describes with wonderful
images: 'These crisp royal blue and Kelly green boxes snap together
like pieces of Lego (the new kind that can make only one thing: the
model fire station or spaceship helpfully pictured on the box)'

(ibid.: 131). The McDonald's, Starbucks and Blockbuster chains sprawl out and intersect with all the other huge corporations, Microsoft, Gap, and Calvin Klein, as 'big-box' malls or 'clusters' to alter the retail landscape and drive out small, independent shops (see www.nologo.org) and it is the pervasive influence of such corporations' advertising that has been the focus for anti-American protest group Adbusters. Using the creativity of design departments, Adbusters turned against the machine to deconstruct and interrogate the 'subconscious' ideologies underpinning the original.

One response to the game-playing of Adbusters is that it is just 'semiotic shadow-boxing' and never gets below the surface, never actually changes anything and can't possibly win out against the wealth and power of corporations (ibid.: 296–7). It is 'more a drop in the bucket than a spanner in the works' (ibid.: 297) for some people and yet, Klein goes on to say, adbusting cannot be seen as an end in itself, but rather as one strategy, 'a tool – one among many – that is being used, loaned and borrowed in a much broader political movement against the branded life' (ibid.: 309). This strategy is necessitated, we might add, by the dominant position that a certain American ideology of consumption has attained. Part of Klein's point is that the brand has annexed dreams of not only personal fulfilment but also social progress, as in the images of 'Cape Cod multiculturalism'. Sometimes then a strategic response is to call for the fulfilment of the brand's claims rather than its abolition, of course in the knowledge that this is not really what is on offer.

A significant aspect of the broader political movement has found a focus in the various anti-globalisation protests with their call to 'reclaim the streets' (RTS) since 'street culture itself is under siege' (ibid.: 311; see also Jordan 1998). RTS (started in London around the rave and DiY cultures) wants uncommercialised space in cities, natural wilderness in the countryside and the seas; it extends culture jamming so that rather than just filling the space left by commerce with advertising parodies, RTSers 'attempt to fill it with an alternative vision of what society might look like in the absence of commercial control' (Klein 2000: 313). Reclaiming public space has become a central issue connecting diverse protest groups who see corporations as controllers and definers of those areas once seen as part of the everyday lives of people. The physical and mental environment – cultural landscapes – became the battlegrounds in this new politics of protest. The 'McWorld' of corporatism was the site of struggle as a new form of 'corporate imperialism', or 'global realization' as McDonald's term it, moved McDonald's into China in 1992 and Kuwait in 1994 (see Schlosser 2001: 229). These increasingly would become the focus for protests against American interests around the world (see Schlosser 2001: 244; Gottdiener 2001; Ritzer 1996, 1998), but after September 11th, American activists have found it more difficult to speak out in quite the same way. Klein writes on her website, 'Our task, never more pressing, is to point out that there are more than two worlds available, to expose all the invisible worlds between the economic fundamentalism of "McWorld" and the religious fundamentalism of "Jihad"' (Klein in the *Observer*, 14 July 2002). The simple binary divisions often associated with discussions of Americanisation are, as we have stressed throughout this introduction, once again revealed as inadequate and in need of revision.

Freedom

For many, America, and therefore Americanisation, has been viewed positively, as constituting a discourse of liberation rather than of imperial domination, connoting dynamism and democracy, and challenging established traditions of cultural and social hierarchy. Its very crudeness (or perceived crudeness) often constitutes this challenge to hierarchy – 'the charm and power of American (un)culture', as Jean Baudrillard nicely puts it (1988: 79), whilst within more overtly political modes of culture America has been read as having a progressive and open political system sustaining freedom, equality and democratic institutions.

In an effort to understand these perceptions of America, we want to examine three ways it presents itself to or is constructed by foreign consumers as what has recently been termed 'Brand America': as zone of liberation or democracy, as locus of pleasure, and as utopia. First, as zone of liberation or democracy, American cultural experimentation, the seemingly democratising juxtaposition of 'King Lear and King Kong, Rimbaud and Rambo, Plato and Puzo', has been explained variously as a form of cultural creolisation or as the cultural logic of replaceable parts (Kroes 1993: 307–8). This 'casual sense of cultural *bricolage*' – producing Baudrillard's (un)culture – is a product of the American liberty and confidence 'to take the European cultural heritage apart and re-arrange it as they see fit' (NIAS 1993: 323). This is effectively a positive gloss on the fear of America discussed earlier in relation to cultural imperialism, a fear partly founded in its culture's capacity to disregard or to threaten a cosy high cultural consensus in Europe.

> One of the signal achievements of American culture was the discovery of its own vernacular form, notably in the poetry of Walt Whitman, which celebrated ordinary men and women, embracing their speech and manners . . . American culture was self-consciously seeking a democratic alternative to [European] elitist forms. Not literature for the few but Whitman's 'the word democratic, the word en masse'. Not classical music, but jazz. Not private palaces but palatial railway stations and movie theatres.
> (ibid.: 324)

In turn, Europe would engage and 'use' American culture in a similarly liberating way, as Gerd Gemunden, writing from the perspective of German and Austrian responses to Americanisation, discusses: artists 'appropriated U.S. culture . . . fusing and refusing, using and abusing, forming and transforming it in order to create a hybrid and genuine form of artistic expression' (Gemunden 1998: 17). To take one example, the music of the Velvet Underground in late-1960s New York was deliberately positioned as dark, introspective, and apolitical, in contrast to the overtly celebratory and progressive soft politics of West Coast music. The group took up an explicitly non-political stance, articulated subsequently by writer, guitarist and singer Lou Reed as 'Gimme an issue, I'll give you a tissue [and] wipe my ass with it' (Reed 1978). Yet for Czech dissidents such as Václav Havel the group's work and clandestinely circulated copies of Reed's lyrics 'played a rather significant role in the development of our country' as a source of inspiration and subversion of the communist status quo (Reed 1992: 152).

Dominic Strinati has pointed out that simple notions of Americanisation-as-domination can be questioned by studies of how American detective fiction opened up for British working-class readers a different and more 'realistic' world from the one they perceived as constrained by the class-bound concerns of classic English detective fiction with its 'corpse in the library, the Colonel's shares on the stock market, and thwarted passion on the Nile' (Worpole cited in Strinati and Wagg 1992: 65–66). American popular culture was seen to offer a fresh, democratic alternative, an experience echoed by film director Wim Wenders as he explains the pull of American pop culture for Germans in the postwar period:

In the early Fifties or even the Sixties, it was American culture. In other words, the need to forget twenty years created a hole, and people tried to cover this . . . by assimilating American culture . . . But the fact that US imperialism was so effective over here was highly favoured by the Germans' own difficulties with their past. One way of forgetting it, and one way of regression, was to accept the American imperialism. (Quoted in Webster 1989, 67; see Gemunden 1998)

For Wenders, German cultural tradition – even Beethoven – was tainted by the Nazi past; American film and popular music on the other hand were free, even innocent. Of course there's a paradox here, as Wenders points out: for postwar Germans, embracing America through its pop culture was both a way of 'forgetting [Nazi] history' and itself a 'way of regression', of moving backwards. Yet central to the sense of liberation Wenders experienced through popular music was the simple fact that it had 'nothing to do with fascism' (quoted in Webster 1989: 68). For Pico Iyer the associations of American things are much more prosaic and yet equally significant:

No one but an American is likely to deny the appeal of American culture, and I can still remember, as a child in Oxford, sitting transfixed before Hanna-Barbera cartoons, or Lucille Ball in all her incarnations, not because they were American but because they were better and more vivid than anything else on TV (and later, in adolescence finding images of possibility and hopefulness in Henry Miller or the Grateful Dead that simply weren't available in England); anyone who's grown up on Wimpy Bars and greasy 'transport caffs' can appreciate how life in Oxford was made unimaginably more pleasant by the advent of the first Baskin-Robbins and then McDonald's in the late seventies, offering clean and dependable places in which to eat that were neither cheap nor expensive. (Iyer 2001: 248)

Second, it is possible via popular culture to view America as locus of pleasure, 'a sense of a culture that is endemically alive and happening . . . with its endless array of choices and the promised excitement and eroticism of opportunity' (Smith 2003: n.p.) The issue here is partly one of the presentation of American self-image. While Baudrillard can view America as New York, all speed, glamour, urban sophistication and decay, others tap into alternative fictions of America. Through visual advertising, for instance, 'we are invited to consume not just an American product but "America" itself' (Webster 1988: 228). This is a point pursued by Dutch academic Ien Ang in her study of the consuming pleasures of American melodrama and soap opera, *Watching Dallas*:

> The hegemony of American television and film has habituated the world public to American production values and American *mises-en-scène*, such as the vast prairies or the big cities, the huge houses with expensive interiors, luxurious and fast cars and, last but not least, the healthy- and good-looking men and women, white, not too young, not too old. Such images have become signs which no longer merely indicate something like 'Americanness' but visual pleasure as such. (Ang, quoted in Webster 1988: 200)

Ang concludes here with the argument that the American popular is now the global popular, that these signs of American pleasure are so dominant today that they effectively function as signs of *universal* visual pleasure. (As we have seen of course, it is problematic to read a process of universalisation as Americanisation by another name.) Mel van Elteren observes, however, that the appeal of America is predicated on local national conditions, so that for Holland he suggests a very specific set of appealing characteristics:

> in a well-regulated and overorganised country as the Netherlands the limitless, expressive individualism embedded in [American] cultural forms is irresistible to particular audiences . . . Here we find an Americanophilia [love of America] which is the expression of a yearning for open spaces, novelty and freedom of action which is to be found among those young and youthful people who want to transcend the boundaries of 'little Holland'. (Van Elteren 1994: 219)

Third, we want to consider the attraction of American popular culture in terms of the construction of America as utopian space, or fantasy zone.[4] We project America in our own (local) images and desires – it becomes what we're not, what we want it to be, what *we* want to be. It doesn't matter whether this bears any similarity to *the real thing*. This utopianism is not a full-blown image of the future-world but rather,

> a longing for a different, and better way of life, a reconciliation of thought and life, desire and the real, in a manner that critiques the

status quo without projecting a full-blown image of what a future society should look like ... [It] is a sensibility ... [formed] as Lefebvre asserts 'as soon as we wish for something different'. (Gardiner 2000: 17–18)

America, in this utopian thinking, therefore, expresses an unwillingness to accept what is 'given' without using it, and possibly transforming it, in our own life's pattern. We can, it claims, all reshape the given norms of existence through acts of material or imaginative change.

The America constructed by producers and consumers of its culture – popular and otherwise – is an imaginary full of images of vast space or super speed, a cinematic, mediated nation (see Chapter 11). But it is also a space that non-Americans design in the image of our own subjective desires. This is the significance of David Forgacs's observation that 'it is more useful to see Americanisation as involving imaginings, myths, subjective perceptions and ascriptions' (Forgacs 1993: 162). Rob Kroes further reminds us that the 'real' America has long been intimately linked with the 'America' produced by European consumers of its popular culture as a realm of desire constructed from without:

To the extent that America holds up a phantasm, a dream world, to the extent that it conjures up a world of freedom, without inhibitions and constraints, we are reading a leaf from our own book. The European imagination had already invented a mythical West before America was discovered ... [America] provides a repertoire for identification with epic worlds that derive their attraction from the fact that 'America' is non-Europe, that it provides a counterpoint to our culture, a utopian realm for our dreams of escape. (Kroes 1993: 313)

But Kroes goes on to emphasise the contradictory nature of Europeans, in his example young musicians in England and the Netherlands in the 1960s, looking to America 'to create a cultural space of their own' (ibid.: 317). A cultural space of their own: this is what many cultural practitioners outside America seek. The paradox of course is that they seek it in the arena of dominant American cultural product. We have almost come full circle, in more ways than one. The connection between superpower and what Christopher Bigsby called 'superculture' remains as problematic as it was when Bigsby wrote about Americanisation and popular culture over twenty years ago. In fact in the intervening period we may well have been seeing the continuing ascendancy of America, of its culture, of its popular culture to a global extent signified by the technological developments of, for instance, satellite broadcasting and the internet. The extent to which Americanisation can be said to constitute a discourse of globalisation seems to be an increasingly insistent question of power at the turn of the millennium.

Notes

1. The processes and problems of 'Americanisation' are considered in different contexts by Webster 1988 (especially Chapter 8); van Elteren 1994 (his introduction); Hebdige 1988 (Chapter 3); Willett 1989; Kroes *et al.* 1993; McKay 1997 and forthcoming; Gemunden 1998; Wagnleitner and Tyler May 2000; Campbell 2003.
2. This can be extended to make it less polite and more political: economic dependency may be covert control; domination by cultural influence may result in destruction of local culture.
3. The casual acceptance of cultural imperialism as simply a symptom of the modern, of global development, might be more worryingly considered if we suggested the same for imperialism itself.
4. As with the problematic and problematically universal rhetoric of the American Dream more generally, positing America as utopia involves long-term amnesia: if it *is* to be viewed as a utopia it's one predicated on the dystopia of the genocide of native Americans and the slavery of Africans.

Bibliography

Anonymous (2003a), 'Outrage at "old Europe" remarks'. http://news.bbc.co.uk/2/hi/europe/2687403.stm

Anonymous (2003b), 'U.S.: Rumsfeld again refers to "old" and "new" Europe'. http://www.rferl.org/features/2003/06/11062003171320.asp

Barthes, Roland [1957] (1973), *Mythologies*, tr. Annette Lavers, London: Paladin.

Baudrillard, Jean [1986] (1988), *America*, tr. Chris Turner, London: Verso.

Baudrillard, Jean (2002), *The Spirit of Terrorism*, London: Verso.

Bhabha, Homi (1994), *The Location of Culture*, London and New York: Routledge.

Campbell, Neil (2003), *Landscapes of Americanisation*, Derby: University of Derby.

Certeau, Michel de (1988), *The Practice of Everyday Life*, Berkeley: University of California Press.

Clifford, James (1997), *Routes: Travel and Translation in the Late Twentieth Century*, Cambridge MA: Harvard University Press.

Crockatt, Richard (2003), *America Embattled: September 11, Anti-Americanism and the Global Order*, London: Routledge.

Davies, Jude (2003), 'Against the Los Angeles Symbolic: Unpacking the Racialised Discourse of the Automobile in 1980s and 1990s Cinema', in Mark Shiel and Tony Fitzmaurice (eds), *Screening the City*, London: Verso, pp. 216–38.

Deleuze, Gilles and Claire Parnet (1987), *Dialogues*, tr. Hugh Tomlinson and Barbara Habberjam, New York: Columbia University Press.

Deleuze, Gilles and Felix Guattari (1996), *Anti-Oedipus: Capitalism and Schizophrenia*, London: Athlone Press.

During, Simon (ed.) (1993), *The Cultural Studies Reader*, London: Routledge.

Eco, Umberto (1986), *Travels in Hyperreality*, San Diego: Harcourt Brace Jovanovich.

Forgacs, David (1993), 'Americanisation: the Italian Case 1938–1954', *Borderlines: Studies in American Culture*, 1:2, 157–69.

Gardiner, Michael (2000), *Critiques of Everyday Life*, London: Routledge.

Gartman, David (1994), *Auto Opium: A Social History of American Automobile Design*, London and New York: Routledge.

Gemunden, Gerd (1998), *Framed Visions: Popular Culture, Americanisation, and the Contemporary German and Austrian Imagination*, Ann Arbor: University of Michigan Press.

Gilroy, Paul (1993), *The Black Atlantic*, London: Verso.

Gilroy, Paul (2000), *Between Camps: Race, Identity and Nationalism at the End of the Colour Line*, London: Allen Lane.

Gottdiener, Matt (2001), *The Theming of America*, Oxford: Westview Press.

Granta (2002), *What We Think of America*, London and New York: Granta.

Hebdige, Dick (1988), *Hiding in the Light: On Images and Things*, London: Routledge.

Hoggart, Richard [1957] (1962), *The Uses of Literacy*, Harmondsworth: Pelican.

Iyer, Pico (2001), *The Global Soul*, London: Bloomsbury.

Jordan, John (1998), 'The Art of Necessity: The Subversive Imagination of Anti-road Protests and Reclaim the Streets', in George McKay (ed.), *DIY Culture: Party and Protest in Nineties Britain*, London: Verso, pp. 129–51.

Klein, Naomi (2000), *No Logo: Taking Aim at the Brand Bullies*, London: Flamingo.

Kroes, Rob (1993), 'Americanisation: What are we Talking about?', in Kroes *et al.* 1993, pp. 302–18.

Kroes, Rob, R. W. Rydell and D. F. J. Bosscher (eds) (1993), *Cultural Transmissions and Receptions: American Mass Culture in Europe*, Amsterdam: VU University Press.

Lasn, Kalle (1999), *Culture Jam: The Uncooling of America*, New York: Eagle Brook.

Lawrence, D. H. [1924] (1965), *Studies in Classic American Literature*, London: Mercury.

McKay, George (ed.) (1997), *Yankee Go Gome (& Take Me with U): Americanization and Popular Culture*, Sheffield: Sheffield Academic Press.

McKay, George (forthcoming), *Circular Breathing: The Cultural Politics of Jazz in Britain*, Durham, NC: Duke University Press.

Mahoney, Elisabeth (1997), 'The People in Parentheses: Space under Pressure in the Post-modern City', in David E. Clarke (ed.), *The Cinematic City*, London: Routledge, pp. 168–85.

Massey, Doreen and Pat Jess (eds) (1995), *A Place in the World?*, Oxford: Oxford University Press.

Mathy, Jean-Philippe (1993), *Extrême-Occident: French Intellectuals and America*, Chicago: University of Chicago Press.

News from Nowhere (ed.) (2003), *We Are Everywhere: The Irresistible Rise of Global Anticapitalism*, London: Verso.

NIAS (Netherlands Institute for Advanced Study) (1993), 'Questions of Cultural Exchange: The NIAS Statement on the European Reception of American Mass Culture', in Kroes *et al.* 1993, pp. 321–33.

Pease, Donald and Robyn Wiegman (eds) (2002), *The Futures of American Studies*, Durham, NC: Duke University Press.

Pells, Richard (1993), 'American Culture Abroad: The European Experience since 1945', in Kroes *et al.* 1993, pp. 67–83.

Pratt, Mary-Louise [1992] (1995), *Imperial Eyes: Travel Writing and Transculturation*, London: Routledge.

Radway, Janice (1999), 'What's in a Name? Presidential Address to the American Studies Association, 20 November 1998', *American Quarterly* 51:1, 1–32.

Reed, Lou (1978), 'Street Hassle', on *Live – Take No Prisoners*, New York: RCA.

Reed, Lou and Václav Havel (1992), 'Interview: To Do the Right Thing', in Lou Reed, *Between Thought and Expression: Selected Lyrics of Lou Reed*, London: Viking, pp. 145–62.

Relph, Edward (1976), *Place and Placelessness*, London: Pion.

Ritzer, George (1996), *The McDonaldisation of Society: An Investigation into the Changing Character of Contemporary Social Life*, rev. ed., Thousand Oaks, CA: Pine Forge Press.

Ritzer, George (1998), *The McDonaldization Thesis*, London: Sage.

Robins, Kevin (2003), 'Encountering Globalization', in David Held and Anthony McGrew (eds), *The Global Transformations Reader: An Introduction to the Globalization Debate*, Cambridge: Polity Press.

Rojeck, Chris and John Urry (eds) (1997), *Touring Cultures*, London: Routledge.

Rutherford, Jonathan (ed.) (1990), *Identity: Community, Culture, Difference*, London: Lawrence and Wishart.

Schlosser, Eric (2001), *Fast Food Nation*, Harmondsworth: Penguin.

Scott-Smith, Giles and Hans Krabbendam (2003), *The Cultural Cold War in Western Europe 1945–1960*, London: Frank Cass.

Smart, Barry (1999), *Resisting McDonaldization*, London: Sage.

Smith, Paul (2003), 'Why "We" Lovehate "You"', Social Science Research Council, http://conconflicts.ssrc.org/usa/smith.

Stein, Gertrude (1935), *Lectures in America*, New York: Random House.

Strinati, Dominic and Stephen Wagg (eds) (1992), *Come On Down? Popular Media Culture*, London: Routledge.

Taylor, Peter J. (1999a), 'Locating the American Century: A World Systems Analysis', in David Slater and Peter J. Taylor (eds), *The American Century: Consensus and Coercion in the Projection of American Power*, Oxford: Blackwell, pp. 3–16.

Taylor, Peter J. (1999b), *Modernities: A Geohistorical Interpretation*, Cambridge: Polity.

Tomlinson, John (1991), *Cultural Imperialism: A Critical Introduction*, London: Pinter.

Van Elteren, Mel (1994), *Imagining America: Dutch Youth and Its Sense of Place*, Tilburg: Tilburg University Press.

Von Eschen, Penny (2000), '"Satchmo Blows Up the World": Jazz, Race and Empire during the Cold War', in Wagnleitner and Tyler May, pp. 163–78.

Wagnleitner, Reinhold and Elaine Tyler May (eds) (2000), *'Here, There and Everywhere': The Foreign Politics of American Popular Culture*, Hanover, NH and London: University Press of New England.

Webster, Duncan (1988), *Looka Yonder! The Imaginary America of Populist Culture*, London: Routledge.

Webster, Duncan (1989), 'Coca-colonisation and National Cultures', *Over Here: Reviews in American Studies*, 9:2, 64–75.

Wenders, Wim (1986), *Emotion Pictures*, London: Faber and Faber.

West, Cornel (1992), 'From an Interview with Cornel West by Anders Stephanson', in Peter Brooker (ed.), *Modernism/Postmodernism*, London: Longman, pp. 213–24.

Woodward, Kathryn (ed.) (1997), *Identity and Difference*, London: Sage.

THEORIES

CHAPTER ONE

Americanisation, McDonaldisation and Globalisation

George Ritzer and Michael Ryan

Globalisation theory has emerged as one of the most discussed perspectives in contemporary social theory. While social theorists have long been interested in globalisation, the recent explosion of work on the topic[1] and the theory reflects what is of concern to, and of significance for, the larger population. Virtually every nation and the lives of billions of people throughout the world are being transformed, often quite dramatically, by globalisation.[2] The degree and significance of its impact is to be seen virtually everywhere one looks, most visibly in the now common protests that accompany high-level meetings of such global organisations as the World Trade Organization, the World Bank and the International Monetary Fund. As both the magnitude of the issues before these organisations and the level of protest against them make clear, people throughout the world feel strongly that they are confronting matters of great importance.

Globalisation theory has also emerged as a result of a series of developments internal to social theory, notably the reaction against such earlier perspectives as modernisation theory (see Tiryakian 1992). Among the defining characteristics of this theory were its western bias, the preeminence it accorded to developments in the West, and the idea that the rest of the world had little choice but to become increasingly like it. While there are many different versions of globalisation theory, there is a tendency in virtually all of them to shift away from a focus on America and the West and to examine transnational processes that not only flow in many different directions, but are also autonomous and independent of any single nation or area of the world (Appadurai 1996).

We can start with a definition of *globalisation* as 'the compression of the world and the intensification of consciousness of the world as a whole' (Robertson 1992: 8). As it has come to be used, the notion of globalisation encompasses a number of transnational processes which, while they can be seen as global in their reach, are separable from each other. It is beyond the scope of this essay to deal with the full range of globalisation processes,[3] but two broad types – glocalisation and grobalisation – that highlight key differences in approaches to this process will be of interest here. The concept of glocalisation gets to the heart of what most contemporary theorists associated with globalisation theory think about the nature of transnational processes (see Robertson 2001). *Glocalisation* can be defined as the fusion of the global and the local, resulting in unique outcomes in different geographic areas. The concept of *grobalisation* (see Ritzer 2004), a much-needed companion to the notion of glocalisation,[4] focuses on the imperialistic ambitions of nations, corporations, organisations and the like, and their desire, indeed need, to impose themselves on various geographic areas. Their main interest is in seeing their power, influence, and in some cases profits *grow* (hence the term 'grobalisation') throughout the world. Grobalisation involves a variety of sub-processes, two of which – Americanisation[5] and McDonaldisation[6] – are of particular interest to the authors and will be dealt with below.

The concept of grobalisation, as well as the sub-processes of McDonaldisation and Americanisation, are at odds, to some degree, with the thrust of the globalisation theories – especially glocalisation – that have the greatest cachet today. There is a gulf between those who emphasise the increasing grobal influence of Americanised and/or McDonaldised interests and those who see the world as growing increasingly pluralistic and indeterminate (see Appadurai 1996). At the risk of being reductive, this divide amounts to a difference in vision between those who see a world that is becoming increasingly grobalized[7] – more Americanised, rationalised, codified and restricted – and those who view it as growing increasingly glocalised – more diverse, effervescent and free.

Grobalisation and glocalisation are rooted in competing visions of modernity. Grobalisation is a very modern view emphasising the growing worldwide ability of largely capitalistic organisations and modern states[8] to increase their power and reach throughout the world. Two of the most preeminent modern theories – those of Karl Marx and Max Weber (and of their followers) – undergird this perspective. Marxian (and neo-Marxian) theory leads to the view that one of the major driving forces behind grobalisation is the corporate need to show increasing profitability through more and more far-reaching economic imperialism. It also demonstrates the need for corporations, and the states and other institutions (media, education) that buttress them, to support efforts at enhancing profitability by increasing their cultural hegemony throughout the world. Thus, from this perspective, the need for (especially) American corporations to show ever-increasing profits, and the related and supporting need of America and American institutions to exert ever-increasing cultural hegemony, go to the core of grobalisation. American corporations aggressively export commodities for their own profit and the nation as a whole is similarly aggressive in the exportation of its ideas in order to gain hegemony over other nations, not only for its own sake, but for the increased ability to market its goods and services that such hegemony yields.

The second modern perspective informing our views on grobalisation is the Weberian (and neo-Weberian) tradition which emphasises the increasing ubiquity of rationalised structures and their growing control over people throughout the world. The Weberian approach attunes us to the grobal spread of these rationalised structures. That is, rationalised structures have a tendency to replicate themselves throughout the world and those nations that do not have them are generally eager to acquire them either because of their perceived benefits or as a defence from being left behind in the irrational dust of the rest of the world. While American corporations, indeed America as a whole, can be seen as highly rationalised, there are, as we will see, many other rationalised structures not only in the United States, but throughout the world.

While modern theories like those associated with the Marxian and Weberian traditions are closely linked to the idea of grobalisation, glocalisation is more in tune with postmodern social theory (see Best and Kellner 1997; Ritzer 1997) and its emphasis on diversity, hybridity and independence. In conjunction with local realities, the globalisation of so many commodities and ideas gives communities, groups and individuals in many parts of the world an unprecedented capacity to fashion distinctive and ever-changing realities and identities. This perspective sees a world of increasing diversity rather than an increasing penetration by capitalist firms and the states that support them, and/or by rationalised structures. Although all nations are likely to be affected by the spread of capitalism and rationalisation, this perspective holds that nations are likely to integrate both of these with local realities to produce distinctively glocal phenomena.

Thus, it should come as no surprise that grobalisation and glocalisation offer very different images of the impact of transnational processes. This is due, in part, to their antithetical bases in modern and postmodern social theory.

Glocalisation and grobalisation

Glocalisation and grobalisation are clearly two very different perspectives on the issue of globalisation. In order to better understand the nuances of each, we will attempt to outline some of the basic tenets inherent in their definitions. Overall, we can, following Robertson (1992), offer the following as the essential elements of glocalisation:

(1) The world is growing more pluralistic. Glocalisation theory is exceptionally sensitive to differences within and between areas of the world.

(2) Individuals and local groups have more power to adapt, innovate and manoeuvre within a glocalised world. Glocalisation theory sees individuals and groups as important and creative agents.

(3) Social processes are relational and contingent. Globalisation provokes a variety of reactions – ranging from nationalist entrenchment to cosmopolitan embrace – that feed back on and transform globalisation and hence lead to glocalisation.

(4) Commodities and the media, arenas and key forces in cultural change in the late twentieth and early twenty-first centuries, are *not* seen as (totally) coercive, but rather as providing material to be used in individual and group creation throughout the glocalised areas of the world.

Naturally, grobalisation leads to a variety of largely antithetical ideas:

(1) The world is growing increasingly similar. Grobalisation theory tends to minimise differences within and between areas of the world.

(2) Individuals and groups have grown less able to adapt, innovate and manoeuvre within a grobalised world. Grobalisation theory

sees larger structures and forces overwhelming the ability of individuals and groups to create themselves and their worlds.

(3) Social processes are largely uni-directional and deterministic. Grobalisation overpowers the local and limits its ability to act and react, let alone act back on the global.

(4) Commodities and the media are the key forces and arenas of cultural change and they *are* seen as largely determining the self and groups throughout the grobalised areas of the world.

Thus, the term 'globalisation' will be employed to encompass all of the transnational processes of concern here, especially glocalisation and grobalisation. 'Glocalisation' will be used to describe the multi-directional global processes that, in conjunction with local processes, produce unique (and very different) cultural, social, political/institutional, economic realities (hybrids). 'Grobalisation' will be used to refer to the (largely) uni-directional global process that is overpowering, and in many cases destroying, the local and producing a world of homogeneous (and largely generic) cultural, social, political/institutional, and economic realities.

Nothing

Much of Americanisation, McDonaldisation and grobalisation involves what we will call here *nothing*, defined as 'social forms that are generally[9] centrally conceived, controlled and comparatively devoid of distinctive substantive content'; forms that are to a large degree substantively generic. This definition carries with it no judgement about the desirability or undesirability of such a social form, or about its increasing prevalence. The notion of nothing requires a parallel concept of something, since one makes little sense without the other, and indeed we will operate here with a something–nothing continuum. *Something* is defined as 'social forms that are generally[10] indigenously conceived, controlled and comparatively rich in distinctive substantive content'; forms that are to a large degree substantively unique.

To further refine our sense of nothing and something, we need to distinguish among places–non-places, things–non-things, people–non-people and services–non-services. Table 1.1 offers an overview of these four sub-continua in the context of the larger something–nothing continuum.

Table 1.1 The four major sub-types of something–nothing (with examples).

SOMETHING..NOTHING
Place (community bank).............................Non-place (credit card company)
Thing (personal loan)..................................Non-thing (credit card loan)
Person (personal banker)...........................Non-person (telemarketer)
Service (individualised assistance).............Non-service (automated, dial-up aid)

Figure 1 outlines the relationship between something–nothing and glocalization–grobalization with representative examples from the four sub-continua outlined above:

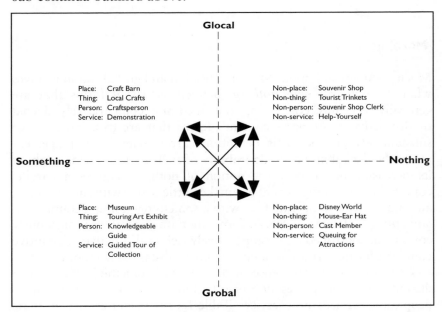

Figure 1.1. The relationship between glocal–grobal and something–nothing (with a few representative examples in each quadrant).

With this general theoretical background we turn now to a discussion of Americanisation and McDonaldisation, both sub-processes of grobalisation.

Americanisation

Americanisation can be defined as 'the propagation of American ideas, customs, social patterns, language, industry and capital around the world' (see Williams 1962). It is a powerful uni-directional process stemming from the United States that tends to overwhelm competing processes (e.g. Britishisation) as well as the strength of local (and glocal) forces that might resist, modify, and/or transform American models into hybrid forms. Moreover, the notion of Americanisation is tied to a particular nation – the United States – but it has a differential impact on many specific nations. It can be subsumed under the heading of grobalisation because it envisions a *growth* in American influence in all realms throughout the world.

Americanisation is inclusive of forms of American cultural, social, institutional/political and economic imperialism. For example, we can include under the heading of Americanisation such things as the world-wide diffusion of the American industrial model and the later global proliferation of the American consumption model; the marketing of American media including Hollywood films and popular music; the selling of American sports like NFL football and NBA basketball abroad; the transnational marketing of American commodities including cola, blue jeans and computer operating systems; the nearly universal adoption of English as a second language, especially in business; the extensive diplomatic and military engagement with Europe, Asia, and South America; the training of the world's military, political, and scientific elites in American universities; the expansion of the American model of democratic politics; and the development and use of the international labour market and natural resources by American corporations.

A particularly good example of Americanisation, and one of particular interest to the authors, is the spread of the 'new means of consumption' (Ritzer 1999: 8), most of which were created in the United States and are now spreading throughout the world. There has been an almost dizzying creation and proliferation of settings that allow, encourage and even compel us to consume innumerable goods and services. These settings have come into existence, or taken revolutionary new forms, in the United States since the close of World War II. Building upon, but going beyond, earlier settings, they have dramatically transformed the nature of consumption.

The following are the major new means of consumption with notable examples and the year in which they began operations: franchises (McDonald's, 1955);[11] shopping malls (the first indoor mall, Edina, Minnesota, 1956); mega-malls (West Edmonton Mall, 1981; Mall of America, 1992); superstores (Toys "Я" Us, 1957); discounters (Target, 1962); home shopping television (Home Shopping Network, 1985); cybermalls (Wal-Mart, 1996); theme parks (Disneyland, 1955); cruise ships (Sunward, 1966); casino-hotels (Flamingo, 1946); eatertainment (Hard Rock Cafe, 1971). With the exception of mega-malls and the West Edmonton Mall (created in Canada) and 'eatertainment' and the Hard Rock Cafe (which was created in London, albeit to bring 'American' food to England), all of these are American innovations that, in recent years, have been aggressively exported to the rest of the world; that is, they have become global phenomena.

What is it about these new means of consumption that make them distinctly American (in Germany, the new Starbucks that are opening there have been described as 'Anywhere USA' (Scally 2002: 14)), and hence excellent examples of Americanisation, when they are exported to other countries? First, and most obviously, they are about consumption and America has been, and is still, the world leader in consumption and in innovations in that realm by a wide margin.[12] When anyone in the world thinks of consumption, a cornucopia of goods and services, and a rate of consumption so frenetic that one can only think of 'hyperconsumption', one thinks of the United States.

Secondly, most of the new means of consumption relate in one way or another to the high rate of mobility associated with American culture. The vast majority of them have to do with the massive addiction of Americans to their automobiles, extensive and frequent automobile travel, and the consequent development of a road and highway system unparalleled in the world. Others relate to other types of mobility by plane (Las Vegas casino hotels; Disney theme parks), boat (cruise ships), and over the Internet (cybershops, cybermalls) that are also more common to American travellers than to most other members of the world community.

Third, the sustenance of these means of consumption requires the level of affluence that is so widely available in the United States. While other nations may have higher average levels of income, no nation has nearly as many people affluent enough to afford to visit and to consume in these sites on a regular basis. Many Americans are so affluent (at least in comparison to those in most other nations) that they can afford to eat more meals out in franchises and eatertainment sites, are able to have drawers full of 'unnecessary' clothing, and are capable of having one (or sometimes more) automobiles, credit cards, and other means facilitating consumption. Only they can afford to descend in droves on meccas of consumption like Las Vegas, Nevada; Orlando, Florida; Pigeon Forge, Tennessee; and Minneapolis, Minnesota. This does not mean that similar means of consumption are not available in other countries, but rather that they are more widely available in and consequently more widely associated with the United States.

Fourth, many of the new means of consumption reflect the American mania for that which is huge, enormous. Many of the cathedrals of consumption reflect this peculiar mania for size – the mega-malls, superstores, theme parks, cruise ships, and casino-hotels all seek to outdo themselves in terms of size. Size is also reflected in the sheer quantity of things available in these settings. Malls and mega-malls are chock full of well-stocked stores (often franchises); superstores have virtually everything one could think of in a particular line of products (sporting goods, athletic shoes, linens, furniture and so on); Disney theme parks, especially Disney World, are characterised by many worlds, tens of thousands of hotel rooms, many restaurants, and much kitsch for sale, and of course Las Vegas is over the top in terms of everything it has to offer and it increasingly seems to offer everything. Then there is, of course, the tendency for fast-food restaurants of all types to be in the business of 'supersizing' everything they possibly can (leading, in many cases, to a supersizing of the customer as well!).

Fifth, these new means of consumption carry with them distinctively American, in other words English, names. Starbucks, McDonald's, Disney, and Wal-Mart are called the same thing in English-, French-, Polish-, and Swahili-speaking countries alike. Therefore, the invasion of these new means of consumption also brings with it a linguistic infusion as well. There are, however, attempts by organisations in many countries, for example the Académie Française in France, to halt the influx of English words and to preserve the sanctity of their own native language.

McDonaldisation

McDonaldisation is the process by which the principles of the fast-food restaurant are coming to dominate more and more sectors of American society and an increasing number of other societies throughout the world. It fits under the heading of grobalisation because it involves the growing power of this model and its increasing influence around the globe. The model's principles are *efficiency, calculability, predictability* and *control*, particularly through the substitution of non-human for human technology, as well as the seemingly inevitable *irrationalities of rationality* that accompany the process (see Ritzer 2000). The basic concept, as well as its fundamental dimensions, are derived from Max Weber's work on formal rationality (Weber 1968). Weber demonstrated that the modern western world (and most especially the United States) was characterised by an increasing tendency towards the predominance of formally rational systems and that the rest of the world was coming under the sway of these systems. Thus, the process of McDonaldisation, or at least its forerunners (increasing formal rationality and bureaucratisation), obviously predates McDonald's as an institution (Weber 1981). However, that franchise is the exemplar (the bureaucracy was the model in Weber's approach) of the contemporary phase of rationalisation. While the fast-food restaurant is the paradigm of this process, the process has by now affected most, if not all, social structures and institutions in the United States, as well as most nations (at least those that are reasonably developed economically) in the world.[13] Thus, McDonaldisation is restricted neither to the fast-food industry nor to the United States. Rather, it is a wide-ranging and far-reaching process of global (even grobal) change.

Recent work has tended to support the McDonaldisation thesis. It has been applied well beyond the fast-food restaurant and even everyday consumption to such areas as higher education ('McUniversity') (see Hayes and Wynyard 2002), politics (see Turner 1999; Beilharz 1999), religion (see Drane 2001), and criminal justice (see Robinson 2002). Of course, not all systems (or nations) are equally McDonaldised; McDonaldisation is a matter of degree with some settings more McDonaldised than others. However, few settings (or nations) have been able to (or even wanted to) escape its influence altogether.

While McDonaldisation is traceable, most proximately, to the United States, especially the founding of the McDonald's chain outside Chicago in the mid-1950s, the process cannot simply be subsumed under the heading of Americanisation. First, it has roots outside the United States, including the German bureaucracies analysed by Weber at the turn of the twentieth century. Second, the process has taken root by now in many nations and at least some of them are in the process of exporting their own McDonaldised systems throughout the world, including back into the United States (for example, the exportation of England's Body Shop or Sweden's Ikea to the United States and many other nations). McDonaldisation can be thought of as a transnational process that is increasingly independent of any particular nation, including even the United States, and therefore is not reducible to a specific form of Americanisation. In the future, paralleling the history of mass manufacturing, we can anticipate that the centre of McDonaldisation might even shift from the United States to other parts of the world.

McDonaldisation is obviously a global perspective, but it is both less than and more than a theory of globalisation. On the one hand, McDonaldisation does not involve anything approaching the full range of global processes. For example, many economic, cultural, social, and political/institutional aspects of globalisation are largely unrelated to McDonaldisation. On the other hand, McDonaldisation involves much more than an analysis of its global impact. For example, much of it involves the manifold transformations taking place within the United States, the source and still the centre of this process. Furthermore, one can analyse the spread of McDonaldisation (once it has arrived) within many other nations and even sub-areas of those nations. In addition, one can, as we have seen, look at the McDonaldisation of various aspects of the social world – religion, higher education, politics, and so on – without considering the global implications for each. Thus, McDonaldisation is not coterminous with globalisation, nor is it solely a global process. What is clear is that McDonaldisation deserves a place in any thoroughgoing account of globalisation.

There can be little doubt that the logic of McDonaldisation generates a set of values and practices that have a competitive advantage over other models. It not only promises many specific advantages, it also reproduces itself more easily than other models of consumption (and in many other areas of society, as well). The success of McDonaldisation in the United States over the past half century, coupled with the international ambitions of McDonald's and its ilk, as well as those of indigenous clones throughout the world, strongly suggest that McDonaldisation will continue to make inroads into the global marketplace not only through the efforts of existing corporations but also via the diffusion of the paradigm.

It should be noted, however, that the continued advance of McDonaldisation, at least in its present form, is far from assured. In fact, there are even signs in the United States, as well as in other parts of the world, of what George Ritzer has previously called *deMcDonaldisation* (see

Ritzer 1998: 174–83). There are, for example, the increasing problems of McDonald's in the American market, where it has recently been forced to close restaurants, fire employees, scale back planned expansion and even let its chief executive go. Internationally, McDonald's restaurants have become targets for various groups with grievances against the restaurant chain, the United States and even globalisation. In light of such international difficulties, McDonald's must be rethinking its plans to expand in certain areas and may even be thinking of scaling back in places where it is particularly likely to be an object of protest and attack. Thus, McDonaldisation is neither inexorable or inevitable, although the same cannot be said of the underlying process of rationalisation (more on this later).

Americanisation, McDonaldisation and nothing

It is grobalisation in general, and McDonaldisation and Americanisation in particular, that are the key forces in the global spread of nothing.[14] While there is not a law-like relationship between grobalisation and nothing, there is an elective affinity between them; one tends to call into existence the other. On the one hand, an increasingly global market insists on large numbers and great varieties of nothing to satisfy the increasing demand for it, at least part of this fabricated (through advertising and marketing) by the forces (corporations, states) that profit from the widespread distribution and sale of nothing. On the other hand, production of so much nothing, and the requirement that it be profitable or successful, leads to increasing pressure to find ever more remote global markets for nothing. It is far easier to grobalise nothing than something and hence the production of nothing, especially in large numbers, is amenable to grobal proliferation. Grobalisation is inherently expansionistic – it is by definition oriented to growth – and a global market offers the largest possible venue for expansionism. And it is far easier to sell (relatively) empty forms – nothing – in diverse settings around the globe than it is to sell phenomena laden with content – something.

As a variant of grobalisation, McDonaldisation expands globally because of a belief in both the host nation[15] and the receiving nations in the basic model and the fact that such a model has demonstrated that it can work everywhere with few, if any, modifications. Behind Americanisation and its spread throughout the world is the belief, again in both host (the United States) and receiving nations, in the American way of doing things; a view that that process has a kind of 'manifest destiny'. While those phenomena that emanate from America are inherently something because they are touched, if not infused with, that which defines America, many of them have shown a peculiar capacity to shuck their American characteristics and become many different things to many different cultures, to melt seamlessly into the culture (Coca-Cola and Levi's jeans in many nations around the world are other excellent examples). The capacity for that which is American to lose its cultural characteristics, to become nothing (or nearly so), is linked to the view that America is everyone's 'second culture' and therefore its exports are easily modified, denuded, and integrated into local culture.[16]

While both McDonaldisation and Americanisation can be seen as key forces in the grobalisation of nothing, McDonaldisation is the purer force because it is by its very nature oriented to the creation of phenomena that are as long on form and as short on content as possible. Americanisation is not nearly as pure a force (its products reflect American culture), but it is the more powerful of the two. In any case, in reality it is difficult, and in some cases impossible, to distinguish between these two processes, with the result that in the real world they are mutually reinforcing. For example, McDonald's, as the paradigm of the process of McDonaldisation, is also intimately associated with Americanisation.

Why does Americanisation lead so easily to nothing?

While Americanisation is not the force that McDonaldisation is (to the degree that they can be distinguished) in the grobalisation of nothing, the issue arises: Why is Americanisation a greater force in the proliferation of nothing than other grobal processes (say, Britishisation)?

First, there is simply much more Americanization than any of the competing grobal processes. As the world's greatest power, especially economically, America simply produces more of virtually everything to offer around the globe than any other nation. America's capitalistic enterprises, as well as many other organisations, churn out Americana of all sorts and there are great pressures, especially the need for ever-escalating profits, to export them throughout the globe. In contrast, a nation such as Brazil, for example, produces far less 'Braziliana' and there is far less pressure to export it globally.

Second, American exporters are more likely to be able to afford to utilise the world's advertising and marketing systems to disseminate their products. Furthermore, advertising and marketing are themselves American specialities, with the result that American products are likely to be presented not only more extensively, but also more expertly.

Third, in order to cater to a global market, American exporters are more likely, at least at times when it suits them, to conceal the roots of these exports and to transform them into ever emptier forms that can adapt to virtually any locale. Bombarded by omnipresent and clever advertisements that may well conceal the American roots of various products, natives are more likely to accept them.

Fourth, and perhaps most importantly, America, as Todd Gitlin has made clear, is everyone's 'second culture' (in Kuisel 1993: 230). That is, even when people are able to distinguish their own culture from American exports, they are likely to be quite comfortable with things American. Since the latter are often relatively empty forms, they are easy to accept and to infuse with whatever meaning the locals desire.

Fifth, the great diplomatic and military strength of the United States leads many nations to desire the fostering of a strong and positive commercial relationship with it in the hope that strong economic ties will also lead to strong political ties and military protection. Additionally, many countries rely heavily on the United States to buy their products, or supply them with economic assistance, so they are more willing to submit to the process of Americanisation.

Anti-Americanism and the global attacks on McDonald's

The thrust of the argument made in this chapter is confirmed, in an odd way, by the recent acceleration of deadly attacks on American interests and on McDonald's restaurants throughout the world. In terms of the former, the most extreme and heinous example is the destruction of the World Trade Center and part of the Pentagon on 11 September 2001.[17] The selection of these two sites reflected a clear desire to strike at the heart of American economic and military power around the world. The assumption that the plane that crashed in Pennsylvania was headed for the White House, the source of American political power around the globe, also supports this view. In addition, McDonald's has become a favourite target around the world with innumerable examples of protests against (José Bové's efforts in France are the best-known example – see Morse 2002: 245–9), and even bombings of, its restaurants around the world. In terms of the arguments being made in this essay, these attacks reflect, at least in part, a growing awareness that Americanisation and McDonaldisation, and more generally the process of grobalisation, under which they can be subsumed, are a threat to local cultures. It is clear to an increasing number of people around the world that ever-increasing and accelerating expansionism lies at the heart of grobalisation and that resistance is necessary if they wish their cultures to survive.

Making this argument should not be construed as a defence of the kinds of deadly actions mentioned above. Clearly, other ways need to be found to oppose these processes. Such responses are far worse than the problems they seek to deal with. Nonetheless, they do make it clear that the processes discussed here have great power and they are being met with strong, albeit sometimes misguided and even downright evil, responses.

This discussion leads to another issue: Does the acceleration of attacks on Americanisation, McDonaldisation, and grobalisation represent the beginning of the decline of these processes? This is a complex question involving multiple, overlapping processes and predictions about the future. We will offer three thumbnail answers to close this discussion and this essay.

First, anti-Americanism is so strong and is growing so fast in many parts of the world that it is possible to conceive of some slowdown in incursions throughout the world. However, there are powerful economic and political forces behind Americanisation, with the result that our view would be that the slowdown is likely to be mild and short-lived. Furthermore, existing side by side with anti-Americanism is widespread and powerful pro-Americanism. Thus, a recent Pew survey found that anti-Americanism was on the rise and that a majority of those surveyed in many countries opposed the spread of American ideas, but they also liked American culture, such as its movies, music and television (see Ross 2002).

Second, a slowdown, even reversal, of the global fortunes of McDonald's is much more likely than a similar development in the realm of Americanisation. This is clearly a corporation not only in trouble in its global operations, but in even more serious difficulties in the American market. However, a slowdown in the global proliferation of McDonald's, or even its disappearance, does not spell the decline or demise of McDonaldisation. While the paradigm may change (Starbucks is the current star in the fast food industry and is undergoing enormous global expansion (it is currently expanding rapidly in Europe and has just announced plans for a massive invasion of heretofore tea-drinking China); can we think in terms of 'Starbuckisation'?), the underlying process of rationalisation, encompassing the basic principles (efficiency and so on) discussed above, is likely not only to continue, but to accelerate.

Finally, grobalisation is the major worldwide development of the age and it is almost impossible to envision a scenario whereby it would slow down, let alone be stopped.[18] There is too much power behind the forces pushing grobalisation, the forces opposing it (at least at the moment) are far too weak, and there are far too many real and imagined gains (Derber 2002: 15). In any case, for most nations of the world, there is little choice. Trying to opt out, even if it was successful (and that's not likely), would push the nations that do so into the backwaters of the global system. A more likely option for most is to become active exporters in the grobal system rather than being passive recipients of that which is created and produced elsewhere, especially in the United States.[19]

Notes

1. A number of leading social theorists have addressed the issue of globalisation including Bauman (1998); Beck(2000); Giddens (2000); Kellner (2002).
2. As we will see, the meaning of this concept is not unambiguous. An effort will be made to sort this out in the ensuing discussion.
3. For an excellent overview see Antonio and Bonanno (2000).
4. We feel apologetic about adding yet another neologism, especially such an ungainly one, to a field already rife with jargon. However, the existence and popularity of the concept of glocalisation requires the creation of the parallel notion of grobalisation in order to emphasise that which the former concept ignores or downplays.
5. The authors would like to point out that this term does not refer to a process radiating from the Americas as a set of contiguous continents, but rather from one country in North America, namely the United States. Hence, perhaps a more appropriate (though unattractive) term would be United Statesisation?
6. We will later discuss the specific elements of McDonaldisation; however, here we discuss it as a process that is sweeping across the globe, as a centrally important grobalisation process.

7. Although everyone recognises that grobalisation, and more generally globalisation, play themselves out differently in various local and national contexts. See Mudimbe-Boyi (2002).

8. States further the interests of capitalist organisations, but also further their own interests, some of which are separable from the capitalist system.

9. There are some forms of nothing that are locally conceived and/or controlled. While the reader should keep this caveat in mind throughout this essay, it will not be repeated in future definitions of 'nothing'.

10. As in the case of the caveat about the definition of nothing, there are some forms of something that are centrally conceived and/or controlled.

11. The inclusion of McDonald's as one of the new means of consumption and as an example of Americanisation helps make it clear that Americanisation and McDonaldisation cannot be clearly and unequivocally distinguished from one another.

12. It is worth remembering that it was not too long ago that the United States was the world leader in production. In many ways, consumption has replaced production as the focus of the American economy and it has become the nation's prime export to the rest of world. It is interesting to ponder the implications of what it means to have gone from the world leader in the production of steel to, say, the world leader in the exportation of fast-food restaurants and shopping malls.

13. It is worth noting that McDonald's now operates in 119 countries around the world so its presence is felt even in those countries that are not economically developed by western standards.

14. Capitalism is another important motor force in the global spread of nothing.

15. In spite of the terminology used here, we do not mean to imply that McDonaldisation is tied to any host nation. It can, in fact, originate in any country and be exported to any other.

16 . This last argument seems to make the case for Americanisation as a glocal process and hence contradicts our earlier assertion that it is a grobal process. While it is true that the two uses of Americanisation are at odds with one another, we believe that the seeming contradiction can be explained in three possible ways. First, Americanisation can be viewed as a dialectical process with two competing sub-components. This parallels our larger notion of globalisation as comprised of the two conflicting notions of glocalisation and grobalisation. Drawing this distinction down to the level of Americanisation, we can see this sub-process in the same light – defined not by one process, but rather by two competing processes. Hence the ideas of Americanisation as a powerful uni-directional process that seems to overwhelm competing processes as well as the strength of local forces *and* as a process whereby those things emanating from America are able to shuck their distinctively American characteristics and melt seamlessly into the local culture are contradictory, yet complimentary, components of the same larger process.

The second possibility is that the process of Americanisation as a grobal

57

phenomenon has already overwhelmed the local to such a degree that what defines the genuinely native, non-American local is no longer discernable. In other words, American phenomena are able to mix with the 'local' culture so easily because some process of Americanisation has already overwhelmed the local, or at least left it with a strong flavour of Americana. The idea of America as the world's second culture would support this viewpoint. American phenomena that are seemingly imploding into the local are really simply augmenting what the process of Americanisation has already begun.

The third possibility for resolving the contradiction inherent in Americanisation as a process requires that we reconceptualise our image of the glocal–grobal/something–nothing continua outlined in Figure 1.1 above. The aforementioned figure seems to indicate that glocal and grobal as well as something and nothing lie on polar ends of a two-dimensional spectrum. It is, however, equally viable to consider the range of these concepts as a three-dimensional ring. That is, what is glocal (or something) melts into what is grobal (or nothing) on two sides. It is a never-ending continuum. Additionally, when the perpendicular ring of something and nothing is added to the glocal–grobal ring, the shape changes from a four-fold table to more of a globe shape (perhaps this is an even more appropriate image!). This further expands the possibilities of any one phenomenon fitting into our model and hence helps explain how Americanisation can appear as both a glocal and a grobal process.

17. For a discussion of this from the perspective of the interests of this essay, see Ritzer in Ritzer (2002).
18. For an alternative view, see James (2001).
19. Thus, for example, in international fine-art sales, Great Britain is poised to supplant the United States as the world leader. See Brewster (2002).

Bibliography

Antonio, Robert J. and Alessandro Bonanno (2000), 'A New Global Capitalism? From "Americanism" and "Fordism" to "Americanization-Globalization"', *American Studies*, 41, 33–77.

Appadurai, Arjun (1996), *Modernity at Large: Cultural Dimensions of Globalization*, Minneapolis: University of Minnesota Press.

Bauman, Zygmunt (1998), *Globalization: The Human Consequences*, New York: Columbia University Press.

Beck, Ulrich (2000), *What is Globalization?*, Cambridge: Polity.

Beilharz, Peter (1999), 'McFascism: Reading Ritzer, Bauman and the Holocaust', in Barry Smart (ed.), *Resisting McDonaldization*, London: Sage, pp. 222–33.

Best, Steven and Douglas Kellner (1997), *The Postmodern Turn*, New York: Guilford Press.

Brewster, Deborah (2002), 'US loses ground to Britain in global art sales', *Financial Times*, 20 September.

Derber, Charles (2002), *People before Profit: The New Globalization in an Age of Terror, Big Money, and Economic Crisis*, New York: St Martin's Press.

Drane, John (2001), *The McDonaldization of the Church*, London: Darton, Longman and Todd.

Giddens, Anthony (2000), *Runaway World: How Globalization Is Reshaping Our Lives*, New York: Routledge.

Hayes, Dennis and Robin Wynyard (eds.) (2002), *The McDonaldization of Higher Education*, Westport, CT: Bergin and Garvey.

James, Harold (2001), *The End of Globalization*, Cambridge, MA: Harvard University Press.

Kellner, Douglas (2002), 'Theorizing Globalization', *Sociological Theory*, 20: 3, 285–305.

Kuisel, Richard (1993), *Seducing the French: The Dilemma of Americanization*, Berkeley: University of California Press.

Morse, David (2002), 'Striking the Golden Arches: French Farmers Protest McD's Globalization', in George Ritzer (ed.), *McDonaldization: The Reader*, Thousand Oaks, CA: Pine Forge Press, pp. 245–9.

Mudimbe-Boyi, Elisabeth (ed.) (2002), *Beyond Dichotomies: Histories, Identities, Cultures, and the Challenge of Globalization*, Albany: State University of New York Press.

Ritzer, George (1997), *Postmodern Social Theory*, New York: McGraw-Hill.

Ritzer, George (1998), *The McDonaldization Thesis*, Thousand Oaks, CA: Pine Forge Press.

Ritzer, George (1999), *Enchanting a Disenchanted World: Revolutionizing the Means of Consumption*, Thousand Oaks, CA: Pine Forge Press.

Ritzer, George (2000), *The McDonaldization of Society*, Thousand Oaks, CA: Pine Forge Press.

Ritzer, George (2002), 'September 11, 2001: Mass Murder and its Roots in American Consumer Culture', in George Ritzer (ed.), *McDonaldization: The Reader*, Thousand Oaks, CA: Pine Forge Press, pp. 213–21.

Ritzer, George (2004), *The Globalization of Nothing*, Thousand Oaks, CA: Pine Forge Press.

Robertson, Roland (1992), *Globalization: Social Theory and Global Culture*, London: Sage.

Robertson, Roland (2001), 'Globalization Theory 2000+: Major Problematics', in George Ritzer and Barry Smart (eds), *Handbook of Social Theory*, London: Sage, pp. 458–71.

Robinson, Matthew B. (2002), 'McDonaldization of America's Police, Courts, and Corrections', in George Ritzer (ed.), *McDonaldization: The Reader*, Thousand Oaks, CA: Pine Forge Press, pp. 77–90.

Ross, Sonya (2002), 'Survey says: Foreigners like U.S. culture but not policies', Associated Press, 4 December; http://abcnews.go.com/sections/world.daily news/survey021204.html.

Scally, Derek (2002), 'Coffee drinkers not swallowing Starbucks line,' *Irish Times*, 5 December, p. 14.

Tiryakian, Edward A. (1992), 'Pathways to Metatheory: Rethinking the Presuppositions of Macrosociology', in George Ritzer (ed.), *Metatheorizing*, Beverly Hills, CA: Sage, pp. 69–87.

Turner, Bryan (1999), 'McCitizens: Risk, Coolness and Irony in Contemporary Politics', in Barry Smart (ed.), *Resisting McDonaldization*, London: Sage, pp. 83–100.

Weber, Max [1921] (1968), *Economy and Society*, 3 vols, Totowa, NJ: Bedminster Press.

Weber, Max [1927] (1981), *General Economic History*, New Brunswick, NJ: Transaction.

Williams, Francis (1962), *The American Invasion*, New York: Crown Williams.

CHAPTER TWO

Freedom, Anger and Global Power: Accusing Others

Victor Seidler

Gore Vidal, in a piece written in the wake of the September 11th attacks on the Twin Towers in New York entitled 'Taking Liberties', recognises that

> for several decades there has been an unrelenting demonisation of the Muslim world in the American media. Since I am a loyal American, I am not supposed to tell you why this had taken place, but then it is not usual for us to examine why anything happens other than to accuse others of motiveless malignancy. 'We are good,' announced a deep thinker on American television, 'they are evil,' which wraps that one up in a neat package. But it was Bush himself who put, as it were, the bow on the package in an address to a joint session of Congress where he shared . . . his profound knowledge of Islam's wiles and ways: 'They hate what they see right here in this chamber.' A million Americans nodded in front of their TV sets. 'Their leaders are self-appointed. They hate our freedoms: our freedom of religion, our freedom of speech, our freedom to vote and assemble and disagree with each other.' (*Guardian* Saturday Review, 27 April 2002: 1)[1]

Vidal then goes on to ask himself the question that emerged in the days after September 11th, when suicide pilots crashed commercial airliners

into crowded American buildings, only to be displaced by talk of war –
So why do Osama Bin Laden and millions of other Muslims hate us?[2]
As Vidal frames it:

> In a 12-page 'declaration of war', Bin Laden presented himself as
> a potential liberator of the Muslim world from the great Satan of
> modern corruption, the US. When Clinton lobbed a missile at a
> Sudanese aspirin factory, Bin Laden blew up two US embassies in
> Africa, put a hole in the side of an American warship off Yemen,
> and so on to the events of Tuesday September 11. Now President
> George W. Bush, in retaliation, has promised us not only a 'new
> war' but a secret war . . . 'We're going to find these evil-doers . . .
> and we're going to hold them accountable.' (ibid.)

As Vidal has it, 'in order to teach them the one lesson that we have
never been able to learn: in history, as in physics, there is not action
without reaction. Or, as Edward Herman puts it, "One of the most
durable features of the US culture is the inability or refusal to recognise
US crimes"' (ibid.).[3]
   Vidal reminds us that

> Bin Laden seemed, from all accounts, no more than a practising,
> as opposed to zealous, Muslim. Ironically, he was trained as an
> engineer. Understandably, he dislikes the United States as symbol
> and as fact. But when our clients, the Saudi Royal family, allowed
> American troops to occupy the Prophet's holy land, Bin Laden
> named the fundamental enemy 'the Crusader-Zionist Alliance'.
> Thus, in a phrase, he defined himself and reminded his critics that
> he is a Wahibi Muslim, a puritan activist. He would go to war
> against the US, 'the head of the serpent'. Even more ambitiously,
> he would rid all the Muslim states of their western supported
> regimes, starting with that of his native land. In the eyes of many
> Muslims, the Christian west, currently in alliance with Zionism,
> has for 1,000 years tried to dominate the lands of the Umma, the
> true believers. (ibid.: 1)

In this way Bin Laden is seen by many Muslims as the true heir of
Saladin, who united and 'purified' the Muslim world. This aspiration
towards purity was given a particular Christian inflection in the vision
of Spain as a Christian state which had to be purified of its Muslim and
Jewish inhabitants. They were to be expelled so that the purity of the

state could be reclaimed. It was only believing Christians who could really 'belong' to this state in which others could not find their place, even if they had been living in these lands for centuries. There is a different vision of 'purity' that is currently at work in post-September 11th United States, in which people have felt forced to present themselves as loyal citizens of the state, fearful of even questioning George W. Bush's 'war against terrorism' so that for almost nine months there was little open dissent.

According to Vidal, 'there have been ominous signs that our fragile liberties have been dramatically at risk since the 1970s, when the white-shirt-and-tie FBI reinvented itself from a corps of "generalists" trained in law and accountancy into a confrontational Special Weapons and Tactics (aka SWAT) green beret-style of warriors'. He recalls how it was an FBI SWAT team which attacked the Branch Davidians – evangelical Christians living peaceably in their own compound at Waco, Texas until they were attacked, illegally using army tanks, killing eighty-two of them, including twenty-five children. This was in 1993. As Vidal explains,

> post-September 11, SWAT teams can now be used to go after suspect Arab-Americans or, indeed anyone who might be guilty of terrorism, a word without legal definition . . . But in the post Oklahoma City trauma, Clinton said that those who did not support his draconian legislation were terrorist co-conspirators who wanted to turn 'America into a safe house for terrorists'. If the cool Clinton could so froth, what are we to expect from the overheated Bush post-September 11? (ibid.: 2)

According to Vidal, 'the awesome physical damage Bin Laden and company did us on Dark Tuesday is as nothing compared to the knock-out blow to our vanishing liberties – the Anti-Terrorism Act of 1991 combined with the recent request by Congress for additional special powers to wire-tap without juridical order; to deport lawful permanent residents, visitors and undocumented immigrants without due process and so on' (ibid.). Things can change quickly and the right has used the events of September 11 to consolidate its powers. According to a November 1995 CNN–*Time* poll, fifty-five per cent of the people believe that 'the federal government has become so powerful that it poses a threat to the rights of ordinary citizens'. Three days after Dark Tuesday seventy-four per cent said they thought 'it would be necessary for Americans to give up some of their personal freedoms'.

Only one congresswoman, Barbara Lee of California, voted against the additional powers granted to the President. Meanwhile a *New York Times*–CBS poll noted that only six per cent opposed military action while a substantial majority favoured war 'even if many thousands of innocent civilians are killed'. As Vidal notes, 'most of this majority are far too young to recall the second world war, Korea, even Vietnam. Simultaneously, Bush's approval rating soared' (ibid.). He also knows that in the United States 'traditionally, in war, the president is totemic, like the flag. When Kennedy got his highest rating after the debacle of the Bay of Pigs he observed, characteristically: "It would seem that the worse you fuck up in this job the more popular you get"' (ibid.).

Since VJ Day 1945 and the end of the Second World War, as Vidal has it,

> we have been engaged in what the great historian Charles Beard called 'perpetual war for perpetual peace'. I have occasionally referred to our 'enemy of the month club': each month a new horrendous enemy at whom we must strike before he destroys us . . . several hundred wars against communism, terrorism, drugs or something nothing much, in which we always struck the first blow. (ibid.)

You could say, following Vidal's line of thought, that the United States only knows itself through the enemies that it defines for itself. As the enemy has become harder to identify within a 'war against terrorism' so anger is often directed within towards those who can be regarded as 'soft on terrorism'. We have the assertion of a hyper-masculinity that is ready to fight the enemy 'wherever they can be found'.

Directing anger

If the events of September 11th were to represent a terrible failure of government, what the government knew and when it knew it was a question that was not allowed to emerge for nearly nine months. Rather, anger was to be directed outwards towards an enemy that had caused such destruction, who was to be fought globally. All the resources of the United States would be needed to defeat this new threat. As George W. Bush made clear, those who were not with us as friends had to be suspected as supporters of our enemies. The world was radically divided between friends and enemies and the anger that was felt was given a clear focus in the war against al-Qaeda and the Taliban in Afghanistan. A war was to be fought against another nation-state, so avoiding difficult questions about whether a 'war' can meaningfully be fought against terrorism. The American empire would take revenge on those who had attacked its symbols of global financial and military power. Citizens would be united as rarely before in this cause to defend its basic democratic values through destroying others who supposedly hated what the United States had come to stand for.

It was crucial for Bush to present the attack on the Twin Towers and the Pentagon not as an attack on the symbols of United States global economic and military power but as an attack on freedom and democracy itself. These were the values that a mythic 'America' represented for the global community so that within the terms of an Enlightenment rationalism America had come to symbolise the aspirations of a universal freedom. 'America' had learnt to identify itself with the aspirations of freedom everywhere. In this way it had refigured freedom as the gift which a mythic 'America' could bring to the world. This was a vision of freedom that supposedly stood in contrast with the freedom and progress that was identified with the European project of colonialism.

The American flag had become totemic so that in the eyes of Americans it had come to represent the aspirations of freedom everywhere. This was part of a secular evangelicalism of freedom that carried its own imperial aspirations. The world was to feel grateful for the freedom that 'America' gifted to them. This was a freedom that was supposedly untainted by colonialism, so that it could speak to postcolonial nations. The flag that survived from the top of one of the Twin Towers achieved the status of a holy relic that was transported throughout the United States as a totem that unified the nation in the face of attack. This worked to displace an extended process of mourning and self-reflection and cut short the early questioning into why other countries could hate the United States so much.

America carried obligations for the global community to defend the freedom that it represented for others. This was part of the shock that made it difficult to reflect upon the causes of such a violent attack. Within days it became difficult to talk about the consequences of United States global power and the ways it was used to exploit others. Very quickly such questioning was cut short with the counter-attack that you must be implying that 'they had it coming to them'. This would seem to justify the killing of innocent civilians in such terrible circumstances. Nothing could justify in any way what happened, which

65

meant there could be no questioning of the consequences of United States global power. Often the notion was invoked that there is a 'slippery slope' so that if you started this questioning it would somehow end up in legitimating the death of innocent civilians. But this is a danger that we must accept if we refuse to be silenced about the abuse of United States global power and the humiliations and sufferings that it has produced over the years, to which the United States' citizens were often blind. Reassured that they were only bringing good things to the table, like freedom and democracy, their power was assumed to be benign.

So questioning could safely be displaced as anger was focused upon 'enemies of freedom' that needed to be defeated. At some level it was assumed that enemies of globalisation were enemies of freedom since within the civil religion of America there was an identification between freedom and the market. People showed their identification with the stricken nation through purchasing flags. There was a shortage because the factory in Shanghai could no longer supply the need. Each day a new group of New York firefighters or police, as the new heroes of the moment, were invited to ring the bell of the New York stock exchange, as Andrew Wernick has written.[4] The bell of the exchange was to be identified in the aftermath of the attack with the freedom bell and the universal idea of 'letting freedom ring everywhere'. The stock exchange became the symbol of normality as it was near to the Twin Towers. As people walked to work on the opening day, America was returning to work to prove to themselves and the world that they had not been defeated by the attack. Mourning was to give way to anger and the 'war on terrorism' was to take shape.

Futures

Nine months after the attack on the Twin Towers when Bush visits Europe, which is supposedly full of allies, he is confronted with a hostile reception. According to Gary Young, writing in the *Guardian*,

> The source of the antagonism is not difficult to divine. Not content with reneging on treaties it doesn't like, threatening countries it doesn't like and ignoring objections to policies it does like, the Bush administration wonders why the rest of the world does not seem to like it. After September 11 commentators pined that

America had lost its innocence. Well, it looks like they have finally got it back again. (*Guardian*, 27 May 2002: 17)

Young goes on to explain crucial differences in perception when he says that 'while Americans interpret the attacks on the World Trade Centre as an assault on the principles of democracy and liberty, a majority in Europe believe the assault was aimed at the United States, not the western world' (ibid.: 17). As Young has it, 'the truth is, so long as Bush pushes ahead with this mindless, murderous military campaign and a world trade regime which discriminates against the poor and undermines democracy, he will remain a legitimate focus for anti-war and anti-globalisation protests'. He insists that one of the few hopeful developments to be salvaged from the wreckage of the World Trade Center 'is for America to wake up from its insularity and understand how little goodwill and how much animosity it has generated' (ibid.).

As *The Times*'s Roger Boyes reported from Bush's visit to Berlin, he was ready to challenge America's sceptical European allies to close ranks in the war against terrorism, declaring: 'We are defending civilization itself' (*The Times*, 24 May 2002: 16). NATO had to transform itself to fight this new war, he insisted in his speech to the German parliament. European allies had expressed opposition to any American-led military action against Iraq and denounced his 'axis of evil' speech against Iraq, Iran and North Korea. He insisted that Europe was as threatened as America, saying: 'Wishful thinking will bring comfort but not security. We do not know where the next threat will come from. We don't know what form it might take. But we must be ready' (cited ibid.). The President's speech was billed in advance as 'historic' and it showed the ways the new post-September 11th global order was being imagined by dominant forces in Washington.

The United States government seems determined to make 9/11 a watershed event which transforms the international order. Bush called September 11th 'a deep dividing line in our history, a change of eras as sharp and clear as Pearl Harbor' (ibid.). The references to the Second World War and the struggles against fascism were intentional, especially with the rise of the new right in Europe in the wake of Jean-Marie Le Pen's showing in the French presidential elections. Again Bush wanted the two continents to realise their common interests. 'Saddam Hussein is a dangerous man, a dictator who gases his people . . . a threat to civilisation,' he said. According to Boyes, 'his point was not only to induce a sense of urgency in Europe but also to put counter-terrorism in the broader context of a changing world, led by the United States and its allies' (ibid.: 16). According to Professor Christian Haake, from Bonn University, Bush was 'trying to complete the work of his father, who proposed a new world order' (ibid.).

Plainly the US leader expected some changes in Europe on the way to his version of the new world order. Defence budgets should rise and focus on modern warfare, such as the need for special commando units. Russia should be transformed from enemy to equal partner with the alliance, since the terms of global conflict had changed with the 'war on terrorism'. Aid was to be given to well-governed societies – Bush's code for those willing to side with the West in closing down terrorist havens. As an editorial in the *International Herald Tribune* made clear,

> it's that unglamorous part of the intelligence game where the United States failed most drastically in the months before September 11. It turns out that US agencies knew nearly every important fact about the al-Qaeda bombers before the tragedy – yet analysts couldn't see the picture.
>
> Contrary to what some in the Pentagon seem to believe, this is not a war in which America can go it alone. Yes, America has leaped a generation ahead of its allies in weapons technology, making it inevitable that there will be more unilateral US military operations. But those weapons won't get America very far without better intelligence, and for that America needs allies.' (*International Herald Tribune*, 25–6 May 2002: 6)

This helps explain the new readiness for the United States to sign a series of agreements in the gilded St Andrew's Hall in the Kremlin to cut by two-thirds the stockpiles of nuclear weapons. Bush on his visit to Moscow hailed the treaty as the end of a long chapter of confrontation and the start of 'an entirely new relationship between our countries' (*The Times*, 25 May 2002: 18). If this treaty was to mark the closing chapter of the Cold War, to prepare the space for the new global war against terrorism, military experts were more sceptical, saying the treaty merely reflected Moscow's decision to reduce stockpiles that it can no longer afford to maintain while allowing Americans to store thousands of warheads that could be brought back into service.

As Bush travelled to Europe he was still having to deal with revelations back home that showed that the administration and intelligence services had either misread or failed to read the clear warning signs that al-Qaeda would strike in exactly the way it did. As Joe Lieberman, the former vice-presidential candidate, framed it, 'the question is if we had been better organised, and all this information had come into one location – was 11 September preventable?' For eight months now, Bush and his presidency had ridden on the political crest of the wave of September 11th, legitimised by its professed defence of America from the global terrorist menace. Historian Robert Dallek saw a return to what he calls the 'imperial' presidencies of Nixon, Johnson and Kennedy; the Bush administration, he concludes, 'has an authoritarian bent'. But Dallek thinks such a style of government ultimately backfires: 'it creates a reaction against the executive,' he says.

As Joe Conason pointed out in the *New York Observer*, 'angry citizens are asking why they have suddenly learnt what George W. Bush knew all along: that weeks before the event, the CIA had warned the President and other top officials of an active plot to seize civilian aircraft' (*New York Observer*, 19 May 2002: 19).

According to Jonathan Freedland these questions are unlikely to bring down the President even if they harm his ratings, not only because

> the chain of command protects the president in cases like this . . . Besides, there is a more basic factor at work: voters' gut instinct says that, if the president could have done anything to prevent the September 11 tragedy, he would have. More deeply people have a fatalistic feeling about that day. Bobbi Rosner, who lost her daughter Sheryl on 9/11, wrote to the *New York Times* yesterday, with astonishing stoicism: 'Could it have been prevented? Probably not . . . Mistakes happen after all.' (*Guardian*, 22 May 2002: 17)

Osama Bin Laden, according to Freedland, has 're-established the old cold war standard of president as protector, and that standard served the Republican party well for decades. That's why any suggestion that Bush failed to protect the American people has to be crushed instantly' (ibid.). But Freedland also recognises that these revelations have hurt the Bush team's ideology. As he remarks,

> to govern is to choose . . . and the Bushies chose to make a priority of everything but domestic terror. Ashcroft was more concerned with drugs and violent crime; Rumsfeld was obsessed with national missile defence; Rice and Cheney were more worried by Saddam than al-Qaeda. (ibid.)

After eight months politics had suddenly returned to Washington with a vengeance. For months very few dared step out of line. They feared offending the dominant mood of the nation. 'You are either with us or against us,' said Bush, ensuring that every critic was branded as a confrere of terrorism. As Freeland reports it, 'it got so bad that even as heartland a figure as Dan Rather, veteran anchor of CBS News, complained to BBC *Newsnight* that the US had developed a near-totalitarian intolerance of dissent' (ibid.). This was a mood which the administration sought to use to its advantage as it reenvisioned the global order post-9/11. They had the power to remake global alliances in their own image. As Gore Vidal imagines the scene,

> thus, as the police state settles comfortably in place, one can imagine Dick Cheney and Donald Rumsfeld studying these figures – (eg 86% favoured guards and metal detectors at public buildings and events) transfixed with joy.
>
> > 'It's what they always wanted, Dick.'
> > 'And to think we never knew, Don.'
> > 'Thanks to those liberals, Dick'
> > 'We'll get those bastards now, Don.'
>
> ('Taking Liberties', *Guardian*, 27 April 2002: 2)

Global power

As Henry Porter, who was introduced as 'a proud friend of America' recognised,

> while Bush was warning the Bundestag that if we ignore the threat presented by the 'axis of evil' we invite certain blackmail and place millions of our citizens in danger, America was gripped by the story that on 6 August last year Bush ignored such a warning. This wasn't by any means a lone briefing. From 22nd June 2001 the Director of the CIA, George Tenet, was 'nearly frantic' with concern and wrote to the national security advisor that 'a significant al-Qaeda attack' was highly likely in the near future, 'within several weeks'. (*Observer*, 26 May 2002: 29)

Porter argues:

What Americans – currently in a more edgy and defensive mood than I can ever remember – do not recognise is that the vast majority of Europeans are not at base anti-American. It's just that we require more in the way of solid reasoning and debate if we are to support serial campaigns against the members of the 'axis of evil' – an awkward phrase which was, incidentally, chosen by the great wordsmith himself. (ibid.)

Porter is ready to acknowledge that

eight months on from the 11 September attacks George Bush's reflections on the grave new world appear to be no more than a couple of slogans deep. The war on terrorism took America just so far, but now Europeans want to see some evidence of thought and leadership beneath the rhetoric, especially because that particular phrase has been readily adapted to neutralise American diplomatic intervention by, for example, Ariel Sharon whose invasion of the Palestinian territories to a shake of the head and a murmured, 'but we didn't quite mean that kind of war on terrorism'. (ibid.)

The US Secretary of State, Colin Powell, as an enthusiast for multi-lateralism, 'nation-building' and mediation in troubled areas, is virtually alone in an administration often dominated by hawks who see Europe as a strategic irrelevance. In an interview he gave in Washington a month after he returned from his mission to the Middle East, when he had been undermined by the Pentagon and the White House, which have their own lines of communication with the Israeli leadership, he said: 'This is an administration and this is a president that has strong beliefs and values . . . And just because we may not be able to reach an agreement, doesn't mean we don't care what everybody else says.' But he also added: 'The evidence is also there that sometimes when we strike what we believe is a correct position and we explain it and people don't agree with us, it turns out a few months or half a year later, maybe we weren't all that wrong' (*Guardian*, 18 May 2002: 5). Here he was partly thinking about the US national missile defence (NMD), which now appears to have been accepted as a fact of life by the Russians, somewhat to the embarrassment of Europeans who had forecast doom. There were also warnings if NATO expanded to include the Baltic states. 'You don't hear that any longer'(ibid.).

As Powell states it somehow defensively, 'we realise that sometimes we Americans speak in certain ways that cause distress, but it's not because we are necessarily wrong' (ibid.). This is partly because Vladimir Putin's Russia has been forced to give up the myth of itself as a global power that can somehow compete with the United States on equal terms. Putin has recognised that more advantage will accrue for the necessary economic development of Russia through a policy of concession to American global power and acceptance as a partner in the 'war against terrorism'. As Julian Boger noted, however, 'paradoxically, the success Mr Powell claimed for the Bush administration's preference for global leadership over negotiation has served to undermine his strength within the Bush administration' (*Guardian*, 18 May 2002: 1). Powell has often found himself in a minority in advocating compromise against hawks who see global accords as unnecessary constraints on US power. They are ready to take whatever advantages they can from the United States' position as the singular superpower, free to sustain its own global empire.

These days, US officials scarcely bother complaining about their European allies' low defence spending. But Gary Schmitt, the head of a conservative Washington think-tank, Project for the New American Century, with close ties to the administration, says silence may be a bad sign.[5] 'It sort of reminds me of a marriage, a bad marriage, in which you know a marriage is over not when people are arguing, but when they stop arguing,' he said. 'It's as though they've decided that, well, it's not worth it.' He continued: 'What really is going on is a fundamental disagreement about strategic matters and how states act on the international stage' (*Guardian*, 22 May 2002: 13).

At the heart of the matter is the 'Bush doctrine', as laid out in the President's State of the Union address on 29 January. It is because it concluded that 9/11 has changed the world fundamentally that muddling through in the alliance between Europe and the United States may not be good enough. The doctrine perceives the greatest threat on the horizon as the combination of terrorist groups and the weapons of mass destruction in the hands of 'rogue states'. It sees fifty years of agreements on arms control as having failed to block that threat, which is now so potent as to justify preemptive military action, most immediately in Iraq. This involves the United States questioning its traditional relationships with Europe. In Afghanistan the Pentagon's view was that Europe simply had no air power to speak of, and it would only start second-guessing decisions and getting in the way.

Philip Gordon, an analyst at the Brookings Institution in Washington, said: 'There's a real question, I think for good reason, about whether the United States thinks NATO is worth anything.' He said: 'You can't unsign the ICC [International Criminal Court], tear up the Kyoto Treaty, call Sharon a man of peace, talk about the axis of evil, disparage NATO, put protection on steel and agriculture and then go make a speech and say, "but everything is fine, right?".' The President's itinerary provides little encouragement for new directions in transatlantic dialogue. His visit to Berlin and a US D-Day cemetery in Normandy in particular were celebrations of US victories in the Cold War and Second World War. The former visit was a very deliberate reminder of America's role in securing Europe's freedom from fascism. Sensitivities are especially sharp on this issue, with the US media interpreting Jean-Marie Le Pen's success in France as a rerun of the 1930s. America has keen perceptions of rampant anti-Semitism in the old continent.

According to Simon Tisdall in a comment piece for the *Guardian*, 'notwithstanding any conciliatory gestures by Mr Bush, his belief that he is doing what is right for America and the world will not change'. His trip reminded Europe's political class of its own relative impotence.

> In speeches since September 11, Mr Bush has articulated a vision that divides the world into good guys and bad guys . . . He has spoken of US values as necessary global values, the chief of which are democracy and free speech, but which also include his government's interpretation of free trade. (*Guardian*, 22 May 2002: 13)

Bush invites Europe and others to follow America's lead. On this basis he rejects accusations of unilateralism. But paradoxically, if and when the US faces opposition, he stresses his determination to go it alone. As Tisdall has it, 'In short, Mr Bush has taken his country's sole superpower status, and using September 11 as a launchpad, is projecting it to further American interests worldwide. He devoutly believes he is right' (ibid.).

Europe as yet has no clear answer to this. Lacking a clear alternative vision and the defence capabilities to sustain it, and divided as ever, according to Tisdall, 'Europe is losing the argument. Many Europeans want their leaders to "stand up" to Mr Bush. But they do not know how' (ibid.). Europe is also in danger of becoming less relevant as America's strategic, military, demographic and economic focus shifts towards Asia, Latin America and the Middle East. As Bush was giving his keynote speech on his European tour in the historically resonant setting of the reconstructed Reichstag building, he told German MPs that it was in their interests to back the broadening US 'war on terror'.

'Those who seek missiles and terrible weapons are familiar with the map of Europe. Like the threats of another era, this threat cannot be appeased and cannot be ignored,' he said. As John Hooper reported from Berlin, the President told his audience: 'Different as we are, we are building and defending the same house of freedom. Its door is open to all Europe's people' – a clear enough indication, according to Hooper, 'that in Washington's view, the US is the host, and maybe the bouncer too' (*Guardian*, 24 May 2002: 2).

Notes

1. Gore Vidal's article is available at http://www.guardian.co.uk; it was also re-published as the first section in his book of essays *Perpetual War for Perpetual Peace* (2002), London: Clairview, re-titled 'September 11, 2001 (A Tuesday)'.
2. On this question, see Ziauddin Sardar and Merryl Wyn Davies, *Why Do People Hate America?* (2003), London: Icon.
3. Edward S. Herman has written a number of books examining US policy and involvement abroad. A useful website is http://www.thirdworldtraveler.com, with articles, books and statements by and about the author.
4. Andrew Wernick, 'Let Freedom Ring: Rebranding America after September 11th', paper given at conference 'Making Sense of 9/11: Teaching American Studies after the Attack on the Twin Towers', University College Winchester, 25 May 2002. Draft essay available at http://www.amatas.org.
5. The Project for the New American Century is also discussed in the conclusion to this book.

HISTORIES

CHAPTER THREE

Jim Crow in Britain in the 1840s and the 1940s

Alasdair Pettinger

Outside South Africa under the apartheid regime in the second half of the twentieth century, systematic racial segregation has been most closely associated with the southern United States, from its introduction in the 1890s until it was gradually dismantled in the wake of the civil-rights movement of the 1950s and 1960s. 'Jim Crow', as it was known, actually emerged in the north in the 1840s, when the term was first used in Massachusetts to refer to the railroad cars reserved for Black passengers. For a century or more, African Americans travelling to Europe often expressed their pleasure at being able – for a time at least – to mingle freely with others in public places.

International condemnation has not prevented 'Jim Crow' exercising its influence beyond the borders of the United States. It has on occasions crossed the Atlantic, when British authorities seemed willing to accommodate the anxieties of those visitors who were fearful of the consequences of racial mixing away from home. This chapter will examine two case studies. Firstly, a much-publicised example of racial discrimination by the Cunard shipping line in the 1840s. Secondly, some responses to the presence of the segregated US army in Britain during World War II. Focusing on the often difficult decisions faced by British politicians, officials and entrepreneurs, these illustrations may help us to identify the conditions under which transatlantic segregation was possible, and the extent to which it was open to challenge. They also contribute to our greater understanding of the export of American socio-political practices to Britain, as a 'negative' version of Americanisation.

Jim Crow on the Cunard line in the 1840s

Instances of segregation on stage coaches and passenger vessels in the US were reported from the 1820s, and the practice was adopted by several railroads built in New England in the 1830s. But it was not until 1841 that the practice was established enough to be given a definite name: 'Jim Crow' – a song and dance routine popularised by the blackface entertainer Thomas Dartmouth Rice – came to be adopted in Massachusetts for the car reserved for Black travellers (Ruchames 1956: 62).

Segregation emerged in response to racial anxieties prompted by the mixing of strangers in urban public spaces where there were significant numbers of free Black people, but especially by the mixing of Black men and white women. The earliest tensions were most keenly felt not in the smoky, all-male environment of the second-class railroad cars but in the more genteel first-class cars in which 'ladies' (white women) travelled (Smith 2002: especially 88–9 and 135–49).

> Consider why, from Jim Crow here up to the bus boycotts of the 1950s in the US South that propelled the Civil Rights movement into a national and international political issue, transport is a critical point for activists. You might explore questions of social mobility and access.

Among the contemporaries who documented the emergence of segregation were the authors of the antebellum slave narratives. Much has been made of the way these narratives 'arose as a reponse to and refutation of claims that Blacks could not write' (Gates 1985: xv). But we might also say that they challenged those who felt they should not be allowed to *travel*: they tell the story of a transformation of the protagonist from one who is moved by others to one who moves of his or her own accord. Many fugitive slave narrators celebrate overcoming restrictions on movement, through their descriptions of clandestine flight, and of victories over segregation in northern cities. But those narratives that told of journeys further afield were able to further taunt their detractors by pointedly dwelling on the pleasures of mixing freely in public places beyond the borders of the United States.

For example, in his second autobiography, *My Bondage and My Freedom*, published in 1855, Frederick Douglass recalls his first trip to Britain ten years previously, touring to promote his first autobiography and to lend his support to the British anti-slavery movement. He quotes from a letter he sent home from Belfast in 1846:

> In the southern part of the United States, I was a slave, thought of and spoken of as property... In the northern states, a fugitive slave, liable to be hunted at any moment, like a felon, and to be hurled into the terrible jaws of slavery – doomed by an inveterate prejudice against color to insult and outrage on every hand [. . .] denied the privileges and courtesies common to others in the use of the most humble means of conveyances – shut out from the cabins on steamboats – refused admission to respectable hotels – caricatured, scorned, scoffed, and maltreated with impunity by any one, (no matter how black his heart,) so he has a white skin. But now behold the change! Eleven days and a half gone, and I have crossed three thousand miles of the perilous deep. Instead of a democratic government, I am under a monarchical government. Instead of the bright, blue sky of America, I am covered with the soft, grey fog of the Emerald Isle. I breathe, and lo! the chattel becomes a man. (Douglass 1969: 370–1; see also Brown 1852: 8–9)

Douglass makes much of the contrast between Great Britain and the United States, setting it up so as to reverse the usual expectations. The monarchy is morally superior to the republic not just because it has abolished slavery, but also because it fully recognises the humanity of its free population.

This 'strategic Anglophilia' (Rice 2003: 180) served an important purpose for the transatlantic anti-slavery movement (winning British support through flattery, North American through shame), although it could only have been convincing if the widespread evidence of racial prejudice in Victorian Britain were conveniently ignored. Some of this prejudice is alluded to (if obliquely) by Douglass himself in his letters, and autobiographies (see e.g. Rice 2003: 172–87), but is addressed most directly in his accounts of his experiences when crossing the ocean on the *Cambria* of the British and North Atlantic Steampacket Company (later known as the Cunard line). On the outward voyage, he found he was barred from dining with other first-class passengers in the saloon; and on the last evening of the voyage he was invited by the captain to deliver a speech on slavery, only to be shouted down by other passengers with a near riot ensuing. Boarding the same vessel in Liverpool two years later, he faced discrimination yet again, as he explained in a letter he wrote to the London *Times*:

Sir, – I take up my pen to lay before you a few facts respecting an unjust proscription by which I find myself subjected on board the steamship Cambria, to sail from this port at 10 o'clock to-morrow morning for Boston, United States.

On the 4th of March last, in company with Mr. George Monbay, of the Hall of Commerce, London, I called upon Mr. Ford, the London agent of the Cunard line of steamers, for the purpose of securing a passage on board the steam ship Cambria to Boston, United States. On inquiring the amount of the passage I was told 40l. 19s [i.e. 40 pounds, 19 shillings, or £40.95]. I inquired further, if a second class passage could be obtained. He answered no, there was but one fare, all distinctions having been abolished. I then gave him 40l. 19s and received from him in return a ticket entitling me to berth No. 72 on board the steam-ship Cambria, at the same time asking him if my colour would prove any barrier to my enjoying all the rights and privileges enjoyed by other passengers. He said, 'No.' I then left the office, supposing all well, and thought nothing more of the matter until this morning, when in company with a few friends, agreeably to public notice, I went on board the Cambria with my luggage, and on inquiring for my berth, found, to my surprise and mortification, that it had been given to another passenger, and was told that the agent in London had acted without authority in selling me the ticket. I expressed my surprise and disappointment to the captain, and inquired what I had better do in the matter. He suggested my accompanying him to the office of the agent in Water Street, Liverpool, for the purpose of ascertaining what could be done. On stating the fact of my having purchased the ticket of the London agent, Mr. McIver (the Liverpool agent) answered that the London agent, in selling me the ticket, had acted without authority, and that I should not go on board the ship unless I agreed to take my meals alone, not to mix with the saloon company, and to give up the berth for which I had paid. Being without legal remedy, and anxious to return to the United States, I have felt it due to my own rights as a man, as well as to the honour and dignity of the British public, to lay these facts before them, sincerely believing that the British public will pronounce a just verdict on such proceedings. I have travelled in this country 19 months, and have always enjoyed equal rights and privileges with other passengers, and it was not until I turned my face towards America that I met anything like proscription on account of my colour. (*The Times* 1847a)

The newspaper takes up his case in an editorial that appeared two days later, expressing its 'disapprobation and disgust at a proceeding wholly repugnant to our English notions of justice and humanity'.

The plain fact of the matter appears to be, that Mr. DOUGLASS being a man of colour, was not allowed to go out on an equal footing with the rest of the passengers on board the Cambria. It signifies very little to us how contemptible the Americans may make themselves by the prejudices they act upon in their own country, and it concerns, perhaps, none but themselves [. . .] We, however, are not in any way bound to tolerate the introduction into this country of any of the degrading peculiarities of society in the United States, nor can we observe with calm indifference any tendency to import among us prejudices utterly at variance with our feelings and character. We therefore do not refrain from expressing our most intense disgust at the conduct of the agents of the Cambria, in having succumbed to a miserable and unmeaning assumption of skin-deep superiority by the American portion of their passengers. (*The Times* 1847b)

A response from Charles Burrop, who describes himself as the US-based 'Head manager of the Cunard Company of Liners', claims that it is not the company that is racially prejudiced – 'the fare of one man is as good as that of another' – but argues that if the majority of its passengers ('particularly of white women') experience 'an absolute and invincible disgust [. . .] to come into close contact with blackamores' to the extent that they would give up their berths, obtain a refund, and sail with a competitor rather than risk such contact, then 'we are compelled by our own interests as a commercial company to place upon the issue of tickets to blacks such restrictions and conditions as were specifically stated to Mr. Douglass' (*The Times* 1847c).

That the newspaper gladly takes up Douglass's assertion of what might be viewed as English exceptionalism suggests how successful his 'strategic Anglophilia' was. But it is also worth noting that the editorial cleverly reworks the sexual and racial rhetoric of 'American' segregation drawn on by Burrop. Against the 'disgust' prompted by mixing, *The Times* expresses 'disgust' at the attempt to prevent it. If in the United States, the duty of white men is to protect white women from the sexual attentions of Black men, on a British ship the duty of the steamship company is to protect Douglass from the intrusive prejudices of American passengers. In failing, the company's masculinity, as it were, is in doubt, as it 'succumbed' to the threat – or, as Douglass put it in a letter to the *Liberator*, 'had not the virtue to resist the demand' (*Liberator* 1847) – and placed the feminised abolitionist in a position of some danger.

Samuel Cunard himself replies next, pointing out that Burrop (whose claim to be connected with the company he refutes) is mistaken, and that this blunt commercial argument is not acceptable. He concludes: 'No-one can regret more than I do the unpleasant circumstances respecting Mr. Douglass's passage; but I can assure you that nothing of the kind will again take place in the steam-ships with which I am connected' (*The Times* 1847c). Cunard's promise to end discrimination – which evidently reassured Douglass (for he warmly commends Cunard's intervention in his autobiography) – proved an empty one. Similar incidents were recorded on his ships until at least the Civil War.

A clue as to why the company was not able to sustain such a principled stand (as Douglass and *The Times* called for) is found in another letter to the paper. Cunard's agent in Liverpool, Charles McIver, argued that the restrictions applied to Douglass were not due to his race, not even to the commercial imperative to pay heed to the prejudices of his fellow passengers. Rather it was prompted by the incident on his outward voyage:

When coming from the United States some months ago in the same vessel, the Cambria, as a steerage passenger, [Douglass] was invited by some of the cabin passengers to enter the saloon, and was the cause, whether intentionally or unintentionally on his part, of producing, by the observations he made use of, serious disturbance on board, which required the authority of the captain to quell, in order to restore peace and safety. Under these circumstances I told Mr. Douglass that had he entered into the arrangements which had been completed, I should undoubtedly have considered it my duty to require of him, before allowing him to embark, a distinct pledge that he would neither of himself, nor at the desire of others, follow such a course as was likely to lead to a repetition of such scenes of confusion as had formerly occurred. I added that, from the conversation that had just taken place between us, it was unnecessary I should act or say more upon the subject. I moreover told him that I should have taken the same course had his name been John Jones, or anything else, instead of Frederick Douglass, or had he been the whitest man in the world. These were my words. (ibid.)

> Consider the complexities of the claims for freedom being made by national practice here: on the one hand the new world of the USA, an independent republic, maintaining slavery and legal racism; on the other, the moral outrage against racial exploitation and segregation of Britain, but with its own imperial and colonial interests to protect and develop.

McIver takes Douglass to task for suppressing this conversation, for this information does complicate the issue. Douglass himself had provided an account of the earlier incident in letters published in the abolitionist press in 1845, where he argued that, having been invited by the captain to address the passengers on the last evening of the voyage, some of them had taken exception to his anti-slavery sentiments, angrily denouncing him as a liar. Although he represents himself as an innocent victim, threatened with being thrown overboard, he does render the tensions of the voyage as an escalating exchange of insults, as if both his supporters and his adversaries were southern 'men of honour' heading for a duel. At any rate, it seems clear that violence was only averted when the 'gallant captain of the ship' threatened to put the 'salt water mobocrats' in irons (Douglass 1969: 366–7).

Jim Crow in Britain during the 1940s

Following the defeat of the Confederacy in the American Civil War, the federal army occupied the south and forced the rebel states to pass legislation allowing Blacks to vote and hold public office, and encouraged the provision of universal education. Nevertheless, customary segregation – which predated the war in some cities – became more, not less, commonplace, as the new Reconstruction governments responded to the exclusions of Blacks from public facilities by promoting the introduction of separate facilities, in order not to overly antagonise whites. With the historic compromise that ended Reconstruction in 1877, southern governments rolled back much of the progressive legislation of the previous decade, and gradually the customary segregation became codified and legally enforced (no doubt partly in response to an increasingly confident Black middle class unwilling to remain 'in their place'). The increasing proliferation of local and state measures were ultimately sanctioned by the Supreme Court decision in *Plessy* v. *Ferguson* (1896), which upheld Louisiana's separate-car law. (Homer Adolph Plessy tested Louisiana segregation laws in 1892 by refusing to move from his seat in a first-class coach. Judge John H. Ferguson rejected his plea that the law was unconstitutional. Plessy's lawyers, supported by the railroad company, took the case to the US Supreme Court, which, however, upheld the original decision by a majority of seven to one). The complex web of segregation legislation that subsequently developed in the south touched almost every aspect of social life, from maternity wards to cemeteries. 'Jim Crow' was the subject of international condemnation, but continued to flourish through the 1950s (see Kennedy 1959).

While the desegregation of the American armed forces began in 1948 – becoming one of the few places of employment for African Americans that afforded some genuine chance of training and advancement – at the time of the entry of the United States in World War II, it was still very much a segregated institution. In 1940, when African Americans made up a tenth of the US population, they represented only 1.5 per cent of the US Army. Political pressure led to the more vigorous recruitment of Blacks, and while this proportion reached 7.4 per cent in 1942 Blacks tended to be allocated service rather than combat roles: drivers, construction workers, cooks, freight handlers, and so on. Furthermore, they were placed in segregated units. There were very few Black officers, and none were in command of white GIs; white officers, however, could command Blacks.

In Britain, US forces grew from 130,000 at the end of 1942 to 1,500,000 by D-Day in June 1944 (of which just under a tenth were Black). Anticipating the tensions that would arise with the arrival of a segregated army into the country, the British government held high-level discussions in 1942 over the official policy to be adopted in relation to the 'American policy of segregation'. Some ministers argued

Figure 1 African American servicemen in Britain, 1940s.

that while this policy was 'the best practical contribution to the avoid-ance of trouble', they nevertheless strongly rejected that 'we ought by any process, visible or invisible, to try to lead our own people to adopt as their own the American social attitude to the American negro; nor should we succeed' (quoted Thorne 1988: 267–8). In the end, however, the Cabinet decided that 'it was desirable that the people of this country should avoid becoming too friendly with coloured troops' (quoted ibid.: 268) and confidential 'Instructions as to the advice which should be given to British Service Personnel' were circulated to senior officers and some newspaper editors (who were asked not to make reference to the existence of the instruction).

This decision effectively endorsed the unofficial notes issued by Major-General Arthur Dowler earlier that year (reprinted in Bousquet and Douglas 1991: 162–5). Dowler was the administrative head of

British Southern Command whose main function was to liaise with US troops in this area. 'Dowler's Notes' – as Smith (1987: 56) points out – could almost have been written by a nineteenth-century southern slave holder. Recommendations include: 'White women should not associate with coloured men' and 'Soldiers should not make intimate friends with them, taking them to cinemas or bars' and 'Avoid such action as would tend to antagonize the white American soldier' (Bousquet and Douglas 1991: 164–5).

So, no official stand was taken by Britain against the racial policies of the US armed forces, which managed to transfer segregation to British soil effectively intact. American commanders provided separate accommodation and canteen facilities in their own camps, and this segregation had ramifications beyond the perimeter fences. Measures were taken by the army to prevent Black and white GIs mixing in neighbouring villages and towns by rotating passes, and local pub and cinema proprietors were encouraged to segregate their facilities, for example. In these ways the social practice of US racial ideology was exported and imposed on largely white Britain.

> Les Back has argued that the correspondence between the practice of the USA, Britain and Germany (that is, Allied and Axis forces alike) worked to confirm a normative whiteness that constructed itself in part via anti-Black racisms, so that there were 'uncomfortable similarities among Jim Crow, John Bull, and the racial phobias of Nazism' (Back 2001: 170). Discuss.

The practical daily consequences of this in civilian life may be gauged in contemporary newspaper accounts, despite wartime censorship. The *Daily Herald* reported that 'coloured American soldiers' in Eye, Suffolk had 'been refused admittance to the town's reading room, which has billiards, ping-pong tables and a dart board, as well as facilities for reading and writing. At the moment they have nowhere to go when off duty' (*Daily Herald* 1942). A British soldier revealed that 'in an English port part of a well-known restaurant is barred to coloured troops' and that his unit was 'instructed . . . not to eat or drink with coloured soldiers' (*New Statesman and Nation* 1942a). In the last month of the war, a meeting of Birmingham City Council discussed a ban imposed by the military authorities on members of the US Women's Army Auxiliary Corps using a particular public baths (*Birmingham Mail* 1945).

If some of these restrictions were imposed by – or under pressure from – the US military authorities, it would be wrong to conclude that they were imposed on a unanimously unwilling public. In Somerset, Mrs May, a vicar's wife, drew up a 'six-point code which would result in the ostracism of American coloured troops if they ever go to the village'. This code, which echoes some of the recommendations made by Dowler, stipulates:

1. If a local woman keeps a shop and a coloured soldier enters, she must serve him, but she must do it as quickly as possible and indicate as quickly as possible that she does not desire him to come there again.
2. If she is in a cinema and notices a coloured soldier next to her, she moves to another seat immediately.
3. If she is walking on the pavement and a coloured soldier is coming towards her, she crosses to the other pavement.
4. If she is in a shop and a coloured soldier enters, she leaves as soon as she has made her purchase or before that, if she is in a queue.
5. White women, of course, must have no social relationship with coloured troops.
6. On no account must coloured troops be invited to the homes of white women. (*Sunday Pictorial* 1942)

Every point of this code – drawn up for a hypothetical eventuality ('if they ever go to the village') – concerns the mixing of Black men and white women, suggesting the significance of the sexual motive behind segregation, the white fear/fantasy of miscegenation. As one journalist was at pains to point out, it was important to understand that the nervousness of the authorities was largely due to the 'feeling of white troops from the "deep South"', who 'take it for granted that it is their duty to interfere if they see black troops with white girls'. He argues that the authorities, in turn, have a duty to 'use every device of persuasion to let white Southern troops know that it is against discipline to treat negro soldiers in a way to which their training and education has accustomed them', but admits that 'discipline and re-education will not work nearly quickly enough'. He concludes that 'very unhappy incidents' will occur for the foreseeable future (*New Statesman and Nation*: 1942a).

One such incident was reported in the same publication the following month. An account of a 'really good dance' at a village hall was followed by reference to a previous occasion, when the band 'contained a

West African'. No one took exception to him while he was on stage, but when he – now referred to as a 'West Indian' – 'took the floor with the wife of one of his colleagues in the band, one of the southern American boys promptly went across the room and struck him' (*New Statesman and Nation*: 1942b). In another episode, some white GIs reacted fiercely when a 'Negro soldier' walked up to the British girl they were talking to and it became clear she was his date. 'One of the white soldiers snatched off his hat and flung it to the ground' (Ottley 1942: 4). In some towns, tensions between Black and white military personnel led to major disturbances, notably in Bamber Bridge, near Preston, in which five soldiers were shot, two of them fatally (Smith 1987: 141–51).

Given that incidents such as this took place, it is not surprising that concern about discipline and public order tended to confirm in the minds of the military authorities the need to separate Black and white US personnel. And British civilians may to some extent have appreciated that segregation – unfair as it was widely perceived to be – had to be tolerated in the interests of military discipline. After all, civilians themselves faced wartime restrictions on their own freedom of speech and movement, and most willingly complied. In that sense, the authorities were in a similar position to the various employees of the Cunard company. If the overriding concern was to avoid conflict on board ship, then they had to risk a practical solution that was unjust but possibly more effective than a more principled stand might have been. And, as with the Cunard line, segregation in World War II had other motivations and excuses too. It was sometimes simply a question of money. Roi Ottley, in Britain as war correspondent for several African American newspapers, reported:

What's true of the United States seems equally true in England: The customer is always right. When the manager of a restaurant was questioned recently about refusing service to a Negro soldier, he had a ready answer. 'White Americans say they will not patronize my place if Negroes were served.' (Ottley 1942: 7)

There is no record of the actual exchange of views in the Birmingham debate over the colour bar imposed on the Kent Street baths, but the conclusion of the Deputy Mayor – who said that 'if military authorities put any place out of bounds the City Council could not put that place in bounds' – may be viewed as a sign of resignation rather than endorsement (*Birmingham Mail* 1945). For 'Jim Crow' was by no means uncritically accepted by the British. The six-point code drawn up by Mrs May in Somerset so shocked her fellow parishioners that 'they told their husbands', and one of them, a local councillor, prepared 'a full statement to be sent to the Ministry of Information'. More importantly, they told the *Sunday Pictorial*, whose reassurances echo those expressed in *The Times* a century before. The article ends:

> *Any coloured soldier who reads this may rest assured that there is no colour bar in this country and that he is as welcome as any other Allied soldier.*
> *He will find that the vast majority of people have nothing but repugnance for the narrow-minded uninformed prejudices expressed by the vicar's wife.*
> *There is – and will be – no persecution of coloured people in Britain.* (*Sunday Pictorial* 1942; italics in original)

And indeed, there were cases of small but heroic cases of resistance to 'the prejudice which certain white soldiers are intent upon imposing', as Ottley was keen to point out. He goes on to tell of an incident in which

> US soldiers boarded a bus in London and tried to eject two Negro soldiers from seats they already occupied.
> 'You can't do that sort of thing here,' a woman conductor protested. 'We won't have it. Either you stand or off you go.'
> They stood. (Ottley 1942: 6–7)

Ottley also refers to the more implicit opposition to Jim Crow that is suggested by the fact that 'every Monday morning the newspapers are filled with reports of Negro activity with the British – such as hikes and picnics. Negroes are seen at churches, groups of them even taking over the choir loft on occasion' (ibid.: 7).

Historians tend to stress the predominantly welcoming attitude of the British. 'I don't mind the Yanks, but I don't care much for the white fellows they've brought with them' was a quip that achieved wide circulation (Reynolds 1995: 303). And official educational programmes suggest that white Americans were not unaware of the need to critically examine their own habits and prejudices. The irony that 'Jim Crow' resembled some of the policies of the fascism the Allies were fighting against was not lost on some. Ottley ends his survey, 'Dixie Invades Britain', with the following overheard conversation:

'Personally,' a town councillor said, 'I have no feeling of race prejudice. I've been led to believe, however, that our relations with American white troops will be better if we conform to what I understand to be American practices of discrimination.'

The answer to that came from a white American officer. 'Discrimination is not American,' he said. 'Even less so today, when we are fighting a war to preserve and extend democratic values in the world.' (Ottley 1942: 8)

> Ottley, who begins his essay with the words 'the noose of prejudice is slowly tightening around the necks of American Negro soldiers' (ibid.: 3), suggests that this exchange 'sums up the situation, tying it in a nice tight knot' (ibid.: 8). Discuss the appropriateness of this lynching metaphor. Could it be said that the different and contested senses of 'American' invoked by the councillor and the officer form strands of a single rope?

Conclusion

These two case studies have examined 'Americanisation' in the form of highly controversial codes regulating public spaces being allowed to take effect in areas beyond the jurisdiction of the United States. By focusing on the way segregationist decisions were made in a local and immediate daily context, it is possible to develop an approach towards 'Americanisation' that avoids trying to make sense of 'Jim Crow in Britain' in terms of the ability of one nation to impose its will on another.

Despite the very different relations of power between Britain and the United States in the 1840s and 1940s, some striking continuities are evident. In each case, the mingling of white and Black Americans in public places was perceived as a potential source of disorder. Wherever they were likely to encounter each other, a wide range of agencies and individuals – from public authorities to those working in the tourist, entertainment and transport sectors – faced difficult decisions: whether to take steps to separate them, by allocating them different spaces or at least different privileges within the same space.

As we have seen, transatlantic segregation was practised unevenly and unpredictably. These decisions took account of a number of factors: the nature of the public space in question (for instance, the availability of resources for containing disorder should it break out), the need to attract future customers (with a certain spending power), knowledge of or assumptions about the character of the individuals concerned, the ideological position and international context, and the existence of official advice, rules and regulations. In any given situation, these factors may have pushed the decision maker towards conflicting courses of action. Where there was a perceived threat of disorder in a place that was hard to police, segregationist practice usually followed. In other cases, British civilians were more likely to stand up and defend the right of African Americans to occupy public spaces on equal terms. The ideal conditions in this case were specific occasions at which hostile white Americans were unlikely to be present (abolitionist meetings, for instance, or private functions to which Black GIs were invited).

The dominant idiom in which direct public statements about segregation were voiced in Britain in both the 1840s and 1940s characterises it as a product of 'American' racial prejudice. Nevertheless, even in the absence of white American soldiers, Black American men still frequently posed a problem for the hosts, especially if they were perceived as mingling too closely with white women. Both Charles Burrop's ventriloquised 'disgust' and Mrs May's six-point code play on the anxieties of *British* readers, even while those who publish their views are at pains to distance themselves from them.

Further reading

Fuller versions of the primary sources quoted here (and others) are included in the web pages on *Jim Crow in Britain* produced in conjunction with the AMATAS project: http://www.bulldozia.com/jimcrow/

Segregation in the United States is the subject of the pioneering study by C. Vann Woodward (1966). Key extracts from this and more recent work by younger scholars may be found in Smith (2002).

Pettinger (2003) offers a more detailed consideration of the experiences of Frederick Douglass and other Black abolitionists crossing the Atlantic in the 1840s and 1850s. For useful background on the mid-century steamship travel across the Atlantic see Hyde (1975) and Babcock (1931).

Smith (1987) is the only book-length study of the impact of the segregated US army on Britain in World War II, but readers unfamiliar with the period may benefit from the wider context provided by Reynolds (1995).

Back (2001) and McKay (forthcoming, chs 2 and 3) consider the place of jazz and dance in the construction of whiteness and blackness during the twentieth century in Britain.

Bibliography

Babcock, F. Lawrence (1931), *Spanning the Atlantic*, New York: Knopf.

Back, Les (2001), 'Syncopated synergy: dance, embodiment, and the call of the jitterbug', in Vron Ware and Les Back, *Out of Whiteness: Colour, Politics and Culture*, London: University of Chicago Press, pp. 169–95.

Birmingham Mail (1945), 'Colour bar: use of the city's amenities', 15 May.

Bousquet, Ben and Colin Douglas (1991), *West Indian Women at War: British Racism in World War II*, London: Lawrence and Wishart.

Brown, William Wells (1852), *Three Years in Europe; or, Places I Have Seen and People I Have Met*, London: Charles Gilpin.

Daily Herald (1942), 'Dance ban on coloured troops', 7 September.

Douglass, Frederick [1855] (1969), *My Bondage and My Freedom*, New York: Dover.

Gates, Henry Louis, Jr (1985), 'Introduction: The Language of Slavery', in Charles T. Davis and Henry Louis Gates, Jr (eds), *The Slave's Narrative*, Oxford and New York: Oxford University Press, pp. xi–xxxiv.

Hyde, Francis (1975), *Cunard and the North Atlantic, 1840–1973*, London: Macmillan.

Kennedy, Stetson (1959), *Jim Crow Guide to the U.S.A.*, London: Lawrence and Wishart.

Liberator (1847), 30 April.

McKay, George (forthcoming), *Circular Breathing: The Cultural Politics of Jazz in Britain*, Durham, NC: Duke University Press.

New Statesman and Nation (1942a), 'A London Diary', 22 August.

New Statesman and Nation (1942b), 'A London Diary', 19 September.

Ottley, Roi (1942), 'Dixie Invades Britain', *Negro Digest*, 2:1, 3–8.

Pettinger, Alasdair (2003), '"At Sea – Coloured Passenger"', in Bernhard Klein and Gesa Mackenthun (eds), *Sea Changes: Historicizing the Ocean*, New York and London: Routledge, pp. 149–66.

Reynolds, David (1995), *Rich Relations: The American Occupation of Britain, 1942–1945*, London: HarperCollins.

Rice, Alan (2003), *Radical Narratives of the Black Atlantic*, London: Continuum.

Ruchames, Louis (1956), 'Jim Crow Railroads in Massachusetts', *American Quarterly*, 8:1, 61–75.

Smith, Graham (1987), *When Jim Crow Met John Bull: Black American Soldiers in World War II in Britain*, London: I. B. Tauris.

Smith, John David (ed.) (2002), *When Did Southern Segregation Begin?*, Boston and New York: Bedford/St Martin's.

Sunday Pictorial (1942), 'Vicar's wife insults our allies', 6 September.

Thorne, Christopher (1988), 'Britain and the Black GI's: Racial Issues and Anglo-American Relations in 1942', in *Border Crossings: Studies in International History*, Oxford: Basil Blackwell, pp. 259–74.

The Times (1847a), 6 April.

The Times (1847b), 8 April.

The Times (1847c), 13 April.

Woodward, C. Vann (1966), *The Strange Career of Jim Crow*, 2nd ed., New York: Oxford University Press.

CHAPTER FOUR

The White Ship *Titanic* and the Transatlantic Imagination: Imperial, National and Racial Perspectives on the Disaster in Film and History

Alan Rice

> There was tension between American ownership and British man-agement of [*Titanic*] and other ships, and nationality of owner-ship itself was ambiguously layered, company within company. Two sets of owners, two main lists of nationals on board, two post-sinking inquiries, two cultures claiming the tragedy: Titanic sailed and sank as an Anglo-American event with all the ambiva-lencies that arose.
>
> John Wilson Foster, *The Titanic Complex* (1997: 35)

This chapter is concerned with exploring and interrogating transat-lantic issues of imperial, national and racial power, culture and identity. It is focused on what was, and still is, resonantly, a traumatic moment in transatlantic sea crossing, the Anglo-American experience of the *Titanic* ship-sinking disaster of April 1912. The boat struck an iceberg at 11.40 on the night of the fourteenth and at 2.20 the following morning the ship's stern sank into the sea. Only 705 people were rescued and 1,503 others went down with the ship. This chapter looks at the his-torical narrative as well as at cultural representations, in particular film revisions of the event.

Figure 2 The *Titanic* Memorial in Liverpool.

The *Titanic* as symbol of imperial shift

On the dockside at Liverpool stands a grand memorial to those engineers and merchant seamen (many of them from the city) who had died in the great *Titanic* disaster. Liverpool, the city where the ship was registered, felt her loss as greatly as Belfast, where she was built, and Southampton, from where she set sail. The memorial, an obelisk with carvings of seamen at its base, was not erected until 1916 so it was made to function as a memorial also to those merchant seamen who had already died in the First World War. The memorial exemplifies the interconnectedness of the civil and military marine in the British formation of imperial power. According to such a narrative RMS *Titanic* was as British and hence almost as laden with patriotic and imperial signifiers as any royal naval ship. At the beginning of the twentieth century this British imperial power was at its zenith. A large proportion of the world was painted red in school atlases, thus illustrating British imperial reach into Asia, Africa, the Americas and Australasia. Hence it is little wonder that at this point in the narrative of the British Empire many contemporary commentators highlighted the phenomenon of the construction of gargantuan vessels (with record-breaking dimensions) to service the transatlantic shipping lines as proof positive of the power and global reach of the British state. Furthermore, their symbolic, classically inspired, grandiose naming – *Titanic* and *Olympic* – seemed also to highlight this imperial might. In the construction yards of the Harland and Wolff shipbuilding company in Belfast, where they were built, the ships towered over the workers who built them, making them appear as tiny ants in comparison to the mighty machines they serviced. The *Titanic* was in fact the largest vessel yet to be built, at the time 'the earth's largest moving manufactured object' (Foster 1997: 55); as John Wilson Foster further comments:

> She was the height of an eleven-storey (high rise) building, her rudder was the height of a house, her length a sixth of a mile. She housed the largest steam engines ever built, before or since; three million rivets went into her hull . . . Combining the statistical superlatives of her dimensions with her innovations in technology and fittings, we see clearly that the *Titanic* was a remarkable product of modernity. (ibid.: 80)

It is little wonder that the *Titanic*, built at the heart of the Empire using the industrial and technological strengths that had contributed to the rapid growth of British power, symbolised for many that Empire's enduring strength and seemed to presage an imperium on which the sun would never set. However, such a simplistic nationalistic narrative to the construction of the ship is undermined by any investigation of its ownership. Far from her portraying the strength of the British imperium, what the *Titanic* actually symbolised was the growing influence of American capital.

There was a subtle change of shift on the bridge of the world capitalist ship in favour of the Americans that had come to fruition in 1902, when control of the White Star Line passed from British into American hands through the machinations of the American financier J. P. Morgan; so that despite the *Titanic*'s appearance as a British ship with British officers and flying a British flag she was absolutely under American financial control. The effective owner of the *Titanic* was the International Mercantile Marine Company, which had eight American directors on its thirteen-man board. Moreover, it operated under seagoing rules drawn up not in Britain but in the United States. Yet, as Michael Davie asserts, the 'appearance of control stayed firmly in Britain' (Davie 1999: 8–9). So firmly in fact that Lord Mersey, the chairman of the Board of Trade inquiry, was visibly shocked to find out the extent of American control (ibid.: 8). So too was the novelist Joseph Conrad, who, in the wake of the disaster, was mortified to discover that British seamen involved would have to answer for their actions at an American inquiry as well as at that of the British Board of Trade. He states the case rhetorically:

> Why an officer of the British merchant service should answer the questions of any king, emperor, autocrat, or senator of any foreign power (as to an event in which a British ship alone was concerned, and which did not even take place in the territorial waters of that power) passes my understanding. (Quoted in Foster 1997: 35)

Obviously, Conrad had not been paying attention to the visible ownership of transatlantic liners. For Morgan himself was highly visible at the launch in Belfast and in deference to its transatlantic provenance the ship on this occasion flew not only the 'British Red Ensign' but 'also the American Stars and Stripes' (Macquitty 1991: 22).

A Night to Remember: a British film version of the disaster

Such a transatlantic sharing of the laurels for her construction is not depicted in the film version of Walter Lord's *A Night to Remember*

(1958), wherein the launch is constructed as an imperial moment with the British flag foregrounded and no American guiding presence imaged. Such a reconstruction suited the nationalist ideology of the film, which portrayed a Britain with its Empire still buoyant at least until the *Titanic* met her doom. With the British character actor Kenneth More playing Officer Lightoller as a no-nonsense, stiff-upper lip representative of British pluck in the face of adversity, the film could be mistaken for a didactic account avoiding the troubling transatlantic discursive dynamic that questions of ownership might have foregrounded. The key scene happens when, with the *Titanic* sunk, Lightoller orders some surviving crew and passengers on an upturned boat to pull themselves together, and there is the authentic voice of British calmness in adversity, evidently to be contrasted with earlier scenes of (apparently un-British) panic. However, the film does exhibit a transatlantic dynamic that exemplifies the changing structure of global power relations. As Thomas Andrews, the ship's Ulster-born engineer, advises a married couple of their best route to salvation when the ship founders, he is placed in a *mise-en-scène* directly in front of an oil painting hanging in the *Titanic* lounge. This painting is called *The Approach to the New World*, and it depicts New York harbour with small boats and tugs and the Statue of Liberty. Quintessentially an American dreamscape of hopes and possibilities, its juxtaposition here with the constructor of the foundering ship foregrounds the message of American futures as the British Empire fades away with its sinking ship.

Before the ship actually sailed, however, owners and builders talked of joint transatlantic triumphs that included lauding a transatlantic relationship 'of British technology and American capital' that foreshadowed the transfer of world leadership from the British to the Americans (Davie 1999: 9). Far from delineating British imperial might, the development of prestige liners by the shipping companies exemplified the British need for American capital to fund its grandiosity. Lord Salisbury, the English Tory peer, railed against this transfer of control and noted how it presaged the economic energy and leadership from across the Atlantic that was to establish the twentieth century as 'the American century'. In a letter to his son-in-law in 1902 he lamented: 'It is very sad, but I am afraid America is bound to forge ahead and nothing can restore the equality between us' (Roberts 1999: 50). If America controlled the greatest vessels on the high seas despite a flagged appearance to the contrary, propagandists for these vessels looked for a new internationalist, yet still xenophobic, language to welcome these ships. At the official launch of RMS *Titanic* in 1911 the language of

Anglo-Saxon triumphalism was pervasive. Such triumphalism was partly puffery in response to the gathering threat to Anglo-Saxon power from the Teutonic Germans; however, the racial underpinnings of transnational English-speaking imperialism are not far from the surface. First, a Mr J. Shelley, representing the owners of the ship, was reported as commenting:

> It seemed to him that as the year passed and the conditions of life changed, the Anglo-Saxon nations became more closely united as a result of such co-operation as was indicated by the building of ships like the *Titanic* and the *Olympic*, which promoted intercourse between the mighty Republic in the West and the United Kingdom. ('The Genius of the Anglo-Saxon' 1999: 254)

In reply, for the shipbuilders, Harland and Wolff, Mr Saxon J. Payne went even further, promoting a white transatlantic racial alliance whose exclusionist racialist dynamic is dynamically foregrounded. The *Belfast Telegraph* reports him as saying that

> he did not recognise any distinctions between the various sections of the Anglo-Saxon race, and they looked upon the building of the *Titanic* and the *Olympic* as a great Anglo-Saxon triumph . . . The two vessels were pre-eminent examples of the vitality and the progressive instincts of the Anglo-Saxon race, and he did not see anything which need give them alarm for the future. As a race they were young and strong and vigorous, and by what it had done in assisting the White Star line in its great and commendable enterprise Belfast could lay claim to no small share in the prosperity of the British Empire. (ibid.: 255)

It was not only at the ship's launch that the promoters of the *Titanic* let their enthusiasm effuse. Promotional literature distributed by the White Star Line in 1911 continued to laud their 'Leviathan' ships, which embodied 'the latest developments in modern propulsion' ('The Progress of the Race' 1999: 256) as symbolic of Anglo-Saxon ingenuity and mercantile and technological achievement. The promotional booklet continues its puffery thus:

> The *Olympic* and *Titanic* are not only the largest vessels in the World; they represent the highest attainments in Naval Architecture and Marine Engineering; they stand for the pre-eminence of

the Anglo-Saxon race on the Ocean; for the 'Command of the Seas' is fast changing from a Naval to a Mercantile idea, and the strength of a maritime race is represented more by its instruments of commerce and less by its weapons of destruction than was formerly supposed. Consequently these two Leviathans add enormously to the potential prosperity and progress of the race. (ibid.: 256–7)

Through such material the White Star Line sought to inculcate its own commercial needs as central to the promotion of white imperial hegemony on both sides of the Atlantic. Out of their own mouths, both the manufacturers and owners of the *Titanic* establish her launch and her subsequent promotion as key to the development of a racialist, imperialist ideology based at the interface of transatlantic travel and technology. Even after the *Titanic* sank appeals were made on the basis of racial exclusion rather than transcendental humanism. A representative of the American Women's Titanic Memorial Fund from the state of Georgia declared: 'Our women can not but appreciate that the memorial is one of, not only national significance, but it will stand for one of the greatest expressions of Anglo-Saxon heroism the world has known' (quoted in Biel 1996: 35).

This discourse of Anglo-Saxon heroism was not all-pervasive: chauvinistic claims were heard on both sides of the Atlantic especially in the wake of the disaster, when the British and American responses exhibited a visceral xenophobia. The epigraph to this chapter, from John Wilson Foster, charts the background to this outbreak of discursive hostilities. All the rhetoric of Anglo-Saxon racial solidarity that accompanied her launch could not survive the sinking. For the American press, and in particular the Hearst newspapers, the Englishman J. Bruce Ismay, the chairman of the White Star Line and a survivor of the wreck, was chief villain, and his nationality was symptomatic to jingoistic journalists who ignored American ownership of the vessel to blame him as the English manager of the company. According to the *San Francisco Examiner*, 'he must be glad he is an Englishman. He is no gladder than we are' (quoted in Biel 1996: 72). The *Denver Post* contrasted his English cowardice with the legendary heroism of the dead American millionaire, John Jacob Astor, who was probably the *Titanic*'s most famous victim: 'Is it better to be a living Ismay or a dead Astor?' it asked (quoted in Biel 1996: 72). Such rhetoric continued despite uncontested testimony that Ismay had helped many onto the lifeboats before finally taking a berth himself.

Titanic: an American film version of the disaster

Ironically, such xenophobically fuelled debate over responsibility for the disaster has survived as an engine for the discursive terrain of 'Titanic' until the present and informs the nationalist pro-American ideology of James Cameron's eponymous 1997 film. This Hollywood blockbuster tells the story of the ship's sinking through the upstairs/downstairs romance of the proletarian, world-travelling American Jack Dawson and the middle-class English woman Rose Dewitt Bukaker, engaged to the immensely rich Cal Hockley. Their relationship breaks the taboos of transatlantic bourgeois society which the ship's social and architectural structure represents by the rigid class divide that separates them into first and third class. Some of the dialogue, characterisations and plot developments that lead to the lovers' *dénouement* highlight the partiality of Cameron's film despite its high-cost striving for verisimilitude.

This is at its most glaring in the characterisation of Second Officer Charles Lightoller, who had epitomised imperial British pluck in *A Night to Remember*. If that had been in tune with a slightly xenophobic pro-British ideology, Cameron's depiction of him as pompous and out of his depth in dealing with loading the lifeboats underpins an anti-British bias that pervades the film. As male passengers try to push forward to indiscriminately load a boat, Lightoller raises his gun and shouts in a plummy English voice, 'Get back, I say, or I'll shoot you all like dogs.' Cameron wants to emphasise this voice as that of a backward-looking empire in comparison to the new American imperium, which is exemplified in the multi-ethnic voices of the third-class American-bound passengers like the Italian Fabrizio, the Irishman Tommy Ryan and the homegrown American son of the soil Jack Dawson. It is particularly disturbing that Cameron emphasises Lightoller's panicking, as most accounts, including the depositions to both the British and American inquiries, have him as keeping remarkably calm despite the panic of the passengers around him. Proof of this comes in his managing to load all the boats under his command with women and children passengers as ordered, whilst only loading one male passenger (a yachtsman to aid the one seaman in No. 6 boat) (Lord 1956: 90).

The new American imperium that Cameron's film promotes as following on the British disaster of the *Titanic* reaches its apotheosis in the scene in which Bukaker, the English wife-to-be of an American millionaire, renames herself Rose Dawson after her proletarian lover Jack Dawson, as the *Carpathia* (the ship that picked up the *Titanic* survivors) steams into Manhattan harbour. She literally remakes herself – escaping the slavery of her English bourgeois name and the marriage she was making to save it. This is done with the Statue of Liberty as background, suggesting the eclipse of British monarchical capitalism in the new democratic American century. *A Night to Remember*, in its seascape which Thomas Andrews is standing in front of, hinted at such changes; *Titanic*, true to its America-first ideology, revels in them. Cameron *does* use a scene of Andrews in front of a similar seascape in *Titanic*'s final minutes; however, the viewer cannot make out the details of the painting. Cameron much prefers to foreground the real statue after the disaster to relate his narrative of American aggrandisement.

> The Statue of Liberty appears in both *A Night to Remember* (1958) and *Titanic* (1997). Consider the use of this (French-donated) American icon in either or both of these films, as well as in other cultural texts, in order to interrogate its various symbolic and ideological meanings.

Nowhere is this more apparent than in the mention (for that is all it is) of the *Titanic*'s construction in the film. Fabrizio, the Italian steerage passenger, riles Tommy Ryan, the stock Irish character, by describing the ship as 'English'. Ryan replies: 'It's an Irish ship. . . . It was built in Ireland, 15,000 Irishmen built this ship – solid as a rock, big Irish hands.' This lauding of Irish workerist values conforms to Cameron's mythology of Irish ethnicity as being a crucial part of the melting pot that makes up the American ethnic kaleidoscope. However, it wilfully ignores the fact that the ship's construction in Ireland might hardly be praised by a southern Irishman like Ryan, as the boat was built by the almost wholly Unionist workforce in the sectarian Harland and Wolff shipyards in Belfast, by workers who would have labelled themselves Ulstermen, British and proud of it. It was workers owing allegiance to the British crown and gaining relatively decent wages, protected from the competition of an Irish Catholic peasantry by a sectarianism that meant the overwhelming majority of the workforce were Protestant, who had lovingly built the ship. Amongst Irish Nationalists, the ship was associated so much with the Protestant pro-British ascendancy that it became symbolic of the ties of Ulster to the British, leading to outrageous myths such as that 'the registration number of Titanic if held up to a mirror revealed the slogan "No Pope"' (Foster 1997: 77). Cameron elides this important history and fundamentally alters the narrative of the building of the ship because it does not suit his retrospective inclusivist agenda, which wants to see a united peasantry desiring to jump ship from the imperial home country to the upstart American state.

The film's manufactured multinational, democratic vision reaches its finale when Rose Calvert (formerly Dawson) looking back from 1996 imagines the *Titanic* passengers alive again, but no longer separated by class and ethnic divides, all milling together in the ballroom of the ship. Never possible under the old class rigidities exemplified by Britain and its Empire, this is now possible, in a modern world brought about by the triumph of American democratic values. Of course, as detailed earlier, the ship with all her faults and foibles was in fact American owned, a fact that Cameron's film, like Roy Baker's before him, chooses to gloss over. Whilst the latter wants to avoid this uncomfortable fact to wallow in the ship's and her crew's last-ditch imperial glory, the former's selectivity with the facts is because he wants to gloat in Britain's imperial class-ridden demise, seemingly exemplified by the ship's sinking under the tutelage of a forever tea-drinking, vacillating captain struck dumb and into inaction by the immensity of the disaster. Never before in cinema has the mere act of drinking a cup of tea been laden with such negativity. Captain Smith's lemon-infected cup is given more airtime than any act of heroism by his crew. The quintessentially British pastime of taking tea is code here surely for the effeteness of late imperialism.

Of course, Cameron is reacting as much to events after the disaster as the sinking itself in his revisionist account. For in the wake of the calamity there were many attempts to foreground the event as being a disaster of which the British should be proud. Smith was lauded in such accounts for having gone down with his ship and music hall songs in his and his ship's honour were published and sung throughout the Empire. These songs often included the supposed final words of the Captain to his men that they should 'be British'.

'Be British,' was the cry as the ship went down,
Everyman was steady at his post,
Captain and crew when they knew the worst
Saving the women and children first
'Be British,' is the cry to everyone . . . (*Sing the Titanic* 1993)

This imperial national arrogance is easy to lampoon and Cameron does so through his depiction of a class-ridden ship of state, steaming to disaster, crewed by rule-based automatons unable to react quickly enough to save the maximum number of passengers. In such a reading, their supposed patriotic heroism is retrospectively accorded to them by a British imperium looking for solace from a disaster that showed the sun was setting on the Empire. Of course, such a reading is particularly tenable for Cameron as it allows him to ignore the consequences of the actual capitalist American imperium the ship represents and to construct his mythology of a foundational transnational peasantry that will emerge in the wake of the disaster to help form a new, seemingly classless, American hegemony. To construct such a narrative from the wreck of the *Titanic*, as I have shown, Cameron distorts the history of the ship's Ulster construction and elides its actual American ownership. What Peter Middleton and Tim Woods have called the 'Titanic history archive' (2001: 522) is salvaged by Cameron but used for narrow nationalist ends.

> A *Night to Remember* (1958) and *Titanic* (1997) promote different ide-
> ological agendas which mean that at times they seem to be narrating dif-
> ferent disasters. Describe these alternative narratives using specific
> examples of characterisation, plot, *mise-en-scène*, etc.

African-American counter-narratives of the disaster

The hubris of James Cameron's adaptation of the *Titanic* legend is satirised most vehemently in an African American response to the film. In Spike Lee's *The Original Kings of Comedy* (2000), for instance, one of the comedians tells a *Titanic* gag. He asks the audience to imagine a *Titanic* peopled by blacks. Would they have stood back and gone down with the ship? Would the black band have kept playing as the ship sank? No, they'd have 'unplugged those speakers' and headed away from that doomed gig. Would the absence of lifeboats have held them back? Hell no, they'd have upturned tables, turned napkins into sails and saved their 'goddam' black asses. As he tells the joke, the comedian mimes their life-saving actions, which is a direct contrast to the torpor depicted in Cameron's film in the immediate aftermath of the collision with the (white) iceberg.

This extended joke, like African American vernacular responses to the disaster ever since the sinking, exemplifies a cynical, anti-heroic, anti-romantic retelling of the narrative, which provides a counter-weight to both imperial British aggrandisement and romanticised notions of America's emerging leadership of the western world. They exhibit a subaltern take on the sinking that critiques white hegemony on both sides of the Atlantic. As such they have provided counter-narratives that foreground the Atlantic as site of a continual racial exclusionism under both British imperial power and American mercantile ownership. An early version of this comes in the African American blues singer Leadbelly's song 'Titanic', which relates the legend that Jack Johnson, the black heavyweight champion of the world, was refused passage on the ship by the British authorities, not wanting to upset the American passengers by having an African American on board. Captain Smith, in this narrative, is a racist, keeping his ship lily white in accordance with early twentieth-century racist ideology in the pay of the aptly named White Star Line. Leadbelly sings:

> Jack Johnson wanted to ge on boa'd;
> Captain Smith hollered, 'I ain' haulin' no coal.'
> Cryin', 'Fare thee Titanic, fare thee well!' (Leadbelly 1998: 814)

Thus when the disaster happens Johnson is safe at home, able to dance to his heart's content: Leadbelly sings:

> Jack Johnson heard the mighty shock,
> Might 'a' seen the black rascal doing th' Eagle Rock
> Cryin', 'Fare thee, Titanic, fare thee well!'

> Black man oughta shout for joy,
> Never lost a girl or either a boy.
> Cryin', 'Fare thee, Titanic, fare thee well!' (ibid.: 815)

The transatlantic Jim Crow response to Johnson's attempt to sail is seen to have its consequence in the sinking of the racially exclusionist ship; almost a divine retribution for the racist ideologies that permeated Anglo-American cultures in the early twentieth century and before. In the dreamscape of Leadbelly's song there is justice for the racists; however, it, like Cameron's film, is based in part on mythology. There is no extant contemporary account of Johnson being refused passage, let alone that Smith himself was instrumental in the deed. However, the song does speak to a history of Jim Crow exclusions and humiliations of famous African Americans on transatlantic ships that extends back to Frederick Douglass on his trips to and from Britain in 1845 and 1847 (as Alasdair Pettinger shows in Chapter 3; see also Pettinger 1999). Also, the *Titanic* was predominantly white, having only one black family on board, the Laroches, and they were Haitians boarded in Cherbourg. Leadbelly did not know of this family as their presence has only recently been uncovered (see Miller 2000). His song then is best seen as outlining not a historical truth, but a crucial African American perspective on a mythology from which British and American myth makers had sought to exclude a black perspective.

Probably the most famous African American perspective on the disaster comes in the oral poems known as 'toasts' still told today in working-class African American communities. These take the Leadbelly line on the sinking and go further. I outline in full the meanings of the many versions of these oral narratives in *Radical Narratives of the Black Atlantic* (Rice 2003). In the context of competing national myths the toasts provide a counter-narrative that emphasises the hubris of ideologies of racial superiority that often underpin such structures. A version told in 1964 in Jefferson City, Mississippi relates as they all do how the black stoker Shine emerges to warn the captain that the famously 'unsinkable' ship is in trouble:

> They tell me on board was a fellow called Shine,
> he was so dark he changed the world's mind.
> Shine came up from the bottom deck below,
> he said, 'Captain, there's water runnin' all in the firebox door,
> and I believe this big motherfucker's gonna overflow.'
> Captain said, 'Shine,' say, 'You go back down,
> I got forty horsepower to keep the water pumped down.'
> Shine went down and came up with a teacup in his hand,
> He said, 'Look here captain,' says, 'I'm a scared man.
> 'I'd rather be out there on that iceberg goin' around and 'round
> than to be on this raggedy motherfucker when it's goin' down.'
> (Jackson 1974: 187)

Shine counterblasts the idea of the technological superiority of the *Titanic*, showing how she is just as vulnerable to natural disaster as any other man-made object. Shine might be the lowest of the low on board ship, a stoker, but he has a wisdom the captain lacks. He turns on their head the usual hierarchies in the myth of the *Titanic*, describing her in the black vernacular and without reverence as 'this big motherfucker'.

He is literally the African American 'so dark he changed the world's mind' as he intervenes in the myth-making of the *Titanic* to give the bottom-up perspective. In introducing his story African Americans are able to subvert the dominating myths of the Anglo-Americans as they revel in their own mythical hero. Not the plucky British captain or officer with his stiff upper lip of the British 1910s and 1950s, nor the romanticised democratic mass of the American 1990s, but an amoral black masculine superhero functioning to outline desperate possibilities for African Americans in a racist world. In this counter-myth even Biblical stories are turned on their head as Shine swims away from the doomed ship:

> Shine took an overhand stroke
> that carried him five miles from that sinkin' boat.
> Up popped a whale with a slimy ass,
> say, 'You a long time coming, but you here at last.'
> Shine said, 'You swallowed old Jonah and spit him on dry land,
> but you'll never swallow me 'cause I'm a hell of a man.'
> (ibid.: 187)

Such a subaltern repositioning means that African Americans, through their retelling of the *Titanic* myth, posit themselves as the unlikely heroes of the disaster. This is emphasised by the radical atheism in the perspective on the final hymn sung on the *Titanic* as she sinks, later in the same toast:

> Folks on the land were singin' 'Nearer my God to thee,'
> The sharks in the ocean were singin', 'Bring your ass to me.'
> (ibid.: 188)

In conclusion, the *Titanic* myth, thus, is a tangled web of national, racial and imperial ideologies, where maybe there is as much 'truth' to be found in the most fantastical and least realistic of the versions as in those that promote themselves as being the height of verisimilitude.

All of the responses discussed in this essay could be said to seek to confine an international disaster to domestic national agendas. Does the persistence of nationalist interpretation into post-1945 texts about the disaster indicate that globalisation is not as powerful as many cultural critics contend? Discuss with reference to British, American and African American nationalist responses to the *Titanic*.

Bibliography

Biel, Steven (1996), *Down with the Old Canoe: A Cultural History of the Titanic*, New York: W. W. Norton.

Davie, Michael [1986] (1999), 'The Starting Point', in John Wilson Foster (ed.), *Titanic*, Harmondsworth: Penguin, pp. 5–9.

Foster, John Wilson (1997), *The Titanic Complex*, Vancouver: Belcouver Press.

'The Genius of the Anglo-Saxon' [1911] (1999), *Belfast Telegraph*, 1 June 1911, in John Wilson Foster (ed.), *Titanic*, Harmondsworth: Penguin, pp. 254–5.

Jackson, Bruce (1974), *Get Your Ass in the Water and Swim Like Me: Narrative Poetry from Black Oral Tradition*, Cambridge, MA: Harvard University Press.

Leadbelly (aka Huddie Ledbetter) [1948] (1998), 'Titanic', in Patricia Liggins Hill (ed.), *Call and Response: The Riverside Anthology of the African American Literary Tradition*, New York: Houghton Mifflin, pp. 814–15.

Lord, Walter [1956] (1976), *A Night to Remember*, Harmondsworth: Penguin.

Macquitty, William [1991] (1999), 'A Launch to Remember', in John Wilson Foster (ed.), *Titanic*, Harmondsworth: Penguin, pp. 21–2.

Middleton, Peter and Tim Woods (2001), 'Textual Memory: The Making of the Titanic's History Archive', *Textual Practice*, 15:3, 507–25.

Miller, Sabrina L. (2000), 'A museum exhibit reveals what many don't know – a black family was on board', *Chicago Tribune*, February 20.

A Night to Remember (1958), dir. Roy J. Baker, Arthur Rank Organisation.

The Original Kings of Comedy (2000), dir. Spike Lee, Forty Acres and A Mule.

Pettinger, Alasdair (1999), 'Send Back the Money: Douglass and the Free Church of Scotland', in Alan J. Rice and Martin Crawford (eds), *Liberating Sojourn: Frederick Douglass and Transatlantic Reform*, Athens, GA: University of Georgia Press.

'The Progress of the Race' [1911] (1999), in John Wilson Foster (ed.), *Titanic*, Harmondsworth: Penguin, pp. 256–7.

Rice, Alan (2003), *Radical Narratives of the Black Atlantic*, London: Continuum.

Roberts, Andrew (1999), *Salisbury: Victorian Titan*, London: Phoenix.

Sing the Titanic (1993), Liverpool: Rare Comic and Curious Records.

Titanic (1997), dir. James Cameron, Twentieth Century Fox.

CULTURAL GEOGRAPHIES

The Transatlantic Seaside from the 1880s to the 1930s: Blackpool and Coney Island

John K. Walton

J. B. Priestley's oft-cited survey of the English provinces, conducted in 1933, had this to say about Blackpool:[1]

> It is not, in my opinion, as good as it used to be. There are various reasons for this. One of them is that like all originators it has suffered from the mere passing of time, during which time others have been able to follow its example . . . There is, however, another and better reason . . . From the few glimpses I have had of the place since the war, I gather the impression that it lacks some of its old genuine gaiety. Its amusements are becoming too mechanised and Americanised. Talkies have replaced the old roaring variety turns. Gangs of carefully drilled young men and women (with nasal accents), employed by the music publishers to 'plug' their 'Hot Broadway Hits', have largely replaced the pierrots and nigger minstrels. The entertainers are more calculating, their shows more standardised, and the audiences more passive. It has developed a pitiful sophistication – machine-made and not really English – that is much worse than the old hearty vulgarity . . . [in the days of the 'energetic old Blackpool', the visitors] had enjoyed, rapturously enjoyed, their Blackpool, and had never once insulted its breezy majesty by singing about their 'blues'. In those days you

did not sing the woes of distant Negroes, probably reduced to such misery by too much gin or cocaine. You sang about dear old Charlie Brown and his pals, and the girls, those with their curly curls. These songs were nonsense too, but they were our own silly innocent nonsense and not another country's jaded weary nonsense; they had a fresh lilting quality, and expressed high spirits not low spirits. The Blackpool that sang about Charlie Brown and the girls with their curly curls was the Mecca of a vulgar but alert and virile democracy. I am not so sure about the new Blackpool of the weary negroid ditties. It would not be difficult, I feel, to impose an autocracy upon young people who sound as tired as that.

We could devote a lot of space to deconstructing this text. Leaving aside the lazy racism, which has additional power to shock when presented so casually in the work of a populist liberal champion of the 'common people',[2] there are plenty of reasons for setting it aside as irrelevant to our understanding of American influences on British popular culture in this most emblematic of settings. Apart from anything else, there was nothing distinctive about the racism: attacks on African American and Jewish contributions to the popular music industry, with clear racist content, were in any case commonplaces of contemporary critiques of a more widespread perceived Americanisation of British popular culture at this time.[3] Priestley hangs his cultural critique on a brief overnight visit to an empty November Blackpool, where the only person he talks to is (perhaps significantly) the barman in his hotel's American bar, who is gently mocked for taking his 'trade of cocktail-shaking' so seriously as to make a tour to assess the comparative state of the trade in different parts of the country: he might have been 'a favourite disciple of Dr [Samuel] Smiles', the great Victorian proponent of self-help. Assiduity in such a trivial cause does not impress Priestley, who does not need it himself as ballast for his strong views on Blackpool: he tells us that his reading of its cultural transformation is based on having '[known] it before the war and . . . seen something of it since', and admits that 'I have never actually been in Blackpool at the crazy height of its season'.[4] But this admitted lack of direct knowledge and experience did not inhibit Priestley from putting forward an articulate, rhetorical critique which was embedded in one of the most influential and enduring texts on the 'condition of England' in the inter-war years; and we need to treat its consequences, if not its content, with respect.

As Britain's most popular resort, a status that went back to mid-Victorian times; as a symbol of the amiable excesses of northern working-class enjoyment; and as a pleasure town of mushroom growth whose ferocious enterprise and grid-plan layout led contemporaries to assume that there was something 'American' about it, Blackpool was an obvious place to look for, and fear, early evidence of that American incursion into British popular culture that was later to become identified with local manifestations of 'globalisation', 'McDonaldisation' and 'McDisneyfication'.[5] What Priestley describes is, indeed, entirely compatible with an anticipation of such concepts. That Disney never got (nor, in fairness, sought) a real foothold in Blackpool, despite the corporation's agreement with Disney in 1952 for exclusive use of the firm's characters in the autumn Illuminations in return for free publicity for Disney films, and despite the efforts of an impressively powerful consortium, led by circus proprietors Billy and Ronald Smart, to get Disney endorsement for a proposed (but aborted) Blackpool version of Disneyland in 1961, does not affect the general issue here. Meanwhile, the Blackpool McDonald's that a hungry Bill Clinton famously visited from the New Labour party conference could have been found, on a smaller scale, almost anywhere in urban Britain by the early twenty-first century.[6] What is at issue is the alleged Americanisation, and associated debilitation, of the entertainment regime (as system both of provision and consumption) of Britain's most popular resort, as the nation's economy began to recover from an American economic event of unchallenged global significance, the Wall Street crash.

How might we test Priestley's tempting assertions? We could begin by comparing his assessment of Blackpool in the 1930s with those of other contemporary observers. Did they, too, find evidence of precocious Americanisation? We can also compare it with the popular resort in the United States that probably bore the closest similarity to it, Coney Island: there was a well-established traffic in amusement devices between the two pleasure centres, and contact with Coney would be the likeliest vector for any creeping Americanisation of Blackpool's amusements during the first third of the twentieth century.

Blackpool and Coney Island are rival aspirants to the label 'world's first working-class seaside resort'. In this guise they are both products of the late nineteenth and early twentieth century. Blackpool was the popular resort of the Lancashire 'cotton towns', and Coney Island that of New York.[7] From the end of the nineteenth century onwards Blackpool and Coney Island became the first great popular playgrounds for the industrial working class in the modern world. Although the working classes at play never completely dominated their beaches, streets and fairgrounds, they quickly came to provide the images that overrode all others, and they became indelibly associated with crowded, noisy, vulgar, unbuttoned, uninhibited enjoyment, for better and worse. They epitomised carnival, saturnalia, the temporary triumph of the periphery over the core, the world turned upside down, the suspension of dignity and inhibitions, the temporary reversal of the civilising process, the reign of gluttony, extravagance and licentiousness, the celebration of the 'collective gaze' rather than the 'romantic gaze', the direction of that gaze at the 'freak' and the sport of nature, the sharing of pleasures communally, and the process of joyful participation in the crowd at play as an end in itself, at once a surrendering and a celebration of self.[8] They were also prominent among the sites of the first great permanent amusement parks, with rides generating physical excitement and appealing to fantasy and wonderment: Blackpool's Pleasure Beach, and the evocative Coney Island trio of Luna Park, Steeplechase and Dreamland. Their place-myths conjure up concepts like popular modernity, mass consumption, and the idea of the 'leisure industries' as well as John Urry's notion of the 'collective gaze'.[9]

Blackpool as a popular resort for the working classes of Lancashire and (especially) the 'cotton towns' began earlier than Coney Island, and even when the latter overtook it in terms of sheer weight of visitor numbers in the late nineteenth or early twentieth century there were important qualitative differences to set against the brute statistics. Blackpool was already attracting around 1.3 million visitors a year in the early 1870s, rising to just under two million in the early 1890s, almost three million at the turn of the century and nearly four million on the eve of the First World War.[10] Coney Island's popularity grew much more explosively even than this; and both Coney's West Brighton and Blackpool's South Beach were making the transition to working-class domination during the 1880s, with a great proliferation of cheap popular amusements and food and drink outlets aimed at (as *Harper's Weekly* said of Coney Island in 1889) 'the great mass of the toilers of the city – not the poorest, but the struggling many'.[11] Democracy soon came to dominate, and by 1910 Coney Island had left Blackpool far behind in terms of sheer visitor numbers, laying claim to twenty million visitors per annum; but the overwhelming majority of them were day-trippers from Greater New York, in contrast to Blackpool where many working-class visitors were travelling longer distances and already staying for a full week by the 1890s.[12] This helps to explain why Coney Island's off-season population grew more slowly than Blackpool's.

Blackpool's inhabitants quadrupled in numbers to more than 47,000 between 1881 and 1901, reaching the 100,000 mark in 1931, while Coney Island, which also had around 12,000 residents in 1880, increased its resident population to around 75,000 by the 1920s and 100,000 in the late 1930s. By this time Blackpool claimed around seven million visitors per season, at least three times as many as any of its British competitors, drawn from all over Britain, but still dominated by the factory and mine workers of Lancashire and Yorkshire.[13]

Blackpool and Coney Island thus had a great deal in common, as transatlantic rivals and counterparts. From time to time they were made aware of each other, as in 1926 when a *New York Herald Tribune* article on 'England's Coney Island' was reprinted in the Blackpool press.[14] The Pleasure Beach amusement park that developed from the turn of the century at the south end of the promenade was often referred to as 'Britain's (or England's) Coney Island', with cross-reference to the great Coney Island pleasure centres that dominated its external image.[15] There was also ample scope for interaction between them, as we shall see. But was this one-way traffic, a series of injections of Americanism into this distinctive northern English setting? Might such developments be a product of the 1920s and 1930s, as Priestley suggests? What did his contemporaries think about this?

There was no shortage of commentators on the Blackpool of the 1930s, which was acknowledged to be a remarkable phenomenon. But, Priestley apart, suggestions of American influence in general, or of that of Coney Island in particular, were at a premium. The emphasis is overwhelmingly on Blackpool as a resort of northern England, and especially of Lancashire. The preferred comparators are European. The international gossip columnist Charles Graves, brother of the poet Robert, waxes eloquent about the sheer vitality of Blackpool and the energy and zest for life of its working-class visitors, comparing its 'tremendous pace' with the 'flabby pulse-beat' of the Continental resort.[16] James Laver, the poet and historian of art and costume, mentions that Blackpool's peep shows are all 'passed by the New York Board of Censors' but otherwise reinforces the town's predominantly Lancashire nature and orientation ('Blackpool is Lancashire on holiday'), with special reference to regional humour, the deflation of pretensions, and the export of female dancers with Lancashire accents to stages all over Europe.[17] The novelists J. L. Hodson and Frank Tilsley hint at some loss of idiosyncrasy and vitality, but only at the margins. Hodson has one of his characters, a likeable impresario rooted in Manchester's Jewish community, bemoan the loss of beach performers of forty years before, 'those people who used to draw your teeth vhile you wait and those who took out your corns', who were no longer tolerated in the more regulated Blackpool of the 1930s; while Tilsley presents us with a fairground barker who regrets a perceived decline, over the years, in the sharpness and repartee of the crowds in front of his booth. But both authors return to the zest for life and colour, and the compulsive holiday spending, of a distinctive Lancashire working-class type, released from the tyranny of the machine and bent on explosive enjoyment, whom Hodson describes as having 'a touch of the wildness and feyness of the Celt, of the recklessness of the Irish, of the venturesomeness of the Vikings'.[18] Another novelist, Anthony Burgess, writing as an autobiographer, also saw Blackpool as above all a Lancashire holiday-place, but with more emphasis on drink, fighting and (reminiscently) sex; but, in contradiction of Priestley, he stressed the Englishness of the promenade song booths and their songs, especially the London firm belonging to Lawrence Wright, who both published and composed (under the name of Horatio Nicholls), and had an interest in shows on the piers.[19] Burgess, unlike Priestley, had been there. So had William Holt, whose descriptions of the Blackpool holiday crowds on August Bank Holiday 1934 reclaimed the despised song booths as quintessential Lancashire institutions, with no trace of racially suspect ditties:

> Gay singing comes from the music bazaars where Lancashire cotton workers are singing the latest songs. If you have not stood among the crowd in one of these Blackpool popular song factories, try it. It is an experience I have never had anywhere else.

His conclusions referred back to popular music even as they returned to the unique Lancashire identity of the Blackpool holiday crowd:

> Blackpool breathes the very spirit of the North. The indomitable spirit of millions of factory workers and those who depend on them for their existence . . . Blackpool is made of the stuff which made Gracie Fields, whose spirit is part of Blackpool though she is a Rochdale lass.[20]

Tom Harrisson's 'anthropological' essays on the Blackpool of the late 1930s, arising out of the Mass Observation project, likewise have very little to say about American influences. The cinemas, of course, showed Spencer Tracy and Clark Gable, but 'the two surest draws', according to the manager of the Imperial, were the Lancashire stars

George Formby and Gracie Fields. On the 'Golden Mile' between Central station and Central Pier in 1937 were small amusement centres called 'Coney Island' and 'Luna Park', named after the second great Coney amusement park, 'a brown stucco Moorish palace dominated by a green half-dome with a crescent moon', which, in true Coney Island style, was consumed by fire during the summer. There was also a stray reference to a 'Disney fantasia' conjured up by the prevalence of grottos among the amusements; but this was Harrisson's own interpretation of what he was seeing.[21] This very full representation of Blackpool's entertainments, indeed, concentrated on their distinctiveness to Blackpool and Lancashire, with emphasis on a home-grown appeal to a sense of the exotic that had its counterparts among the Coney Island attractions, but did not demonstrably derive from them. Mass Observation noted a widespread fascination with the 'oriental', especially when presenting itself as Indian mysticism; with the occult, including astrology, palmistry, lucky charms and tea-leaf readings; with dubious or equivocal sexuality or transgressive sexual behaviour; with torture, horror and deformity; with gambling in a small way on slot-machines; and with futuristic machines with inscrutable powers. What it did not comment on was anything that might be thought to be particularly 'American' about these preoccupations.[22]

Since the 1870s, Blackpool had acquired a more mainstream entertainment industry, the late Victorian pleasure palaces of the Winter Gardens, the Tower and the Alhambra, later the Palace, as well as an array of lesser theatres and music halls. They were based on popular capitalism and shareholder democracy, much of it Lancashire based, and had to avoid outraging sensibilities to keep the huge audiences that paid their dividends. As Mass Observation showed, they relied on innuendo and an expanded tolerance among visitors whose moral antennae were relaxed by the holiday environment. Coney Island had nothing on this scale or of this type, although it did share the growing Blackpool obsession with dancing. What it did have, and what made it internationally famous, was the three great amusement parks: Steeplechase, Luna Park and the short-lived but lastingly famous Dreamland. The place to look for American influences at Blackpool was not in the song booths or at the Tower or Winter Gardens, despite the lasting popularity of 'minstrel' shows (an import of the 1840s) and circus acts that harked back to Buffalo Bill and the Wild West Show. It was the Pleasure Beach, which after all drew comparative attention to the Coney Island parallel. Here were the real transatlantic links. They also dated back to a period that predated Priestley's argument, and they were more ambiguous and negotiated than his indictment suggests; but the agenda he introduced requires their investigation. He himself referred to it as 'the enormous amusement park, with its terrifying giant coasters and other fantastic idiocies'; but in November it, like the rest of the 'great roaring spangled beast', was hibernating.[23] By the time of Priestley's 1933 visit, however, it was an essential element in Blackpool's menu of attractions, having come a very long way since its foundation by an 'Anglo-American syndicate' on sand dunes occupied by gypsies at the turn of the century.

The pioneering seaside amusement parks, Paul Boyton's short-lived Sea Lion Park, which opened in 1895, and George Tilyou's long-lived Steeplechase two years later, built on and pulled together existing technologies of pleasure in a new setting. They depended on and made use of the traditions of the travelling fairground and circus; the novel (and transatlantic) genre of the travelling 'Wild West Show' of the later nineteenth century; the exhibitions of panoramas and dioramas; the fairground amusement areas of international exhibitions and World's Fairs; the developing fascination exerted by the zoo and aquarium; and the new technology of the roller coaster, growing out of the European idea of the 'Russian mountain' and the American exploitation of old mine railway inclines for tourist purposes, bearing fruit in La Marcus Thompson's Coney Island switchback of 1884, to which steam power had been applied a year later. The first scenic railway was inaugurated in Atlantic City in 1886, joining the steam roundabout or carousel which had been developed in England from the early 1860s, manufactured at Coney Island since 1876, and was already an established pleasure and problem at Blackpool in the 1880s.[24] What was new about the developments of the mid-1890s at Coney Island was the grouping of such attractions on a single site, to cater for reliable flows of visitors from an accessible conurbation. The Pleasure Beach followed soon afterwards; and, significantly, the leading figures in its development, J. W. Outhwaite and (especially and enduringly) W. G. Bean, had strong connections with the American amusement machine and amusement park industry. Albert Ellis, a locally based phrenologist and stall owner on the emergent central 'Golden Mile', was another early fairground speculator among the southern sand dunes, but it may be significant that he did not last the distance: he was very much a local figure. Early rides drew heavily on American innovations: the carousel that Outhwaite brought to the business, the bicycle railway that was Bean's original dowry, the early switchback railway and the Sir Hiram Maxim Captive Flying Machine, an innovation of 1904 that was the brainchild of the American inventor of the Maxim gun, now based in Britain. The scenic railway of 1907 was La Marcus Thompson's of Coney Island fame. The arrivals of the 'Gee Whiz' and the 'Brooklyn Cake Walk' in 1908 told their own story, and from 1910 there was even a 'Monitor and Merrimac' battle show, drawing on the American Civil War. But, just as the emblematic Blackpool Tower of 1894 had adapted a structural theme from a Paris exposition to the needs of the Lancashire entertainment industry, so the Pleasure Beach also took European innovations by way of the London exhibition grounds, and used European, imperial and even British motifs in décor and representations. Within four years the Monitor and Merrimac show had a Spithead review of the British Navy added on, and in 1922 the British attack on Zeebrugge in the First World War took centre stage. What also mattered, of course, was the nature of the Blackpool crowd itself, and how it used these attractions. What we see here is far removed from the hypodermic model of cultural injection assumed by Priestley: it is about selection, negotiation and accommodation.[25]

Transatlantic comparisons, in practice, produce complex results. The Pleasure Beach was much less central to Blackpool's core identity as a resort than were Steeplechase, Dreamland and Luna Park to Coney Island's developing place-myth, although even twentieth-century Coney offered plenty of other pleasures and its beach could be even more crowded than Blackpool's, especially on a hot summer Sunday.[26] But the Pleasure Beach's concern for 'respectability' of a distinctive northern English provincial kind matched the dominant preferences of its visiting public, and it is significant that it did not provide the more 'extreme' forms of fantasy entertainment that the Coney Island amusement parks traded in. It was selective in its transatlantic borrowings. There were no epic trips to the Moon, Midget Cities, displays of babies in incubators, reconstructions of flood disasters or dramatic daily rescues from tenement fires, or (above all) still more epic depictions of the Creation or journeys to Hell at Blackpool: this was a more prosaic and a more uniformly religious visiting constituency, with widespread Nonconformist susceptibilities which rarely extended to obsessive abstemiousness or Sunday observance, but still had to be treated with caution. The Pleasure Beach had its exciting rides, its roller coasters, water chutes and scenic railways, its helter-skelter and Joy Wheel, all enhancing intimacy between the sexes that could be continued or resumed in the dance halls and shows during the evening. War, historical fantasy, journeys through scenic splendours and imperial spectacle were all acceptable; but the Pleasure Beach was less challenging or 'in your face' than Steeplechase, Luna Park or even self-consciously respectable (and short-lived, despite its kitsch magnificence) Dreamland, which had specialised in Biblical spectacles before being itself consumed in an inferno that attracted its own huge crowds of spectators from central New York.[27] As, from a very early stage, the only operation of its kind in Blackpool, the Pleasure Beach lacked the sort of competition that might have persuaded it to take risks by opting for potentially controversial sensationalism. The more challenging kind of Coney Island show had its Blackpool counterparts in the stalls of the Golden Mile, but on a much smaller scale (matching the similar sideshows in the warren of narrow streets behind the Coney Island beaches, even after the realignment on a more generous scale that accompanied the building of the Boardwalk), aiming at more limited markets and with less for the proprietors to lose.[28]

In some senses Coney Island had already reached its peak as amusement capital by the First World War. It had already lost one of its most impressive amusement parks as early as 1911; but Dreamland had already suffered one bankruptcy before the fire consumed it. Luna Park struggled on through bankruptcy, increasing dilapidation and a hand-to-mouth existence through the Depression of the 1930s, and making one last throw of the dice by taking a clutch of new rides from the World's Fair, only to be itself consumed by fire in 1944.[29] This vulnerability to fire reflected a culture of ephemeral showiness rather than the durable solidity that characterised Blackpool, not excepting the Pleasure Beach, whose Moorish 'Casino' of 1913 defied conventional demolition techniques when it was replaced by today's Art Deco construction in 1937. This was part of a general makeover of the Pleasure Beach on modernist lines from the mid-1930s, supervised by the architect Joseph Emberton, which completed, under a new generation of the ruling family, the park's inter-war transition to permanence, respectability, clean lines and tidiness.[30]

The contrasting nature of the crowd at Blackpool and Coney Island was crucial to these outcomes. Blackpool's visiting public was far more stable, more homogeneous and, already at the turn of the century, more tradition bound than that of Coney Island. It was firmly grounded in the working and lower middle classes of the textile-manufacturing districts of Lancashire and Yorkshire, and when it extended its catchment area through the Midlands in the early twentieth century, and then became a genuinely national resort in the inter-war years, it still recruited from industrial towns with strong, stable neighbourhood associational cultures and traditions of regular, disciplined, well-paid work and relatively high family incomes. The Depression forced some people to lower their aspirations, and kept most of the unemployed away altogether, but the important point is that Blackpool was essentially a regional resort for industrial workers and (increasingly) their families, large numbers of whom came for a week after saving through the rest of the year to afford the visit. These visitors were overwhelmingly white Anglo-Saxon Protestants, with a small leavening of Catholics of Irish or Italian descent and even smaller numbers drawn from other ethnic minorities. This picture did not even begin to change until the end of the twentieth century.[31]

So Blackpool was an ethnically and culturally homogeneous resort, attracted by novelty but resistant to destabilising innovation, whose visitors came predominantly from the better-off strata of the working class, and from towns whose systems of shared holiday weeks ensured that the crowd was anything but anonymous and was likely to contain relatives, neighbours, workmates and minor authority figures. There was no hint of the melting pot about Blackpool; and very few of its visitors came from the metropolitan and seaport environments of places like London and Liverpool that bore a closer resemblance to New York. Coney Island was very different. From an early stage it drew in wave after successive wave of new migrants, at that expansive period in American history at which the Statue of Liberty was erected: there were (among others) British, Irish, Italians, Germans, Scandinavians, Greeks, Eastern Europeans, and Russians. Many of the latter, especially, were Jewish, complicating an ethnic and religious mix that extended from Episcopalians and other Protestant groups through Roman Catholics, Greek, Russian and other Orthodox persuasions and various sects.[32] The different groups tended to gravitate to bathhouses and sections of the beach that they made their own.[33] There were also African Americans, in small but growing numbers, adding a dimension that was completely absent from Blackpool until the Second World War.[34] The beach might be territorial, but the streets and amusement parks brought together all groups that could afford their services, and this was potentially a tenser and less biddable crowd than the Blackpool ones. Michael Immerso argues that rather than a melting pot, this 'multi-ethnic canvas' was 'variegated. Its colors, smells and sounds did not blend or meld together, they collided and recompounded.' But, in apparent contradiction, 'the crowd with its immense numbers assumed an identity that, in the end, trumped ethnicity or neighborhood loyalty by imposing a common identity more closely linked to class'.[35] Much the same might be said of Blackpool, except that there was less to divide, apart from the eternal rivalry between Lancashire and Yorkshire; but Coney's was, increasingly, a poorer and much more heterogeneous visiting public than Blackpool's, and it displayed less continuity or consumer loyalty, although there was of course an extensive core of multiple repeat visitors. Above all, by the 1920s there was much less purchasing power per capita, which is why Nathan's five-cent hot dogs did so well out of very small profits and enormous turnover; but there was also a much greater variety of fast food on offer, from knishes to salt water taffy.[36] The crucial differences, which undoubtedly contributed to the longevity and resilience of Blackpool's popularity, were that visitors to the Lancashire resort, although less numerous, travelled longer distances, stayed longer, had much more in common with each other and had more to spend.

By the 1930s, in fact, Coney Island was already beginning its long decline. Prohibition between 1920 and 1933 had been difficult to cope with, and competition from new, more respectable, family resorts reached by car and promoted by New York City's parks commissioner Robert Moses, who hated Coney Island passionately, turned it increasingly into a resort for the city poor who arrived by subway and spent as little as possible. While Blackpool was going up-market in the inter-war years, with extensive new investment in parks, gardens and planning, Coney Island's impressive boardwalk of 1923 merely brought its beach access and promenading space to the stage Blackpool had reached in 1870. Priestley had got it precisely and diametrically wrong: all the evidence we can marshal suggests that Blackpool was still as vital, lively and distinctively North Country English as ever in 1933, while the likeliest source of any creeping Americanisation, its transatlantic alter ego Coney Island, was losing its identity and prosperity as a popular resort, despite a continuing and still growing capacity for attracting huge crowds to its beaches on hot summer Sundays.[37] The main transatlantic traffic had come at the turn of the century, although the Pleasure Beach's W. G. Bean had made regular trips to catch up with developments until his untimely death in mid-Atlantic on just such an errand in 1929. His successor, his son-in-law Leonard Thompson, hired American architects and roller coaster designers for the start of his Pleasure Beach improvements in the early 1930s.[38] Most (but not all) of the actual movement had been eastwards, but in use and practice the American motifs and technology had been selectively adapted for northern English tastes, as the local synthesised with the global and created new cultural hybrids. This transatlantic story is much more complicated than a flying visit from an influential commentator made it seem; and this in turn confirms that there was, and has been, nothing linear or straightforward about transatlantic cultural transmission in the twentieth century.

Notes

1. J. B. Priestley, *English Journey* (London: Heinemann, 1934), pp. 267–8.
2. For Priestley's generalised nostalgia for an idealised pre-1914 industrial England, and his conception of 'the people' as the real nation, see John Baxendale, '"I had seen a lot of Englands": J. B. Priestley, Englishness and the People', *History Workshop Journal*, 51 (2001), 87–111.
3. James J. Nott, *Music for the People: Popular Music and Dance in Interwar Britain* (Oxford: Oxford University Press, 2002), pp. 209–11, 230–3.
4. Priestley, *English Journey*, pp. 263–9.
5. For an accessible introduction to Blackpool, see J. K. Walton, *Blackpool* (Edinburgh: Edinburgh University Press, 1998). For ways into McDonaldisation and McDisneyfication, see George Ritzer, *The McDonaldization of Society* (Thousand Oaks, CA: Pine Forge Press, 1993); idem, *The Globalization of Nothing* (Thousand Oaks, CA: Pine Forge Press, 2003); Barry Smart (ed.), *Resisting McDonaldization* (London: Sage, 1999).
6. Peter Marsden, *Lighting the Waves: A Pictorial Social History of Blackpool Illuminations 1912–2003* (Preston: Laughing Donkey, 2004), p. 16; National Fairground Archive, Sheffield, Smart Family Collection, 'Themeland' file: many thanks to the Smart family and to Dr Vanessa Toulmin for letting me see this material, which will be discussed further (along with other themes of this chapter) in Gary Cross and John K. Walton, *The Playful Crowd* (forthcoming).
7. For Blackpool, in context, see J. K. Walton, *The British Seaside: Holidays and Resorts in the Twentieth Century* (Manchester: Manchester University Press, 2000); Helen Meller, *European Cities 1890–1930s* (Chichester: John Wiley and Sons, 2001), ch. 5; Peter Bennett, *A Century of Fun* (Blackpool: Blackpool Pleasure Beach, 1996). For Coney Island, see most recently Michael Immerso, *Coney Island: The People's Playground* (Piscataway, NJ: Rutgers University Press, 2002); Charles Denson, *Coney Island Lost and Found* (Berkeley, CA: Ten Speed Press, 2002); and also J. F. Kasson, *Amusing the Million* (New York: Hill and Wang, 1978).
8. Rob Shields, *Places on the Margin* (London: Routledge, 1991); Tony Bennett, Colin Mercer and Janet Woollacott (eds), *Popular Culture and Social Relations* (Milton Keynes: Open University Press, 1986); John Urry, *Consuming Places* (London: Routledge, 1995); Gary Cross (ed.), *Worktowners at Blackpool* (London: Routledge, 1990); Rachel Adams, *Sideshow USA* (Chicago: University of Chicago Press, 2001).
9. John Urry, 'Cultural Change and the Seaside Resort', in Gareth Shaw and

Allan Williams (eds), *The Rise and Fall of British Coastal Resorts* (London: Mansell, 1997), pp. 102–13.

10. J. K. Walton, 'The Social Development of Blackpool, 1788–1914', Ph.D. thesis, Lancaster University, 1974, p. 263.

11. Immerso, *Coney Island*, pp. 41–2.

12. Immerso, *Coney Island*, p. 167; Denson, *Coney Island*, p. 41; John Walton, 'The Blackpool landlady revisited', *Manchester Region Historical Review*, 8, 1994, 23–31.

13. Comparisons are complicated by the fact that Coney Island was not a separate local government district. Immerso, *Coney Island*, p. 127; Denson, *Coney Island*, p. 65; J. K. Walton and C. O'Neill, 'Numbering the Holidaymakers', *Local Historian*, 23 (1993), 205–16.

14. Newspaper cutting in author's possession, by courtesy of Shirley Clarke.

15. *Blackpool Official Guide 1924: The Home of Health, Pleasure, Fun and Fancy* (Blackpool: Blackpool Corporation, 1924); *Blackpool: Britain's Playground* (Blackpool: Blackpool Corporation, 1928), p. 51.

16. Charles Graves, *– and the Greeks* (London: Geoffrey Bles, 1930), p. 190.

17. James Laver, 'Blackpool', in Yvonne Cloud (ed.), *Beside the Seaside*, 2nd edn. (Birmingham: The Kynoch Press, 1938), pp. 171, 176–80.

18. J. L. Hodson, *Carnival at Blackport* (London: Victor Gollancz, 1937), pp. 56, 181; Frank Tilsley, *Pleasure Beach* (London: Collins, 1944), pp. 19, 35, 291.

19. Anthony Burgess, *Little Wilson and Big God* (Harmondsworth: Penguin, 1988), pp. 127–32; and see also Cross (ed.), *Worktowners at Blackpool*, pp. 170–1.

20. *Daily Dispatch*, 3, 4, 6 August 1934.

21. Cross, *Worktowners at Blackpool*, pp. 99, 104, 135.

22. Ibid., especially pp. 75–83, 110–27, 192–201.

23. Priestley, *English Journey*, p. 263.

24. Immerso, *Coney Island*, ch. 5; Vanessa Toulmin (ed.), *Pleasurelands* (Sheffield: National Fairground Archive, exhibition catalogue, 2003); eadem., 'The History of Fairground Rides', http://www.shef.ac.uk/nfa/history/rides/index.php

25. Bennett, *Century of Fun*, ch. 1; Ted Lightbown, 'Blackpool Pleasure Beach: Its Buildings and Rides', Blackpool Pleasure Beach archives; Arthur Hawkey, *The Amazing Hiram Maxim* (Staplehurst: Spellmount, 2001); and for Ellis see Cross, *Worktowners at Blackpool*, pp. 116–18, and Owen Davies, *Witchcraft, Magic and Culture 1736–1951* (Manchester: Manchester University Press, 1999), pp. 254–8.

26. Bennett, *Century of Fun*.

27. Immerso, *Coney Island*, ch. 4.

28. Denson, *Coney Island*, ch. 4.

29. Immerso, *Coney Island*, pp. 161–3.

30. Bennett, *Century of Fun*, pp. 36–8.

31. Walton, 'Social Development of Blackpool', pp. 266–9, 272–8.

32. Immerso, *Coney Island*, p. 149.

33. Joseph Heller, *Now and Then* (London: Simon and Schuster, 1998), pp. 32–3, 44.
34. Immerso, *Coney Island*, pp. 150–5.
35. Ibid., p. 153.
36. Denson, *Coney Island*, pp. 65, 274; Heller, *Now and then*, p. 51.
37. Immerso, *Coney Island*, chs 7–8.
38. Bennett, *Century of Fun*, p. 58.

CHAPTER SIX

Landscapes of Americanisation in Britain: Learning from the 1950s

Neil Campbell

> Cultural landscape studies focus most on the history of how people have used everyday space – buildings, rooms, streets, fields, or yards – to establish their identity, articulate their social relations, and derive cultural meaning. (Groth and Bressi 1997: 1–2)

Cultural landscapes have often been the unwitting focal sites for debates about American influence upon British life, using discussions about material change as the platform for broader arguments about what has become known as 'Americanisation'. In the immediate post-World War II culture I will examine here, it was often the shock of Americanised cultural forms, products and attitudes that were felt most where they impacted upon everyday life. In so many ways, in the days before mass television and the fears of 'wall-to-wall *Dallas*', early reactions to 'landscape' shaped the future analyses and helped to form the more generalised approach to Americanisation. This chapter will examine some of these positive and negative post-war responses and begin to project these forwards to our contemporary situation as consumers and producers of a so-called Americanised McWorld.

David Chaney argues that 'places encapsulate and communicate identity' and that this 'interest in the cultural meanings of the physical environment . . . has become one of the defining features of the turn to culture' (Chaney 1994: 147). In casting our minds back to the 1950s we can see how the beginnings of the 'cultural turn', usually associated with an interest in popular cultural forms, were commensurate with a deep suspicion of the products of America's mass culture. When a character in Wim Wenders's film *Kings of the Road* says, 'The Americans have colonised our sub-conscious,' he overlooks the signs of American presence rooted in the material and embodied in the everyday cultural landscape itself. Perhaps to examine these relations of exchange one needs something more complex than the metaphors of imposition and colonisation. What I propose here is to examine cultural landscape as a marker of ideological change and, in particular, as a means of analysing the impacts and responses to issues of Americanisation within Britain.

As James Corner reminds us,

landscape is an *ongoing medium of exchange*, a medium that is embedded and evolved within the imaginative and material practices of different societies at different times. Over time, landscapes accrue layers with every new representation, and these inevitably thicken and enrich the range of interpretations and possibilities. (Corner 1999: 5 – my emphasis)

In this palimpsestic 'exchange' there is an 'inextricable bond' between landscape and 'cultural ideas' (ibid.: 7), between landscape's significance and its presence as an arena for critical, creative thought and action. Quite often this sense of 'exchange', or what James Clifford has usefully termed 'cultural import-export' (Clifford 1988: 147), is too easily omitted in favour of metaphors of invasion, conquest and imperialism.

> An interesting project is to go out and record as a visual diary every contact with 'America' as part of your everyday life. Analyse and comment on the findings.

For some in Europe after World War II there was a growing sense of 'placelessness' (see Relph 1976) emerging as a response to mass culture or the 'commodification of culture', whereby the 'local' and 'regional' were seen as being overrun by mass-produced commercial goods and 'lifestyles'. This form of mass culture had, as Crang (1998: 115) puts it, a 'particular symbolic [American] geography' existing in tension with a more romantic relationship to American space and influence defined in road movies, westerns and rock and roll. The threat, it was felt by some, was national culture, heritage and 'authentic' Britishness being colonised by American influences, goods and attitudes. Typically, cultural identity is often 'anchored' through place, a 'landscape' that defines it through a sense of rootedness and belonging:

> To think of oneself as 'English' or 'British' is inevitably to place oneself within a set of meanings that have a long history and continuity. . . They seem to provide a frame of reference or a tradition which connects one's present mode of existence to the way of life of one's ancestors, thereby giving a culture a distinctive coherence and shape over time and making it internally homogeneous. (Hall 1995: 176)

Such a 'frame of reference' is place-image, meaning that 'when we think of or imagine cultural identity, we tend to "see" it in a place, in a setting, as part of an imaginary landscape or "scene". We give it a background, we put it in a frame, in order to make sense of it' (ibid.: 181). Such a vision of 'culture' as 'place' anchored in tradition, continuity and distinction seems under threat when confronted by different practices, values, products and styles that arrive from 'outside'. This reaction is often explained in terms of an imperialist assault on 'national' integrity defined by authentic place-imagery.

Hoskins and Hoggart

The threatened national identity is clearly articulated in the 1950s as American influence became increasingly apparent in Britain, in works like W. G. Hoskins's *The Making of the English Landscape* (originally 1955), a classic study of the relationship between landscape and national identity, whose final chapter, 'The Landscape Today', states that since '1914, every single change in the English landscape has either uglified it or destroyed its meaning, or both . . . It is a distasteful subject but it must be faced for a few moments' (Hoskins 1985: 298). He sees the English countryside as a 'symphony' with a *'logic that lies behind the beautiful whole'* (ibid., my emphasis), the product of continuity and an organic and timeless tradition, now at risk from the 'incessant noise, speed, and all the other acids of modernity' (in Meinig 1979: 207), seen most evidently in the American military's colonisation of landscape (in Norfolk and Lincolnshire): 'Airfields have flayed it bare wherever there are level, well-drained stretches of land . . . Over them drones, day after day, the obscene shape of the atom-bomber, laying a trail like a filthy slug upon Constable's and Gainsborough's sky' (Hoskins 1985: 299).

Writing in the village of Steeple Barton, with planes flying close overhead from the US Air Force base at Upper Heyford, Hoskins condemned all 'modern' (i.e. American) consumerism such as 'the harsh chromium plate, television, and tubular lighting' of a devastating 'new age' which he clearly envisaged as despoiling the landscape, replacing his village 'England' with a trashy, harsh Americanised alternative (Meinig 1979: 207). For Hoskins, the Cold War era marked the transformation of the English rural idyll by a stealthy Americanisation, into a landscape of 'new ranch farming' and the 'nissen hut, the "prefab", and the electric fence . . . England of the by-pass . . . the bombing-range where there was once silence . . . England of the battle-training areas . . . Barbaric England of scientists, the military men, and the politicians' (Hoskins 1985: 299).

Hoskins presents an 'anti-modern, anti-state, anti-progress culture of landscape' (Matless 1998: 274), rejecting notions of 'internationalism' or the hybridisation of landscape, claiming in 1959 that

> we are not born internationalists and there comes a time when the complexity and size of modern problems leave us cold. We belong to a particular place and the bigger and more incomprehensible the world grows the more people will turn to study something of which they can grasp the scale and in which they can find a personal and individual meaning. (Cited ibid.: 198)

The intimations of a global age of transnational corporations and their consequent influences upon the landscape are viewed only as threats to his particular view of a rooted, stable identity; however, as Morley and Robins point out, 'contemporary cultural identities must also be about internationalism in a direct sense, about our positions in transnational spaces . . . to achieve other forms of dialogue and collectivity' through reaching out beyond the local to the global perspective (Morley and Robins 1995: 41). Of course, to hold fast to a particular, rooted and essential sense of the English landscape, which in reality is an evolving accumulation of layers and histories and identities, is in danger of becoming an overly nationalistic England transposed into 'Little England', an imagined community in which the complex mongrelisation of place and identity is wilfully overlooked. As Morley and Robins put it, 'the defence of a given "cultural identity" easily slips into the most hackneyed nationalism, or even racism, and the nationalist affirmation of the superiority of one group over another' (ibid.: 47). Although rarely stated as such, Hoskins's refusal to consider the 'international' dimensions of today's landscape cuts him off from any consideration of issues such ethnicity and landscape, for his work assumes an 'unproblematically white', preindustrial, rural England (ibid.: 49).

American geographer D. W. Meinig's criticism of Hoskins's antimodernism centres on whether 'he has considered the difference between looking at a landscape and living in it' (Meinig 1979: 208). This sense of a living landscape rather than a 'deep' England of tradition, order and unanimity does return us to the issue of nostalgia and the desire to repeat only those elements of landscape rooted in a certain 'vision of Britain' with its comforting looking back to an imagined wholeness and harmony. Hoskins, writing after the Second World War, wanted the reassurance of traditional landscape and historical continuity as a restatement of the English 'homeland' in a world increasingly 'homeless' and internationalised. It's no surprise that Sigmund Freud's essay 'The Uncanny' (the un-homely), written in 1919, was in part a response to the First World War and the terrible loss of 'home' and the destabilising consequences of the disruption of the familiar. 'Homelessness', Martin Heidegger wrote in 1947, 'is coming to be the destiny of the world' and landscape offered the possibility of what Heidegger called 'dwelling' in opposition to this loss of home (cited Vidler 1992: 65). Indeed, the sense of alienation and loss felt after these two wars often found expression as a destruction of tradition, home, rootedness and land, and the subsequent fear of a nomadic, 'modern', rootless world 'diasporized' by war and national disaster (ibid.). The landscape in ruins symbolised the loss of security and identity associated with the traditional, harmonious 'place-image' and modern humanity faced a life of fragmented primitivism 'living in *bidonvilles*, bungalows, and no doubt the garden huts, caravans, or even cars of the near future' (ibid.: 66). Such a vision mixing the primitive past with the horror of the future is very much in keeping with Hoskins's view of the 'landscape today' falling (in every sense) into a placeless American primitivist future where legacy and continuity are displaced by immediacy, rootlessness and popular taste. Conventionally, America is often denigrated as a country with 'no History' and therefore shallow and rootless.

This postwar 'spectre of Americanisation' (Hebdige 1988: 52) found further expression in Richard Hoggart's *The Uses of Literacy* (originally 1957), whose ideas were primarily articulated, like Hoskins's, through a deep concern over the loss of particular 'homely' cultural landscapes. In the year that Harold Macmillan spoke of 'never having it so good', Hoggart recognised vital British working-class cultural 'roots' as threatened, like Hoskins's Oxfordshire fields, by an encroaching Americanisation. Fearing, like his colleague Raymond Williams, that 'at certain levels, we are culturally an American colony' (Williams 1966: 109), Hoggart's emphasis right from the start is on place-image and the particular qualities and attributes of its cultural landscape. Indeed his second chapter is called 'Landscapes with Figures – Setting', beginning with the spatial, territorial proverb 'There's no place like home', and proceeding to examine those invading, 'un-homely' forces disrupting its coherence with 'shiny barbarism' (Hoggart 1962: 33). In Hoggart's vision of working-class life people move only small distances between familiar places, home, work, pub and the 'home-place' – 'the warm heart of the family' – living static and fast-disappearing existences under an encroaching spatiality defined not by slowness and tradition but by its antithesis, the new rhythmic impulses of America's endlessly promising 'Candy-Floss World' (ibid.: 68, 206).

Associated with 'Progressivism' and the future 'shot through with suggestions of skyscrapers, neon-lighting, and space-ships', Hoggart's Americanising forces produce a 'new callowness' that 'debases' older values as the working classes 'take up these things just as they appear and use them in the manner of the child in the fairy-tale, who found toys hanging from the trees and lollipops by the roadside' (ibid.: 190–3). Unlike more recent notions of people 'using' and even subverting popular cultural forms (see work by Michel de Certeau and Ien Ang discussed elsewhere in this volume), Hoggart portrays a compliant and powerless working class in thrall to American hegemonic power and ideology, simply jumping on the 'band-wagon mentality' and finding themselves confronted by 'the wagon loaded with its barbarians in wonderland, [as it] moves irresistibly forward: not forward to anywhere, but simply forward for forwardness's sake' (ibid.: 193–4).

Hoggart's Americanised landscape of mass-market magazines or paperbacks infiltrates his ordered home-place of tradition with 'brash confidence', 'cheap gum-chewing pert glibness and a streamlining which mark[s] it at once as mid-twentieth-century popular writing' (ibid.: 235). Its inhabitants are the pulp fiction-reading British 'juke-box boys', existing in 'harshly-lit milk-bars', whose 'clothes, . . . hair-styles . . . facial

expressions all indicate [they] are living . . . in a myth-world compounded of a few simple elements which they take to be those of
American life' (ibid.: 247–8). Here the boys navigate a terrain of

> modernistic knick-knacks, their glaring showiness, an *aesthetic
> breakdown* so complete that, in comparison with them the lay-out
> of the living-rooms in some of the poor homes from which the
> customers come seems to speak of a *tradition* as *balanced and
> civilized* as an eighteenth century town-house. (ibid.: 248 – my
> emphases)

Hoggart's sense of chaos with its 'aesthetic breakdown' is in contrast
to an idealised, 'balanced and civilized' home-place of 'tradition' that
it has superseded. Although championing a 'working-class', he applies
the very same criteria as Hoskins to think about the English rural
tradition being destroyed by the chaotic appearance and values of the
bombing ranges of Norfolk. The boys have 'an American slouch',
listen to the 'mechanical record-player', play records that 'almost all
are American', with their 'hollow-cosmos effect', 'great precision and
competence', and sit on 'tubular chairs' and stare 'as desperately as
Humphrey Bogart' (ibid.: 248). This Americanised cultural landscape –
'a peculiarly thin and pallid form of dissipation, a sort of spiritual
dry-rot' – is compared unfavourably by Hoggart with the traditional
'pub', and he condemns it all as a 'myth-world compounded of a few
simple elements which they take to be those of American life' (ibid.).
Barely existing in this demi-world, Hoggart's representative boys are
'less intelligent than the average', otherwise why would they live like
this, he seems to suggest, having 'no aim, no ambition, no protection,
no belief', becoming as machine-like as the landscape through which
they define themselves: 'the directionless and tamed helots of a
machine-minding class . . . the hedonistic but passive barbarian who
rides in a fifty-horsepower bus for threepence, to see a five-million-
dollar film for one-and-eight pence', and who 'is not simply a social
oddity; he is a portent' of the growing, dangerous influence of a 'Candy
Floss World' (meaning presumably frothy, cheap, sweet, sickly and
without real substance) – defined by 'American or pseudo-American'
cultural landscapes (ibid.: 250, 259).

Like Hoskins, Hoggart consistently overlooks the capacity for consumers to also 'produce' identities under such conditions and not
simply to be 'colonised' in a one-way process. He refuses to acknowledge
the possibility for 'exchange', for 'import-export', for the potential

'dialogue' taking place as two (or more) cultures collide. This production process demonstrates de Certeau's arguments about how we 'write' (produce) as we 'read' (consume), creating rather than simply receiving a defined image: 'each individual is a locus in which an incoherent (and often contradictory) plurality of such relational determinations interact' (de Certeau 1988: xi). As 'consumers' of Americanised space it is possible to be 'producers' too – makers of pleasure and meaning – since 'users make (*bricolent*) innumerable and infinitesimal transformations of and within the dominant cultural economy in order to adapt it to their own interests and their own rules' (ibid.: xiii–xiv). Deriving his ideas, like Stuart Hall and Mary-Louise Pratt later, from examining colonial relations, de Certeau sees ways in which such 'uses' are tactical subversions of the dominant order for 'they were *other* within the very colonisation that outwardly assimilated them . . . they escaped without leaving it' (ibid.: xiii). If America is seen as a colonial power whose culture was swamping postwar Europe (as Hoggart and Hoskins suggest), then what is omitted is precisely how people 'used' and would continue to use these American traces in their everyday lives in all kinds of ways and for all kinds of different purposes.

By 1962 and Anthony Sampson's *Anatomy of Britain*, America is seen as having more of a dialogic relationship:

Within two years the credit squeeze ended, skyscrapers rushed up, supermarkets spread over cities, newspapers became fatter or died, commercial TV began making millions, shops, airlines, even coal and banks had to fight for their lives. After the big sleep many people welcomed any novelty; any piece of Americanization seemed an enterprising change . . . Only now, is Britain becoming *visually* aware of living in a state of perpetual and perilous change (Sampson 1962, cited in Hewison 1987: 4).

Here 'the new classless Americanized world of Wimpy bars, coffee-bars, television, mini-motors, pre-packaged food, ice-skating, Marks & Spencers, Vespas and airport lounges' (ibid.) is no longer seen exclusively as a threat, but as the potential source of creative energy, questioning, or new hybrid relations – 'a space in which oppositional meanings (in relation to dominant traditions of British culture) could be negotiated and expressed' (Morley and Robins 1995: 55). For many in postwar Britain, America's 'dream-world' represented a positive alternative to the stuffy establishment values of conservatism, rationing and repression, a short-term, low-rent, chromium utopia. As Dick Hebdige makes clear in his discussion of the rise of pop art in the 1960s, America represented 'a repressed, potentially fertile realm invoked against the grain' in the work of Europeans, symbolising transgressive, alternative energies – 'a productive clash of opposing forces' – in the face of official discourses (Hebdige 1988: 128–9).

These images emerged from the 'use' and experience of the very cultural landscapes that Hoskins and Hoggart criticised and can be seen most clearly in the work of the Independent Group (IG) of artists, architects and designers (Peter Reyner Banham, Richard Hamilton, Alison and Peter Smithson, John McHale, Magda Cordell, Nigel Henderson, Lawrence Alloway and Eduardo Paolozzi), reacting with 'none of the dislike of commercial culture standard among most intellectuals', preferring instead to accept it, discuss it in detail, consume and 'use' it enthusiastically and dialogically since

> Hollywood, Detroit, and Madison Avenue were, in terms of our interests, producing the best popular culture. Thus expendable art was proposed as no less serious than permanent art; an aesthetics of expendability . . . aggressively countered idealist and absolutist art theories . . . We assumed an anthropological definition of culture, in which all types of human activity were the object of aesthetic judgment and attention. (Alloway in Lippard 1991: 32, 36)

Like the Pop Art they influenced, the IG utilised the commercial iconography of pulp fiction, advertising, signs and the everyday – the very things Hoskins and Hoggart rejected – to unsettle established art practices by including previously marginal or excluded visual codes in the creation of new works and ideas. On the meeting grounds of cultural landscape postwar Britain entered more fully into an exchange, a '*dialogue* between British and American perspectives', or, as Alloway put it, 'If the IG, or I, was accused of Americanization, the spiritless character of the British art scene may have been the real fault' and the alternative was to take 'pleasure in the *aesthetics of plenty*' and to be 'engaged in *a game* derived from its American possibilities' (Robbins 1990: 9, 49, my emphasis).

The collage form epitomised this fascination with cultural recombination, multilayeredness and hybridisation, rejecting a fixed and rooted cultural landscape for something more 'routed' and mobile (see Gilroy 1993):

Acceptance of mass media entails a shift in our notion of 'what culture is'. Instead of reserving the word for the highest artifacts and the noblest thoughts of history's top ten, it needs to be used more widely as the description of 'what a society does'. Then, unique oil paintings and highly personal poems as well as mass-distributed films and group-aimed magazines can be placed within a continuum rather than frozen in layers in a pyramid. (Alloway in Robbins 1990: 165)

Similarly, instead of fearing a loss of national identity and a dissolution of authenticity at the hands of American mass culture, Alloway saw a creative potential as in his 'City Notes' (1959), where Piccadilly Circus is not 'architectural squalor' but rather 'the best night-sight in London' with

drug stores, with dense displays of small bright packages, arrayed in systems to throw the categorist. The LP [sic] environment at airports, restaurants, bars, and hotel lounges, of light and long-lived pop music that extends radio and TV sound outside the house and into a larger environment. (Robbins 1990: 167)

Peter Reyner Banham

Crucial to these shifts in thinking about cultural landscape was Peter Reyner Banham, who maintained an interest in American culture whilst retaining a 'leftist' view of politics and art. In his 'An Alphabetical Chronicle of Landmarks and Influences, 1951–61' under 'Detroit' he demonstrated his strong dualistic feelings, ranging from 'Detroit-Machiavellismus' ('everything that was thought to be hateful about U.S. design') to those who admired its automotive products for their 'unconventionality and boldness' (Banham 1996: 70). Indeed, argues Banham, Detroit represented the 'War of the Generations', for its language became the 'language of revolt among the young', contributing also to major shifts in aesthetics, away from 'subjective standards like "good taste"' and towards 'objective research into consumers' preference and motivations' (ibid.). What Banham identified throughout his career was a constant friction, an intense dialogue, over issues of taste and aesthetics, seen as primarily productive, between British and

American design traditions, played out across everyday cultural land-scapes and involving active 'consumption'. As Nigel Whiteley argues, the 'popular culture generated by consumer capitalism was, IG members claimed, enhancing democracy, not undermining it . . . Others were less convinced, and interpreted the IG's ideas as naïve enthusiasm for things American' (Whiteley 2002: 98).

The American popular forms criticised by Richard Hoggart were intrinsic to Banham's working-class 'live culture', as he called it – 'American pulps, things like *Mechanix Illustrated* and the comic books (we were all great Betty Boop fans), and the penny pictures on Saturday mornings' – and yet he was only too aware of how this sat uncomfortably with his leftist political position (Banham 1981: 84). The 1950s became for Banham and the IG a transatlantic 'contact zone' in which 'disparate cultures meet, clash and grapple with each other' and 'subjects are constituted in and by their relations to each other . . . in terms of co-presence, interaction, interlocking understand-ings and practices' (Pratt 1995: 6–7). This productive and creative encounter, its 'cultural import-export' of American things, was far from one-sided, for, as Banham has written, it was often difficult to admit to any interest in America as although 'one's natural leanings in the world of entertainment, and so on, were to the States . . . one's political philosophy seemed to require one to turn one's back to the States', leaving many with the 'curiously divided mind' that 'wondered just whose side you were on' (Banham 1981: 85). Banham was fully aware of this strange dichotomy and once expressed it as the tension between 'unavoidable admiration' for American 'creative power' and production and the 'equally unavoidable disgust at the system that was producing it' (cited in Webster 1988: 247). Living through the Cold War in the 1950s, Banham felt the

> division which runs right through English thinking, and indeed much American thinking (people like Dwight MacDonald): that to accept, to enjoy, the products of Pop, the products of the enter-tainment industry, Detroit-styling and such things, was to betray one's political position. (Banham 1981: 85)

Yet American energy was critical for Banham, a corrective to the 'sloppy provincialism' of postwar Britain, as he wrote of the 'gusto and pro-fessionalism' of American design as an antidote to the 'Moore-ish yokelry of British sculpture, of the affected Piperish gloom of British painting'; indeed, 'the average Playtex or Maidenform ad in American

Vogue was an instant deflater of the reputations of most artists then in Arts Council vogue' (in Webster 1988: 247). In a very powerful phrase, Banham referred to American pop culture as 'the day of the outsider' because it offered so much energy and expression to those in Britain who had been defined and delimited as 'working class' (in Whiteley 2002: 380). The appeal of the 'outside' draws us to Mikhail Bakhtin's comment that 'outsideness' is a 'most powerful factor in understanding' since

> it is only in the eyes of another culture that foreign culture reveals itself fully and profoundly... A meaning only reveals its depths once it has encountered and come into contact with another, foreign meaning: they engage in a kind of dialogue, which surmounts the closedness and one-sidedness of these particular meanings, these cultures... Such a dialogic encounter of two cultures does not result in merging or mixing. Each retains its own unity and open totality, but they are mutually enriched. (Bakhtin 1990: 7)

Banham explored these dialogical tensions, utilising their energies to challenge both sides and thereby existing 'with one foot on either side of the dividing line that had been drawn through the culture of the West' (Banham 1981: 85). Unlike Hoggart's and W. G. Hoskins's fear of loss, Banham felt that 'the public... cannot be... manipulated to that extent' and what was required was the 'need to redefine [the progressive middle and Left's] relationship to the live culture of the working classes as it exists' (ibid.: 85, 87). Banham analysed the changes he witnessed from 'new' America rather than rejecting them as inferior to the well-established 'old' culture of Britain, and this meant shifting towards concepts like 'expendability' and a willingness to engage with the commercial design process. Above all, he refused to be 'isolated from humanity by the Humanities', as he put it (in Whiteley 2002: 94).

The 'popular', wherever he found it, was not automatically denied, but took on a role in his expanding vision of the relations between Britain and America that led him in his later career to write two great books on America – *Los Angeles: The Architecture of Four Ecologies* (originally 1971) and *Scenes in America Deserta* (1982). Both books are the consequence of Banham's earliest productive collision with the USA and his refusal, as he puts it in *Los Angeles*, 'to reject the inscrutable, to hurl the unknown in the ocean' (Banham 1973: 23). In fact, much of Banham's general uncertainty about being of the British

'Left' and still taking pleasure from America is suggested by the introduction to *Scenes*, where he writes of his views that 'alternated between
elation and bewilderment' and his 'confusions as well as . . . enthusiasms'
(Banham 1982: 3). But as I have maintained throughout, it is precisely
out of this uneasy and suspicious relationship that Banham is able to
comprehend the complex nature of the overall UK/US relationship in
all its tension and irresolution. Banham's reputation and influence on
both sides of the Atlantic is exemplified in Peirce Lewis's belief that
he was one of the few 'glorious exceptions' in the academic world
who took 'landscape-reading' seriously and had a major impact on the
writings that went into *The Interpretation of Ordinary Landscapes*
(Meinig 1979: 14). In this respect, Banham provides a model for the
'shifting frontier' of UK/US relations, in which pragmatism replaced
the dogmatism often associated with much modernist thinking and
allowed him to travel between cultures and disciplines in a productive
and provocative manner. Indeed Whiteley argues that Banham thrived
on 'the combination of being an outsider and being an insider', contributing to his 'ambivalent relationship with the architectural history
Establishment'; however, one might go further to see these characteristics
as a vital approach to studying US/UK relations as well (Whiteley
2002: 410, 399). Banham referred in 1959 to his 'prophet-without-
honour-in-own-country complex', identifying himself as being at odds
with the established views of the age – one of which was a fear of
Americanisation – and, as Whiteley puts it, 'perhaps the outsider-insider
was one of the most impressive achievements of a "both/and" approach'
(Whiteley 2002: 400). To be 'both/and' is an inclusive vision that
rejects binary oppositions, close to Bakhtin's notion of multi-accented,
unfinished dialogue, an attitude that Banham certainly brought in so
many ways to his appreciation of the possibilities of Britain's multiple
social and cultural relationships with the USA. Banham's vision and
his perspective on UK/US relations provide an approach to cultural
landscape that is innovative and refreshing, concerned as it is with the
'traces' we leave in the process of intersection and contact, an attitude
summarised in this short section from *Scenes from America Deserta*:

> Where I differ is that the works of man always interest me as
> much as the landscapes in which they are wrought. The tire tracks
> in the sand, the old arastra by the gold mine's mouth, the grove
> where the station used to be, the shiny power pylons marching
> over the horizon, the old windmill in the canyon and the new
> telephone repeater on the peak, the Indian pictograph and the war

graffiti, the trailer home parked in the middle of nothing, the fragment of Coalport china found in the sand at the bottom of the wash. (Banham 1982: 199–200)

Conclusion: diasporised cultural landscapes

The counterpoint between Hoskins, Hoggart and Banham tells an exemplary story about the approaches to and fears over Americanisation and reminds us that today, in the twenty-first century, there is much to learn from these tensions and arguments. As we survey our contemporary cultural landscapes infused with McDonald's, KFC and Burger King, with Nike, O'Neill and Timberland, with theme parks and malls and the Atkins Diet, are we not still encouraged to see this as a colonisation, as an over-running of the 'true' British tradition?

To borrow some ideas from the work of James Clifford, we could learn from this moment in the 1950s, seeing it as a time of 'traveling cultures' in which 'the "chronotope" of culture . . . comes to resemble as much a site of travel encounters as of residence; it is less like a tent in a village or a controlled laboratory or a site of initiation and inhabitation, and more like a hotel lobby, urban café, ship, or bus', and in so doing move away from the idea of culture as fixed, 'as a rooted body that grows, lives, dies and so on' and see instead spaces of 'constructed and disputed historicities, sites of displacement, interference, and interaction' (Clifford 1997: 25). Suddenly, a simple singular notion of place, nation and identity is no longer sufficient and can be supplemented with the idea of hybridity, creolisation or mixing: 'Across a whole range of cultural forms [or cultural landscapes] there is a powerfully *syncretic* dynamic which critically appropriates elements from the master-codes of the dominant culture and *creolizes* them, disarticulating given signs and rearticulating their symbolic meaning otherwise' (Mercer 1994: 63). Hence, the Americanising presence is not necessarily an imposition on passive recipients, but can rather be *used* or appropriated in a variety of creative, hybrid forms or experiences that may indeed subvert, transform or translate any original. Thus cultural landscapes are best seen as complex, hybrid contact zones as defined by Mary-Louise Pratt (see earlier) 'where disparate cultures meet, clash and grapple with each other, often in highly asymmetrical relations of domination and subordination – like colonialism, slavery, or their aftermaths', and through these 'ongoing relations' emerges a 'co-presence of subjects previously separated by geographic and historical disjunctures

[UK/USA] . . . whose trajectories now intersect' with the possibility of productive dialogical, hybridised encounters (Pratt 1995: 6–7, 4).

> Examine an 'Americanised' cultural landscape – a local restaurant or mall – as a 'contact zone', as defined by Pratt (above) and comment on and assess the 'exchanges' that take place there. How is the space 'used'?

> Examine the advertisement below, for the 'Frontierland' theme park in Lancashire, as an example of an 'Americanised' / hybridised cultural landscape. How do elements of American and British mythology mix here? What kind of a 'dialogue' exists here?

Paul Gilroy's work on the 'Black Atlantic' employs such tensions to productively rethink how essential, racial 'roots' can be dialogised by the acceptance of 'routes' and the hybrid quality of encounter. His work is based upon an interrogation of 'essences' and 'absolutist discourses' and an interest in 'the space between them' as a means of questioning the fixed and 'overintegrated conceptions of culture' that promulgate nationalistic and essentialist notions of identity (Gilroy 1993: 1–2). These ideas can be helpfully applied to this shifting sense of cultural landscape 'relations' as multiple and hybrid – as 'stereophonic, bilingual, or bifocal cultural forms' (ibid.: 3). Gilroy employs the concept of *diaspora* as a 'more worldly sense of culture than the characteristic notions of soil, landscape and rootedness' that often fix national identity in very specific, boundaried concepts of place, such as 'Merry England' (in Woodward 1997: 328). Diaspora (that is, migratory movement, dispersal, contact) re-assesses this thinking about place and identity as essential and absolute, and 'problematizes the cultural and historical mechanics of belonging' by disrupting the mythic, explanatory 'links between place, location and consciousness' (ibid.). Hence, Hoskins's and Hoggart's myth-ideals of England are questioned under diasporic thinking, since cultural landscape is constructed as dynamic, interlinked and relational, formed by the 'routes' it travels (tourism, imagination, mediation, etc.) and the contacts it makes in that process as much as by any fixed settlement or 'essence'. This new geography explores the possibility of interactive, hybrid landscapes as 'sites of

Figure 3 'Frontierland' advertisement.

collision' where 'American culture is not monolithic and homogenous' but is 'used and enjoyed' in many complex and unexpected ways (Webster 1988: 72).

As Homi Bhabha has argued, there is a 'need to think beyond narratives of originary and initial subjectivities and to focus on those moments or processes that are produced in the articulation of cultural differences', since it is in these 'in-between spaces' that 'new signs of identity, and innovative sites of collaboration' are initiated (Bhabha 1994: 1–2). Cultural landscapes, even at their most commercialised and commodified, present hybrid contact zones in which a dialogised 'battle' takes place between cultures, architectures, desires and ideologies representing 'practices of crossing and interaction that troubled the localism of many common assumptions about culture' (Clifford 1997: 3). Perhaps allowing ourselves to think of these cultural landscapes as Clifford does will reveal new and different stories about the relations of culture, place and identity and, specifically in this case, relations of Americanisation beyond cultural imperialist models and closer to what Gilroy terms 'one fragile moment in the dialogic circuits' that constitute our lives (Gilroy 2000: 109–10).

Bibliography

Bakhtin, Mikhail (1990), *Speech Genres*, Austin: University of Texas Press.

Banham, Peter Reyner [1971] (1973), *Los Angeles: The Architecture of Four Ecologies*, Harmondsworth: Pelican.

Banham, Peter Reyner (1981), *Design by Choice*, London: Academy Editions.

Banham, Peter Reyner (1982), *Scenes in America Deserta*, London: Thames and Hudson.

Banham, Peter Reyner (1996), *A Critic Writes*, Berkeley: University of California Press.

Bhabha, Homi (1994), *The Location of Culture*, London: Routledge.

Certeau, Michel de [1984] (1988), *The Practice of Everyday Life*, Berkeley: University of California Press.

Chaney, David (1994), *The Cultural Turn*, London: Routledge.

Clifford, James (1988), *The Predicament of Culture*, Cambridge, MA: Harvard University Press.

Clifford, James (1997), *Routes: Travel and Translation in the Late Twentieth Century*, Cambridge, MA: Harvard University Press.

Corner, James (1999), *Recovering Landscape: Essays in Contemporary Landscape Architecture*, New York: Princeton Architectural Press.

Crang, Mike (1998), *Cultural Geography*, London: Routledge.

Gilroy, Paul (1993), *The Black Atlantic*, London: Verso.

Gilroy, Paul (2000), *Between Camps*, Harmondsworth: Penguin.

Groth, Paul and Todd Bressi (eds) (1997), *Understanding Ordinary Landscapes*, New Haven: Yale University Press.

Hall, Stuart (1995), 'New Cultures for Old', in Doreen Massey and Pat Jess (eds), *A Place in the World?*, Oxford: Oxford University Press.

Hebdige, Dick (1988), *Hiding in the Light*, London: Routledge.

Hewison, Robert (1987), *Too Much: Art and Society in the Sixties*, London: Methuen.

Hoggart, Richard [1957] (1962), *The Uses of Literacy*, Harmondsworth: Pelican.

Hoskins, W. G. [1955] (1985), *The Making of the English Landscape*, London: Penguin.

Lippard, Lucy (1991), *Pop Art*, London: Thames and Hudson.

Matless, David (1998), *Landscape and Englishness*, London: Reaktion.

Meinig, D. W. (ed.) (1979), *The Interpretation of Ordinary Landscapes*, New York: Oxford University Press.

Mercer, Kobena (1994), *Welcome to the Jungle*, London: Routledge.

Morley, David and Kevin Robins (1995), *Spaces of Identity*, London: Routledge.

Pratt, Mary-Louise (1995), *Imperial Eyes: Studies in Travel Writing and Transculturation*, London: Routledge.

Relph, Edward (1976), *Place and Placelessness*, London: Pion.

Robbins, David (ed.) (1990), *The Independent Group*, Cambridge, MA: MIT Press.

Sampson, Anthony (1962), *The Anatomy of Britain*, London: Hodder and Stoughton.

Vidler, Anthony (1992), *The Architectural Uncanny*, Cambridge, MA: MIT Press.

Webster, Duncan (1988), *Looka Yonder! The Imaginary America of Populist Culture*, London: Routledge.

Whiteley, Nigel (2002), *Reyner Banham: Historian of the Immediate Future*, Cambridge, MA: MIT Press.

Williams, Raymond (1966), *Communications*, London: Chatto and Windus.

Woodward, Kathryn (ed.) (1997), *Identity and Difference*, London: Sage.

POPULAR MUSIC

CHAPTER SEVEN

Americanisation and Popular Music in Britain

Andrew Blake

It is the purpose of this chapter to explore the Americanisation of music – and its discontents. The chapter discusses preliminary issues and goes on to offer a historical outline which is in two parts, divided roughly at 1960. The focus of the outline is popular music (including jazz) in Britain and the USA; there is a brief appendix devoted to classical composition and performance. It is the intention to propose the critical use of music as evidence, by exploring ways in which music contributes to the political and cultural shifts which contemporary Britons and their forebears have experienced.

Preliminary issues

Such an exercise necessitates that we develop our faculties of critical listening to music. This is particularly important in classroom contexts. Playing any undigested sequence of sonic events can all too easily make music into part of the 'background noise' of the real object of study, whether that be political or cultural shifts.

The first issue, then, in approaching the use of music as evidence is that we have to learn to listen. We exist in a world in which music is part of the background noise of contemporary culture – in bars, shopping malls, and domestic spaces alike – and most of us have a strongly developed expertise in ignoring it and talking over it without paying more than cursory attention to this routine sonic environment. We need, therefore, to pay attention to the very real problems involved in using music as evidence and to try and develop the skill of listening. This means firstly acknowledging that most people do not have this skill. Unless this is done, as soon as a teacher turns from audio-visual delivery to the purely sonic (i.e. whenever s/he first turns to playing music examples rather than talking or using visual aids), *students will start to talk to each other, and will lose focus on the task at hand.* The point needs to be made, and repeated at the start of any session in which music is to be used, that the music played during the class is there to be listened to.

In order to be able to listen, and then to discuss music intelligently, we must share some very basic analytical language – in effect, a *musicology* – as well as knowledge of the history and economics of the music business, and biographical and discographical information on key artists. We need to be able to recognise and identify the organisational components of sound, and relate the basic qualities and quantities of timbre and pitch as they change over time to the ways in which such sounds are structured. A teacher who wishes to *use* music must, in other words, identify voices and individual instruments and groups of instruments, and the ways in which they are recorded, sampled and balanced, and go on to identify the deployment of those voices and instruments in rhythm, harmony and melody – the structures of sound in time and space.

The second prerequisite is some basic sense of the sounds of musics (in particular, of popular musics) in Europe *before* the impact of American recordings and performance practices. Students might be played (or if possible, perform themselves) some or all of: Strauss family waltzes and polkas; music hall songs; hymns, for instance well-known Christmas carols such as Felix Mendelssohn's tune *Adeste Fideles* ('O Come, All Ye Faithful'); and folk songs from the collections made at the turn of the twentieth century by Cecil Sharp and his followers. This might be backed up by reference to for example Dave Russell's survey of popular music in nineteenth-century England (Russell 2001). Without this knowledge students will be unable to make any assessment as to whether sonic Americanisation had in fact occurred.

Thirdly, students will need to be aware – and, again, to be reminded at various salient moments – that the diffusion of cultural forms is not a magical uni-directional process in which local differences are system-atically erased by dominant forms imposed by industrial capitalism. American music is itself far from monocultural, and has evolved and is evolving now in relation to the musics of the world whose peoples have contributed to the formation of the American population. Students will probably already be aware of the magisterial account of one crucial aspect of this process given by Paul Gilroy (Gilroy 1987). They should be made aware firstly that there are many other, parallel aspects of the development of music in the USA, and secondly that musics also continue to evolve elsewhere despite the global success of American capitalism and the pervasive global presence of popular music with lyrics in English, rock and r'n'b beats, and harmony based on the European system of tempered tuning, major and minor scales and their African-American derivations (Born and Hesmondhalgh 2000; van der Merwe 1989; Negus 1999: 131–72).

A final preliminary point is to emphasise the very substantial cultural paradox which qualifies any simple story of the development of American musical hegemony. Musics such as jazz and blues, which are largely African-American in genesis and development if not always in delivery, had a more positive reception history in the UK and Europe than in the USA. Jazz musicians such as Sidney Bechet (1897–1959) and Dexter Gordon (1923–1990) spent substantial parts of their careers in Europe, because they found it to be more welcoming than the more overtly racist USA, and because it developed a strong sense of 'their' jazz as art music, and the blues as an authentic folk music, well before such a position was encouraged in the USA by the Civil Rights movement (Godbolt 1984; Hodeir 1956; Jackson 2003). It is arguable that the blues-based music the Beatles and the Rolling Stones proudly took to the USA in the early 1960s helped to produce a more positive view of Black American musics within the (white) USA mainstream. Meanwhile in the USA itself, a premium was paid on the musical traditions of Europe. Until the mid-twentieth century at least, the European composed music of the 'classical' tradition was considered to be the highest form of music, and many American film scores, musicals, and compositional structures such as big-band jazz owe something to those European traditions.

The Americanisation, and anti-Americanisation, of popular music before 'pop'

From this appropriately qualified basis it can be proposed that nonetheless, musically, the twentieth was the American century. Any satisfactory account of this phenomenon has to mix cultural and economic history along with music examples, and an introductory survey might start from the invention of sound recording (Chanan 1995). The gramophone appeared at the end of the nineteenth century, and in its spread, led by American capitalism, an American musical sensibility was inculcated in many parts of the world. From the turn of the twentieth century American music was welcomed by an Old World whose composed art music was becoming increasingly self-referential and elitist, while its popular musics (folk songs, hymns, the waltz and other dance music, the participant choruses of music hall songs and so on) lacked the melodic sinuosity, rhythmic punch and improvisatory freedom for the performer which was found in spirituals, ragtime, jazz and blues.

One familiar master narrative of Americanisation simply assumes that all popular music was quickly and completely Americanised. Edward Lee, for example, reviews British popular music from the Anglo-Saxons onwards; but as soon as the story reaches the twentieth century, Lee's attention is diverted to the story of American popular music (Lee 1970). Similarly Donald Clarke looks at Anglo-Euro-American musical interaction up to around 1900, followed by the history of American popular music and jazz, until the narrative reaches the 1960s – when the international success of British pop makes an America-centred history impossible, and we return to interaction (Clarke 1995). British music and musicians are mentioned before this point; but Clarke offers no narrative, let alone analysis, of popular music in twentieth century Britain before rock'n'roll. Such accounts necessarily leave out not only the persistence of local forms, but also the recurrent resistance to sonic Americanisation based on the hostility expressed by many who saw themselves as guardians of British musical culture.

British popular music has been connected with American musics since the settlement of British people in the Americas from the sixteenth century – they took their hymns and psalms, and in return the first visits of Black entertainers to Britain occurred in the middle of the nineteenth century. Several indigenous forms have influenced subsequent development in parallel with the Anglo-American story. Music hall is arguably the most important of these forms since it involves a tradition of songwriting and performing which can be traced through bands such as the Small Faces and the Kinks in the 1960s, the pantomimic camp of Roxy Music and David Bowie in the 1970s, the witty stories of Squeeze and Chas 'n' Dave in the early 1980s, and to their very aware inheritors such as Pulp and Blur in the 1990s (Sinker 1995: 107–8; Blake 1996: 197–214). Many of the British music hall entertainers received star status within their communities, a few such as Marie Lloyd and Charles Lauder were popular tourists in the USA, and of course Charlie Chaplin built an important second career there as a film actor.

Mention should also be made of the indigenous 'musical comedy', including shows by Vivian Ellis and Noel Coward, which always had a very aware relationship with American models (Russell 2001: 72; Pearsall 1975, 1976). One of the best known of these shows, Coward's *Bittersweet* (1929), was a response to, in his words, 'the endless succession of slick American Vo-do-deo-do musical farces in which the speed was fast, the invention complicated, and the sentimental value negligible' (Lee 1970: 139) – such as Jerome Kern's 1928 success *Showboat*. This anxious isolationism was common among British musicians wishing to promote their own goods in a market constantly threatened by American imports. Well into the 1950s the Songwriters' Guild of Great Britain was pressing the BBC to play a part in 'the creation of a specifically British culture in the realm of the song' (Briggs 1979: 692).

This indicates that there was dialogue, differentiation and divergence, rather than the simple adoption of American models. This occurred partly through the maintenance of traditions, or through a more diffuse sense of cultural resistance, and partly because of the specific protection afforded the British musicians' union. Resistance in general often took the form of specifically racialised discourses: hot jazz in the 1920s, swing in the 1930s and rock'n'roll in the 1950s were all resisted from within the British musical establishment on the grounds that these were Black or Black-derived forms, and that Black music was dangerous: it would infect the white 'race' through its open eroticism and its association with illegal narcotic drugs. There was a particular fear that eroticised and narcotised music would make white women open to the sexual advances of Black men, the common fear of 'miscegenation' around which many forms of racism have been organised (Kohn 1993).

Resistance in particular was crystallised when in 1930 the dance band section of the Musicians' Union was set up specifically to police the membership of dance bands plying their trade in Britain. The chief purpose was to exclude Americans. In connection with this, 'needle time' agreements were negotiated with the BBC, which restricted the amount of recorded material the organisation could broadcast (most recordings then as now were American in origin) and therefore guaranteed the BBC's continuing employment of British musicians. Licences were needed for visiting American artists. These protective measures were matched in the USA with reciprocal arrangements, though until the 1960s the loss appeared to be to British audiences rather than Americans. Exceptions such as the 1955 visit to America of the Ted Heath Band attracted national newspaper headlines (Briggs 1979: 684). The strategy did not protect an isolated British popular music, which continued to adopt and adapt American forms; it protected British *performance*, and in this case helped to protect a lengthy tradition of British-played but musically (Latin-)American dance band music: the BBC Big Band was disbanded only in 1993.

The various acts of cultural and political resistance alongside American music's popularity resulted in cultural schizophrenia, as seen through the reception of jazz. Some Europeans saw jazz as an art form, a parallel with classical music. But many moments of public interest in jazz have enthused over its danceability – the rhythm or groove, rather than the technical ability revered by musicians. And indeed from the 1920s to the end of the Second World War the principal meaning of jazz was precisely as dance music. Jazz variants such as the big band swing which American soldiers brought with them during the 1939–45 war remained desirable. After the war trad jazz, a form related to the early days of the music in New Orleans, was (re)constructed, and at its high point of popularity in Britain played its part alongside folk music in the CND protests of the early 1960s (Hobsbawm 1961: 245; McKay, forthcoming). Meanwhile the modern jazz of soul/funk grooves and the Hammond organ-based sound made by players like Jimmy Smith was also popular in early 1960s Britain – and gave the name 'modernist' to the 'mods'. The James Taylor Quartet was performing very similar material in the 1990s, when 'acid jazz' became a category including almost any post-war jazz which people *could* dance to, including 'modernist' hard bop – but also some music in which the rhythm section (bass, drums, keyboards) was produced by sequencers and samplers, while soloists used traditional instruments (one example, guitarist Ronny Jordan's 1992 album *The Antidote*, charted). Through such reinventions jazz remained culturally available as dance or background music despite the continuing tendency also to value it as 'art' (concert) music.

So from the 1930s on there was a large, protected group of English musicians playing some or all of music hall/musical comedy, and American or American-influenced jazz, dance music and popular songs, and by the 1940s big band swing; and despite the attentions of the Musicians' Union, recordings of American music were popular. The coincidence of this music, these musicians, and the Second World War is noteworthy. Because of the proximity of this music and the war, the conservative anti-European magazine *This England* promotes nostalgic recordings of American and Anglo-American dance bands (including much Black music) with the same vigour it devotes to the promotion of cottage gardens, cricket on the village green, fox-hunting and other traditional English pastimes. There can be no greater index to the success of sonic Americanisation before rock'n'roll.

A similar, and similarly surprising, process of adoption of American music happened on the left – whose tendency had been to blanket American music as the cultural arm of consumer capitalism. After the Second World War, the political imperative and source material of folk music changed, principally through the dominance of organised communism. A. L. Lloyd and Ewan MacColl promoted the songs of the industrial working class (especially of the north of England, Scotland and Wales) as folk songs. To these were added the political songs of the American radical elite (those of Pete Seeger in particular) and the folk-blues of the American Deep South. The enthusiasts for the latter virtually created, and certainly rechristened as 'authentic', a form that had long ceased to have any provenance in America: visiting blues musicians from the USA were criticised if they used electric guitars, to their confusion (Boyes 1995: 213).

The 1960s and after: Anglo-American pop and the study of culture

The emergence of rock'n'roll in late-1950s Britain was shadowed by a connoisseur's appreciation of both country blues and urban rhythm 'n' blues, which complemented the politicised folk movement which had helped to promote interest in the rural blues (Bradley 1992; Lister 1991; Mackinnon 1993). It is easy to illustrate the ways in which early-1960s British pop was sonically Americanised through the basic rock'n'roll twelve-bar chord sequence, whether played with blues or rockabilly rhythms. One obvious example would be Bo Diddley's insistently repeated shuffle rhythm, via his own track 'Bo Diddley', in the 1964 Rolling Stones hit 'Not Fade Away'. While representable as 'theft', this is part of a connection with blues and r'n'b which the band itself always scrupulously acknowledged, and which could be illustrated in their guest performers: for example, bluesman Taj Mahal was an onstage guest artist on the Stones' 1998 *Bridges to Babylon* tour.

Consider this kind of 'sonic Americanisation' by listening to the early Beatles and Rolling Stones albums in relation to those of Buddy Holly and Chuck Berry, and to Tamla Motown and Phil Spector-produced girl group singles. Further, in what ways did John Lennon, Mick Jagger and others of their ilk try to sound *vocally* American, and subsequently, in what ways did Ray Davies and David Bowie try *not* to?

The Lennon–McCartney songwriting partnership emerged from a band which at first copied American models. In Dave Harker's retelling of their story, there is a deliberate taming of the more raucous elements of r'n'b as the band becomes successful, with the tone of voice used by both Lennon and Paul McCartney becoming softer and smoother (Harker 1980: 83). One could equally say that the band moved away from a single, limited means of vocal realisation, based on the mimicking of r'n'b performers, as it quite literally began to find its own voice; and that the raucousness was still available for numbers like 'Helter Skelter' on the 1968 *White Album*. Nonetheless arguably the band did become *less* 'American' in sound as it developed – and became *more* successful in the USA.

The very success of the early-1960s pop groups made first Liverpool and then London into world musical centres. It was to the 'swinging' London mythologised as the place of classless social mobility where young talent could find its true reward that Jimi Hendrix came in 1966, to escape from the stereotyped role of the Black r'n'b guitarist which was all that had been afforded him in the United States, and to forge a new expressive language of guitar-playing. Hendrix developed this from r'n'b, the solo guitar voices of American urban-blues players like B. B. King and Buddy Guy, and English guitarists such as Peter Green, Jimmy Page and Eric Clapton. Working outside the cultural, ethnic, political and legal constraints which had made the blues and r'n'b in the USA, but inside the cultural constraints defining musical value in Britain, guitarists working in British blues bands such as the Graham Bond Organisation, John Mayall's Bluesbreakers, the Alexis Korner band and the Yardbirds first abstracted and reified the virtuosity, and romanticised the position, of the musician, then pushed the barriers of song structure further away from blues in outfits such as Cream and Led Zeppelin. They saw themselves through the eyes of a culture dominated by the idea of the romantic artist as an inspired commentator separate from the common herd, rather than, say, the dance band leader as servant of popular entertainment (Heckstall-Smith 1988).

Thanks to this process, as with many jazz musicians who left the United States to work in France or Scandinavia, where they were treated with far more public respect than in their native land, Hendrix in London could more easily become the inspired solo voice. This solo voice was developed within a songwriting context which did not rely merely on blues harmonies or the controlled rhythmic repetition of r'n'b or soul, but also paid respect to white popular musics from both sides of the Atlantic – white English musicians Noel Redding and Mitch Mitchell played in the Jimi Hendrix Experience, and the debt to Bob Dylan as songwriter and lyricist is celebrated in Hendrix's version of Dylan's 'All Along the Watchtower'. Hendrix's role in the emergence of rock music alongside Clapton, Page et al. has been emphasised by Charles Shaar Murray. Here the importance of London should be stressed again: without living there, he would probably have remained another Buddy Guy (a Chicago blues musician and virtuoso guitarist who has been lionised in Britain by musicians, but who did not become a major-label success as a recording artist). Singer Marsha Hunt followed the same path in order to realise her ambition:

> The American music scene was still severely segregated. They wanted me to be a soul singer, but I wasn't into bubble haircuts and short dresses, I wore leather and I had a large Afro. I said, I wanna sing rock. They said, black women don't sing rock. So I had to come to London to do it. (O'Brien 1995: 294)

What we have here, then, is not one-way traffic but *cultural exchange*. There is more to sonic Americanisation than the parroting of American songs learned from vinyl, and the academic discipline of cultural studies has explored the cultural transformations of which these musics were a part. Cultural studies started at the moment of the impact of rock'n'roll in the late 1950s and early 1960s, with its accompanying Americanisation – of which it was at first deeply suspicious. Richard Hoggart's 1957 book *The Uses of Literacy* warned against Americanisation, offering instead a nostalgic celebration of inter-war northern English working-class culture which paralleled the contemporary, Communist Party-inspired and deeply anti-American (re)creation of 'folk' music.

Paradoxically, though, Hoggart's hatred of the symbols of American 'mass culture' – hard-boiled detective fiction, the milk bar, the juke box and rock'n'roll – was matched by insistence that these forms should be studied. Bringing these aspects of culture into academic discussion then made it possible for the negative critique to be engaged with and refused, in studies which are more positive about the cultural products valued by the working class. Dick Hebdige's 1978 book *Subculture: The Meaning of Style*, among the most influential of these studies, argues that British youth subcultures are engaged in a long imaginary 'phantom dialogue' with Black American (and Caribbean) culture, a dialogue focused around dress and music, and embracing the marginality of those cultures against mainstream white culture.

> Consider the use made, for example, of the musics of Miles Davis and Art Blakey in the British jazz revival of the late 1980s – an important moment for Black British identity – or the use of samples from 1960s records by James Brown in contemporary dance music in contributing to a more inclusively 'multicultural' sense of contemporary British culture.

However, there are problems here which any student of Americanisation must address. Hebdige romantically overstates the importance of punk rock, then as now a tenacious but marginal Anglo-American movement. And he ignores another concurrent weekend alternative culture, the disco boom, which forms an important component in the continuing story of sonic Americanisation. Punk was hardly a mass movement by the side of the disco boom of the late 1970s – *Saturday Night Fever* (featuring the British band the Bee Gees) and the hits of the Swedish band ABBA, not punk, dominated the British charts in 1978. And there *was* a disco subculture. All-night dances and their apotheosis, 'soul weekenders' (in which entrepreneurs hired holiday camps such as Caister in Norfolk, and large groups of young people danced the weekend away), were a challenge to parental orthodoxy in their hedonism; they routinely involved gay as well as heterosexual people; they were most definitely part of the urban engagement between Black and white cultures around imported American music. They had a well-defined supporting cultural apparatus, including, as well as the various parties and weekenders, record stores importing 'rare grooves' from America, and illegal pirate radio stations, which were necessary (and popular) because the official broadcasting apparatus ignored their music, and which brought them into clear and continuous conflict with the state. So while, if you see them as leisure practices, the soul weekenders offered no resistance to the mainstream values of consumer capitalism, as conflicting centres of power and pleasure – involving illegal entrepreneurship around drugs, parties and broadcasting – and thereby as oppositional to the official economy, they were at least as subversive as punks (Chambers 1985: 187–9; Dyer 1990: 410–18). Isaac Julien's 1990 film *Young Soul Rebels* tried to capture the spirit of this moment.

This particular British–American musical dialogue remained important in the emergence and development of British hip-hop, house and techno musics. The disco boom's party culture, based around gay and mixed venues and DJs with new skills in mixing, spread from New York to Chicago and Detroit where by the middle of the 1980s house and techno styles had emerged (Lawrence 2004). Although the party culture of the Balearic Islands helped the formation of the wider dance culture of outdoor 'raves' in the UK, musically it was in fact Chicago house and Detroit techno which provided the foundation for the dance phenomenon of the late 1980s and thereafter. British dance musics, however, also draw on the distinctive development of UK Black music – Caribbean-derived forms like reggae and ragga are influential in drum 'n' bass and UK garage. Likewise bhangra and other British Asian pop and dance musics are partially American and partly subcontinental, but just as stridently local, in inspiration.

Rock and pop, too, continue to exist in transatlantic dialogue rather than one-way traffic. The nostalgia for the 1960s expressed in 'Britpop' was in part a reaction to the early-1990s dominance of the charts by American phenomena such as grunge (for which there was no simple British equivalent).

As the millennium dawned, however, another form of cultural nostalgia emerged temporarily victorious, as pop demonstrated its continued interest in the lowest common denominator through transatlantically successful series such as *Pop Idol*.

By the mid-1980s, in fact, television had become a major carrier of pop music, establishing itself through MTV and its derivatives, which at first provided sequences of generic material provided for them by the record companies. This has had a spinoff back into terrestrial television, with more use of video and video-related material in youth programming, films, and advertising.

Since the early 1980s advertising has used popular music as a deliberate part of its ploy to draw in, not young people, but as wide a consumership as possible: and the consumer-citizen is usually aurally imagined as American. 'Classic' popular songs have been used to advertise car tyres (the Velvet Underground's 'Venus in Furs'), jeans (a lovingly re-recorded pastiche of Marvin Gaye's version of 'I Heard it

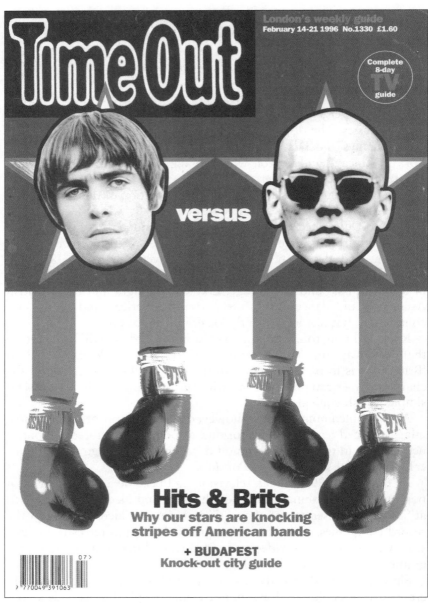

Figure 4 Anglo-American ambivalence in a nutshell. In 1995–6 'Britpop' tried to relaunch the British music business by returning to the sounds of the 1960s, when the 'British Invasion' had challenged American hegemony. Oasis sounded like the Beatles, who launched the 'invasion'. But the Beatles started out trying to sound American . . .

Through the Grapevine') and insurance services (Nat 'King' Cole singing 'Let's Face the Music and Dance'). The implication is that enough people will be drawn into making purchases through the use of such music – most of which is American or Americanised – for the royalty costs to be worthwhile. Since the mass manipulation of debt via hire purchase and credit are American contributions to the development of consumer capitalism we are all, apparently, Americans now, as we listen and spend.

However, as usual there is resistance to this manifestation of music as consumer manipulator, though now the resistance comes from file-sharing Internet software programmes following the example of Napster (Alderman 2001). Though the reaction against this free exchange of musical information has been led by the Recording Institute of America Association, file-sharing is another form of Americanisation, this time drawn from the libertarian ideology of personal computer use which helped to establish companies like Apple (Barbrook et al. 1995). Thanks to peer-to-peer software, whatever the fate of the global music industry, it is likely that the ambivalently dialogic processes of sonic Americanisation will continue in the twenty-first century.

Appendix – classical music: Americanisation within European hegemony

In the USA the musical traditions of Europe were, until the mid-twentieth century at least, considered the highest of the sonic arts. Wealthy Americans founded symphony orchestras and hired Europeans such as Arturo Toscanini (1867–1957) and Leopold Stokowski (1882–1987) to conduct them. Film music, whether written by émigrés such as Erich Wolfgang Korngold (1897–1957) or American-born composers such as John Williams (b. 1932), continually referred to the work of Europeans as both structural and emotional authority (compare, for example, Williams's *Jaws* main theme with Stravinsky's *Rite of Spring*, or his *Star Wars* theme with 'Mars' from Gustav Holst's *The Planets*). Meanwhile harmonically rich 32-bar songs were written for musicals by composers such as Jerome Kern (1885–1945), George Gershwin (1898–1937) and Richard Rogers (1902–79), and jazz musicians such as Charlie Parker (1920–55) and John Coltrane (1926–67) tried to learn aspects of Western composition – all evidence that European composed music was influential in the USA at all levels.

Apart from Hollywood, 'classical' composition in the USA was dominated by those who modified European forms, usually through more vigorous and repetitive rhythmic writing, such as Aaron Copland (1900–1988), Leonard Bernstein (1918–1990) and more recently the post-minimalist John Adams (b. 1947).

Again, however, this is not the story of a one-way relationship, and those interested might wish to explore the sonic Americanisation of composed classical music as a particular case study. Composition within the USA itself was moved in more avowedly American directions by the most eccentric of composers, such as Charles Ives (1874–1954), Edgard Varèse (1883–1965), Harry Partch (1901–74) and Conlon Nancarrow (1912–2002) – each of whom was largely a prophet without honour in their own lifetime – and by the globally influential experimenter John Cage (1912–99). While Cage's philosophy of composition has probably been more influential than the actual sounds of his music, the 'minimalists' such as Steve Reich (b. 1936), Philip Glass (b. 1937) and Laurie Anderson (b. 1949) have had a much more easily demonstrable influence over European composers such as Michael Nyman (b. 1944) or Louis Andriessen (b. 1939). European composers have also responded to jazz – by trying to write down its sounds and rhythms: obvious examples such as Darius Milhaud's (1892–1974) *Le Boeuf sur le toit* could be played alongside Ralph Vaughan Williams's (1872–1958) Sixth or Ninth Symphonies, each of which has prominent saxophone parts, or *Blood on the Floor* by Mark-Anthony Turnage (b. 1960), in which improvising jazz musicians are integrated into the orchestra in an affectionate pastiche of big-band jazz. Turnage acknowledges Miles Davis as his greatest musical influence.

Bibliography and further reading

Alderman, John (2001), *Sonic Boom: Napster, MP3 and the New Pioneers of Music*, Cambridge, MA: Perseus Publishing.

Barbrook, Richard and Andy Cameron (1995), 'The Californian Ideology', *Mute* 3, Autumn.

Blake, Andrew (1996), 'The Echoing Corridor: Music in the Postmodern East End', in Tim Butler and Michael Rustin (eds), *Rising in the East? The Regeneration of East London*, London: Lawrence and Wishart, pp. 197–214.

Born, Georgina and David Hesmondhalgh (2000), *Western Music and Its Others*, Berkeley: University of California Press.

Boyes, Georgina (1995), *The Imagined Village*, Manchester: Manchester University Press.

Bradley, Dick (1992), *Understanding Rock 'n' Roll: Popular Music in Britain 1955–1964*, Buckingham: Open University Press.

Briggs, Asa (1979), *A History of Broadcasting in the United Kingdom*, Oxford: Oxford University Press, vol. 4.

Chambers, Iain (1985), *Urban Rhythms: Pop Music and Popular Culture*, Basingstoke: Macmillan.

Chanan, Michael (1995), *Repeated Takes*, London: Verso.

Clarke, Donald (1995), *The Rise and Fall of Popular Music*, London: Viking.

Dyer, Richard (1990), 'In Defence of Disco', in Simon Frith and Andrew Goodwin (eds), *On Record*, London: Routledge, pp. 410–18.

Gilroy, Paul (1987), *The Black Atlantic*, London: Verso.

Godbolt, Jim (1984), *A History of Jazz in Britain*, London: Quartet.

Harker, Dave (1980), *One for the Money*, London: Hutchinson.

Heckstall-Smith, Dick (1988), *The Safest Place to Be*, London: Quartet.

Hobsbawm, Eric, writing as Francis Newton (1961), *The Jazz Scene*, London: Weidenfeld and Nicolson.

Hodeir, André (1956), *Jazz: Its Evolution and Essence*, London: Secker and Warburg.

Jackson, Jeffrey (2003), *Making Jazz French: Music and Modern Life in Interwar Paris*, Durham, NC and London: Duke University Press.

Kohn, Marek (1993), *Dope Girls*, London: Lawrence and Wishart.

Lawrence, Tim (2003), *Love Saves the Day: A History of American Dance Music Culture 1970–1979*, Durham, NC and London: Duke University Press.

Lee, Edward (1970), *Music of the People*, London: Barrie and Jenkins.

Lister, Derek (1991), *Bradford's Rock'n'Roll*, Bradford: Bradford Libraries and Information Service.

McKay, George (forthcoming), *Circular Breathing*, Durham, NC and London: Duke University Press.

Mackinnon, Niall (1993), *The British Folk Scene*, Buckingham: Open University Press.

Murray, Charles Shaar (1989), *Crosstown Traffic: Jimi Hendrix and Post-War Pop*, London: Faber and Faber.

Negus, Keith (1999), *Music Genres and Corporate Cultures*, London: Routledge.

O'Brien, Lucy (1995), *She Bop: The Definitive History of Women in Rock, Pop and Soul*, London: Penguin.

Pearsall, Ronald (1975), *Edwardian Popular Music*, Newton Abbot: David and Charles.

Pearsall, Ronald (1976), *Popular Music of the Twenties*, Newton Abbot: David and Charles.

Russell, Dave (2001), *Popular Music in England*, 2nd ed., Manchester: Manchester University Press.

Sharp, Cecil (1902), *A Book of British Song for Home and School*, London: John Murray.

Sinker, Mark (1995), 'Music as Film', in Jonathan Romney and Adrian Wootton (eds), *The Celluloid Jukebox*, London: BFI, pp. 105–18.
Van der Merwe, Peter (1989), *Origins of the Popular Style: The Antecedents of Twentieth-Century Popular Music*, Oxford: Oxford University Press.

CHAPTER EIGHT

Sign of a Black Planet:
Hip-hop and Globalisation

Russell White

Over the course of the last twenty-five years, rap music and the hip-hop culture[1] of which it is part have spread from the South Bronx across the United States, and to many parts of the globe. In its edition for January 1998, hip-hop magazine the *Source* published a series of reports documenting what the magazine described as 'burgeoning' hip-hop 'scenes' in London, Kingston, Vancouver, Paris, Dakar, Milan, Tokyo, Amsterdam, Barcelona, Madrid, the Hawaiian Islands and Cuba. Under the title 'Round the Globe at 100BPM', Tracii McGregor noted that 'hip-hop is practically everywhere. In fact, it can easily be said that no country in the world – from Germany to Ghana – remains untouched by this incredibly powerful and prolific medium' (McGregor 1998: 100). The globalisation of this specifically African American cultural form has been the subject of much discussion in this vein, fuelled by debates over the status of hip-hop as a racial and as a national culture. As with other forms of cultural Americanisation, its qualities of having 'power' and being 'prolific' hint at the importance of its resignification outside America, so suggesting the inadequacy of simply categorising it as a cultural export. But the status of hip-hop as a Black cultural form means that there is more at stake than merely national differences. Depending on one's point of view, the globalisation of hip-hop could be regarded as promising an international popular culture of the Black diaspora, or seen as diffusing the authentic culture of urban blue-collar African Americans into a deracialised free-for-all colonised by people with no connection to these roots, as embodied graphically by abject figures such as the 1990s white rappers Milli Vanilli. While this chapter will ultimately argue against these extremes, the intense investments which generate them underline the importance, and the difficulty, of Paul Gilroy's question in *The Black Atlantic*, of 'how we are to deal with black cultural forms [that] originated [in Black communities], but are no longer the exclusive property of blacks dispersed within the black Atlantic' (Gilroy 1993: 3). Gilroy's own answers to this question have successively questioned the utility of the nation (in *The Black Atlantic*) and of essentialist forms of race (in *Between Camps*), in the process demonstrating the crucial importance of interactions between race, culture, and location. Warily entering this fraught arena, this chapter proceeds in the spirit of tracking these interactions, by examining how and with what results forms of Blackness and Americanness that were produced out of Black and Latino experiences of life in New York's South Bronx during the 1970s have been reproduced and renegotiated in different national and regional contexts. After outlining the issues at stake in the globalisation of hip-hop, the essay moves to discuss and compare the different ways in which British and French artists and audiences have reinterpreted it.

Globalisation and racial, local and national authenticity in hip-hop

Of course, hip-hop is hardly the first form of African American music to be exported across America and the globe. Indeed, there is a long and well-documented history of both Black and non-Black audiences outside the United States and non-Black audiences within the United States adopting African American-identified music, language and fashion, and mining them for what Naomi Klein refers to as 'borrowed "meaning" and identity' (Klein 2000: 73). The embracing of hip-hop 'style' by non-African American audiences thus represents the latest example of what could be called African Americanisation – the processes by which African American cultural forms and their attendant (sub)cultures have been exported to and received by the rest of America and the rest of the world. Such is the kudos given to forms of African American *popular* culture that Klein is moved to assert that 'the history of cool in America is . . . a history of African American culture' (ibid.: 74). The parallels with the consumption of American popular culture overseas are obvious. However, unlike most forms of Americanisation, African Americanisation has generally been structured by a fundamental – and quite vicious – paradox. While African American culture has been a pivotal influence on wider American – and global – popular culture, the majority of African Americans continued to be generally excluded from mainstream social, economic and political institutions. The failure to accord critical acclaim (at least in their lifetimes) or remotely equitable financial reward to African American jazz and blues performers is just one aspect of these conditions, albeit one of the most visible.

The coupling of cultural influence with the persistence of social and economic disadvantage makes the appropriation of Black cultural forms by others highly problematic. For critics of African American popular music such as Nelson George and Greg Tate, appropriation is a form of cultural piracy. A dominant culture borrows certain aspects of African American culture without giving anything back in return, such that the economic exploitation of Black performers is reflected in the cultural sphere. George's highly regarded *The Death of Rhythm and Blues* (1988) is indicative of the way in which these critics therefore present a revisionist history of African American music in order to accord previously excluded Black recording labels and musicians the attention and respect they deserve.

From its first inception, via the formal strategies of toasting and sampling, hip-hop music and culture has demonstrated a high degree of self-consciousness about issues of appropriation. This self-consciousness was made explicit in work such as Eric B and Rakim's 'Paid In Full', which presented hip-hop as both the epitome of African American culture and the moment at which that culture finally received its economic due. Accounts of hip-hop's globalisation in US newspapers and magazines tended to elaborate this racial narrative in national terms. The early 1990s saw a number of articles document the emergence and development of hip-hop 'scenes' in Europe, Africa, Asia and Oceania. As critics like Tony Mitchell and Adam Krims have observed, many American commentators took the view that, while these 'scenes' showed just how far hip-hop culture had spread, the musics produced by non-American rap artists were nevertheless wholly derivative and thus inferior to their African American equivalents. Mitchell cites James Bernard's 1992 article 'A newcomer abroad, rap speaks up' as one of the most forthright assertions of the American roots of hip-hop.

Labelling rap music an 'American artform', Bernard questioned how well rap had 'translated outside the American context where rap and race are inextricably bound' (Bernard 1992: 1). The negative reception given non-American hip-hop scenes by American critics such as Bernard comes about, Krims argues, because such scenes raise 'the spectre of what to some would be a politically frightening prospect, namely the erasure of the specifically African American origins and cultural embeddedness of rap' (Krims 2000: 6).

The unease with which Bernard and others view hip-hop's globalisation has its roots in the specific ways that authenticity is constructed and validated in the immediate regional and national context of African American popular culture. As Stuart Hall has suggested, authenticity in Black popular culture is contingent upon lived experience. In hip-hop culture, this manifests itself in the premium placed by artists and audiences on maintaining links to the local, normatively configured as the 'street' or the '(neighbour)hood'. The globalisation of hip-hop puts this model of authenticity under new pressures, as when the 'authenticity of experience' is related to locations in for example Dakar, Paris or London. In response, the proprietory discourse of Bernard and others tends to translate the highly racialised terms of social and geographical origin (the Bronx, or South Central LA) into national terms. 'America' is thus called upon to police a racial and class-based claim to cultural authority, which is to say that, under the condition of globalisation, the discourse of localised identity is explicitly reframed within nationalistic cultural paradigms. The result is to privilege the American experience – as Coco Fusco has suggested, the African American experience comes to represent the 'prototype of blackness' (Fusco 1992: 282).

PROVOCATIVE THOUGHT:
The point here is not to scorn the strategies by which Black popular culture has won overdue validation, but to suggest the importance of resisting the nationalistic frameworks which can circumscribe such strategies. The example of Paul Gilroy is again instructive, not simply for his insistence on cross-national frameworks for a full appreciation of racialised cultures, but also for the resistance encountered by Gilroy in some parts of the academy in the USA.

It can be seen then that American interpretations of non-African-American rap music, whether 'Black' or not, as lacking authenticity, are overdetermined by struggles over racial identity and status within the USA. They should therefore be seen in parallel with responses to attempts by white Americans to establish themselves as rap artists. White rap artists have long found it difficult to gain a foothold within hip-hop culture. Indeed, the history of hip-hop in America is littered with white artists that have failed to make the grade. Poor Righteous Teachers, Young Black Teenagers and 3rd Bass are all groups that, despite considerable investment from their respective record companies, have been unable to achieve lasting success. The hostility shown white rap artists is, in part, attributable to Vanilla Ice and the controversy that was generated by his exposure as a middle-class white kid from the suburbs rather than the ghettos of Miami as he had claimed. Once exposed, of course, Ice's credibility evaporated and his career went into terminal decline. The fact that Ice felt the need to construct a fictional biography illustrates both how important issues of identity and background are in the construction of rap authenticity and also the importance of location as the central and privileged identity for the producer of rap music.

If the unmasking of Vanilla Ice's fabricated social roots fuelled the unease with which Black cultural critics viewed white rap artists, the emergence of Eminem in the late 1990s provides a contrasting example, which nevertheless reiterates the importance of geographical location in authenticating the hip-hop voice. Unlike previous white rap artists, Eminem has successfully negotiated the thorny issue of authenticity. The fact that Eminem is considered 'authentic' by hip-hop fans in America and elsewhere is due in part to the patronage of Dr Dre, one of hip-hop's most influential record producers. Eminem's inclusion on the Dre-promoted Up in Smoke tour, in particular, contributed to his acceptance by the hip-hop community at large. Secondly, and more important in the context of this discussion, is the fact that Eminem hails from inner-city Detroit, a biographically authentic urban landscape which is understandable as 'Black' in social and cultural terms. This is reinforced through his coding as trailer park trash, an identity that as the Race Traitor and Bad Subjects collectives have suggested, is a form of white racial identity that lacks much of the economic and cultural status associated with whiteness in America.

The example of Eminem therefore bears out Hall's claim that Blackness is a politically and culturally constructed category. With all its tensions and problematics (violence, anti-feminism, homophobia) hip-hop has elaborated a powerful cultural location for Blackness, one which resonates with various marginalised groups both within and outside the United States. Other communities in other parts of the

167

world have used rap as a means of expressing their own sense of exclusion and alienation. For many of these groups and communities, rap serves an explicitly political function. Rap's political reputation dates to the 1980s, the decade in which groups such as Public Enemy and Boogie Down Productions, following the lead of Grandmaster Melle Mel and the Furious Five and fuelled by a Black Nationalist agenda, explored the problems facing Black America. Although the critical consensus suggests that American rap music abandoned its political aspirations during the 1990s in favour of the much more nihilistic sensibility of gangsta rap and, later, the conspicuous consumption represented by Sean Combs's 'Gucci and girls' aesthetic, extra-American rap scenes have not always followed suit. As I will show in the next section, the work of many French rap artists evinces the political and social engagement apparently declining in US hip-hop.

The implication of hip-hop's globalisation for notions of authenticity is something that is addressed by Paul Gilroy. The 'diasporic'[2] perspective offered by Gilroy stands in marked contrast to the more insular approaches to Black music offered by many American commentators. Whereas many American and African American critics tend to view appropriation as a betrayal of musical and cultural origins, Gilroy's approach reframes such relationship in cross-national perspective. The theory of the Black Atlantic is based on identifying the existence of a global diasporic Black culture that links Africa, America, the Caribbean, Brazil and Britain. In the context of popular music, Gilroy's theory throws into relief a system of cultural exchange in which different music cultures from different parts of the Black diaspora cross-fertilise one another. In other words, Gilroy's theory looks beyond the confines of the nation-state to consider the various thematic and musical connections that exist not only between local manifestations of hip-hop but also between hip-hop and other diasporic music forms such as UK garage, drum 'n' bass and dancehall.

The sort of transnational framework that underpins Gilroy's take on popular music also informs George Lipsitz's *Dangerous Crossroads*. Whereas Gilroy generally sticks to examining the connections that exist between different Black music cultures, Lipsitz has a much wider brief, analysing the relationship between Black music forms like hip-hop and music cultures that are not identified as Black. Drawing on a range of critical models (for example those formulated by Arjun Appadurai and Manuel Castells) that have questioned and reconceptualised the link between culture, community and location, Lipsitz examines the 'poetics of place' in the context of globalisation. Increased global integration has, as several critics have argued, loosened the links between particular music cultures and specific racially defined communities. Indeed, as Gregory Stephens suggests, 'once music enters the marketplace, it is all but impossible to claim any kind of racial ownership' (Stephens 1992: 66). While it is obviously true that music 'circulates as an interchangeable commodity marketed to consumers all over the globe', it is also the case that music cultures 'never completely lose the concerns and cultural qualities that give them determinate shape in their places of origin' (Lipsitz 1997: 4). As such, and as Mitchell acknowledges, it is perhaps best to think of extra-American manifestations of hip-hop culture as 'transnational hybrids which are interfaces between African American and other local practices' (Mitchell 1996: 12).

Though their approaches differ, both Gilroy and Lipsitz privilege notions of hybridity and cultural fusion. These critics thus provide a genuinely global and multiethnic perspective on Black-identified music cultures like rap and in so doing articulate a useful framework for analysing both the globalisation of hip-hop and, by extension, the globalisation of Blackness. Moreover, both critics recognise the fact that, in recent years, many of these extra-American hip-hop scenes have developed beyond the point of merely imitating African American rap music. Such arguments draw attention to the need to historicise the development of these extra-American rap 'scenes', rather than seeing them merely as one-dimensional copies. Indeed, the notion that non-American adaptations of hip-hop are inherently inferior does a disservice to those communities who have utilised hip-hop culture as a means of voicing concerns specific to the contexts in which they live, and limits our understanding of the complexity and historical development of such forms. While engaging with American-led global trends in hip-hop, these communities have adapted African American hip-hop for their own purposes. As such, although individual hip-hop scenes form part of a transnational hip-hop community, each scene has its own identity, addresses nationally specific issues and employs its own culturally and linguistically specific markers.

Boyz in the *banlieues*: studying French hip-hop

French hip-hop affords us an opportunity to explore the complex relationship between French audiences and critics and American popular culture. On the one hand, French metropolitan audiences in particular have actively embraced American cultural forms. Westerns, detective films, jazz, rock'n'roll, folk music and disco have all been well received in France. In this context hip-hop is simply the latest in a long line of (African) American music cultures to be popular with metropolitan French audiences. On the other hand, within certain academic and political circles long-standing reservations about the influx of American culture remain. Fuelling this is a fear that American consumer culture is replacing indigenous French forms, a fear which has resulted in various legislative moves to protect French culture, including notably films and popular music, and language. French legislation mandates forty per cent minima for film presentation and music broadcast. A comparable measure with respect to language itself is the Loi Toubon, passed in August 1994, which attempts to eradicate Anglicisms in the French language and replace them with French equivalents.

André Prévos has documented the historical development of hip-hop in France, from an initial period of uncritical copying of American forms to a more mature, diverse, and creative ownership of the form. Prévos argues that during the 1980s French rap artists were content to copy both the self-aggrandisement and 'street reportage' that were the most prominent features of American hip-hop (Prévos 1997: 149–50). While such themes and elements remain a central part of French hip-hop, the late 1980s and early 1990s 'marks', in the words of Prévos, 'the end of a period of uncritical adoption of African American music styles and repertoires by French rappers' (ibid.: 151). The subsequent success of French rap is measured in the fact that, as has been acknowledged by several critics, France has become the second largest consumer and producer of hip-hop in the world after the United States. The French rap scene has generated an industry that encompasses magazines, radio stations and record labels. Moreover, artists like Doc Gynéco, MC Solaar and IAM sell hundreds of thousands of records in France and in other countries, such as Belgium and Switzerland, where a significant part of the population speak French.

France's hip-hop scene is now the most developmentally mature and independent in Europe, and there are signs that it is increasingly defining itself with respect to an international sense of Black diaspora rather than simply with respect to American models. Recently, a number of French artists have attempted to 'break' the Anglo-American music market. Saïan Supa Crew, for example, have released both a French and an 'international' version of their *X Raisons* album. The 'international version' features collaborations with American rappers Brand Nubian, Dwellas and the Arsonists, Britain's Roots Manuva and reggae star Ky-Mani Marley. In many ways, *X Raisons* embodies Paul Gilroy's notion of a diasporic Black culture, linking together Africa, America, the Caribbean and Britain. The album also illustrates the way in which different Black music cultures (hip-hop and reggae) and different rap scenes (Britain, France and the United States) are in dialogue with one another. However, by far the majority of international collaborations are with Americans. French artists MC Solaar and Suprême NTM have performed alongside Gang Starr and Wu-Tang Clan respectively. Such collaborations allow French artists the opportunity to 'pay their respects' (or, as the culture would have it, give 'props') to African American hip-hop culture and receive in return the cultural capital that comes with performing with American rap stars. This cultural capital has yet to recross the Atlantic. While both Solaar and Saïan Supa Crew have achieved a measure of success (albeit limited) in Britain, no French rapper has, as yet, made much of an impact in the United States.

The displaced position of French rap has enabled the cross-mutation of styles that remain somewhat separate in the USA. Thus Rupa Huq distinguishes between two different styles of French rap – 'hardcore', represented by the likes of Suprême NTM and Ministère Amer, and 'pacifist cool' rap, represented by artists such as MC Solaar and Alliance Ethnik (Huq 1999: 136). The former is ostensibly, a French reinterpretation of African American gangsta rap, the latter a reinterpretation of the sort of laid back hip-hop associated with Gang Starr and with such 'native tongues' groups as De La Soul and A Tribe Called Quest. Despite these very different delivery styles, both rap genres share a similar emphasis on addressing the various social problems facing modern France. Where the raps of MC Solaar and Alliance Ethnik are underpinned by a pacifist sensibility, the raps of Suprême NTM and Ministère Amer are much more violent. Tracks like Ministère Amer's 'Sacrifice de poulets' ('Sacrificing Pigs') and Suprême NTM's 'Police' echo recordings like Body Count's 'Cop Killer', NWA's 'Fuck tha Police' and Cypress Hill's 'Pigs' in outlining the consequences for the police of accosting and tangling with the rapper or his group. Moreover, like their American counterparts, such recordings have been heavily criticised by the media and by certain politicians. 'Sacrifice de poulets', for example, was banned on French radio upon release, while a live performance of 'Police' by Supreme NTN saw the group fined 50,000 francs and disbanded for six months by a French court (the latter was reduced to two months on appeal).

To a much greater extent than in the USA, in France hip-hop has been adopted by performers and audiences from 'varied musical and social backgrounds' (Prévos 1997: 146). While it is predominantly identified with France's African, West Indian and Arab immigrant communities, one of the most noticeable things about French rap music, and something that sets it apart from its American counterpart, is that many of the groups and crews are multiethnic. IAM provide an instructive example here. The various members are of Malian, Algerian, Spanish and Italian origin. Still, and as stated above, hip-hop has been primarily adopted and championed by communities that live in the *banlieues*, run-down districts of high-rise housing that encircle some French cities. Such areas have become synonymous with such problems as crime, delinquency, unemployment, racial conflict, social exclusion and (sub)urban decay. Given that this is the case, it is easy to see why young Arab and African immigrants have made a connection between their own situation and that facing young working-class African Americans living in the inner city. To an extent, rap music has enabled French hip-hop performers and their audiences to understand life in the *banlieues* of France in terms of the inner-city ghettos of America. Hence rap exemplifies George Lipsitz's suggestion that music facilitates a 'poly-lateral dialogue among aggrieved populations' (Lipsitz 1997: 7). At the same, however, through the re-interpretation of styles and tropes associated with African American rap music, French rappers have been able to assert a distinctive identity that addresses 'French societal and popular environments' (Prévos 1997: 146).

Mathieu Kassovitz's 1995 film *La Haine* (Hate) provides an interesting representation of life in the *banlieues* of Paris. The deployment of rap music throughout the movie is one of the strategies used by Kassovitz to make a connection between the themes explored in his film and those explored in films by African American film directors such as John Singleton and Matty Rich. Indeed, the film's soundtrack features some of the 'leading lights' of the French hip-hop scene including Ministère Amer, Sens Unik, IAM, MC Solaar and Assassin. Whereas most French cinema of the 1980s and 1990s tended to ignore and gloss over the problems facing French society, Kassovitz chose to tackle issues of poverty, police violence and race head on. As such, his film became one of the most controversial and talked-about films of recent times in France.

How does *La Haine* compare to such 'gangsploitation' films as *Boyz N The Hood* (John Singleton, 1991) and *Straight Outta Brooklyn* (Matty

Rich, 1991) which purport to document life in America's black inner-city ghettos?

Suggested Reading

Diawara, Manthia (1993), *Black American Cinema*, New York and London: Routledge.

Farred, Grant (1996), '*Menace II Society*: No way out for Boys in the Hood', in Laurence Goldstein and Ira Konigsberg (eds), *The Movies: Texts, Receptions, Exposures*, Ann Arbor: University of Michigan Press.

Konstantarakos, Myrto (1999), 'What Mapping of the City? *La Haine* and the Cinéma du Banlieue', in Phil Powrie (ed.), *French Cinema in the 1990s: Continuity and Difference*, Oxford: Oxford University Press, pp.160–71.

Reader, Keith (1995), 'After the Riot', *Sight and Sound,* November.

Watkins, S. Craig (1998), *Representing: Hip-Hop Culture and the Production of Black Cinema*, Chicago: University of Chicago Press.

Zissermand, Katya and Colin Nettelbeck (1997), 'Social Exclusion and Artistic Inclusiveness: The Quest for Integrity in Mathieu Kassovitz's *La Haine*', *Nottingham French Studies*, 36:2, 83–98.

The desire to assert a sense of regional, local and national identity manifests itself in a number of ways. French rap artists deploy a range of visual and linguistic markers in an attempt to 'represent' their locale (normatively configured in hip-hop culture as the 'hood). Such markers can be found in the lyrics, videos, album art and even in some groups' names. Their purpose is to establish the artist's credibility and authenticity. As such, these markers assure the audience that the artist is in a position of authority relative to the material. For example, the acronym IAM can be interpreted as *Invasion Arrivant de Mars* (Mars is a slang term for Marseille) and *Indépendantistes Autonomes Marseillais*,[3] while Suprême NTM's name can be interpreted as *Le Nord Transmet le Message* (a reference to the Paris suburb that the group are from) as well as *Nique Ta Mere* (literally translated as 'fuck your mother' and the closest French approximation of the word 'motherfucker').

Perhaps the most interesting cultural marker and one of the most distinctive features of French hip-hop culture is the use of *verlan*, a form of French slang that involves reversing letter orders and playing around with syllables. According to Huq, *verlan* has its roots in 'French, English, Arabic, gypsy languages and certain African languages' (Huq 1999: 142). As a non-standard language, *verlan* has certain things in common with hip-hop slang and with African American Vernacular English (AAVE) more generally. Like AAVE, *verlan* was designed to exclude certain constituencies (the mainstream, the authorities). However, and again in common with AAVE and hip-hop slang, it has been adopted by the very communities it was designed to exclude and, as such, has to some extent entered into mainstream usage. If by rapping in their native tongue, French artists seek independence from African American forms of expression, the use of *verlan* represents a rejection of the nationalistic hierarchies enshrined in the Loi Toubon and a much more hybrid sense of the French language. The use of locally and nationally specific visual, linguistic and sartorial markers is central to the process of 'indigenization' which sees, in the words of James Lull, 'imported cultural elements take on local features' and 'the exotic, unfamiliar and foreign . . . domesticated' (Lull 1995: 244). Seen in a narrowly national context, French hip-hop artists have developed a youth culture that, while inspired by African American tropes, is nevertheless independent and distinctively French. Through hip-hop music and culture excluded *banlieusards* have been able to assert their cultural and social identities. Moreover, part of this challenge to and reformulation of Frenchness takes place in the name, not of Americanisation, but of other globally distributed identities such as the Black diaspora or a multiethnic underclass.

The view from Britain

As with other European hip-hop scenes, African American hip-hop culture provided the model upon which a British hip-hop scene was based. Films like *Wildstyle* (Charlie Ahearn, 1982), *Breakdance* (Joel Silberg, 1984) and *Beat Street* (Stan Lathan, 1984) together with artists such as Blondie, Malcolm McLaren, The Sugarhill Gang, Grandmaster Flash, Grandmaster Melle Mel and Run DMC provided many prospective British rappers, breakdancers and writers with their first exposure to hip-hop. Over the course of the 1980s, hip-hop established itself as perhaps the major influence on British urban youth culture, a position it continues to hold. In parallel with the French experience in that decade, the attempts of British rap artists to establish a distinctively

British hip-hop scene largely failed. But unlike the French experience of the 1990s, in Britain the sense that hip-hop is something African Americans simply do better has remained strong.

America's hip-hop hegemony in Britain has been reinforced through magazines like *Hip-Hop Connection* and through radio shows such as Tim Westwood's *The Radio 1 Rap Show*, both of which have tended to privilege American rap music over indigenous product. Moreover, and in contrast to French hip-hop, which regularly features in the French charts, British hip-hop acts rarely impact on the UK top 40 singles or albums charts. This comparative immaturity of British hip-hop is largely attributable to language.

Recent commentaries have suggested that all this is about to change. Indeed, many critics have argued that the emergence of such artists as Roots Manuva and Blade marks a renaissance in British hip-hop. While recordings made by these artists have not sold in anything like the quantities regularly achieved by top American performers or even by French rappers, these artists have nevertheless shown that it is at least possible for British rap artists to achieve a measure of success. Mark B and Blade's debut album *The Unknown* (2003), for example, has sold in excess of 40,000 copies, while Roots Manuva's *Run Come Save Me* (2003) has garnered considerable praise from critics. Moreover, these albums signal a new maturity in British hip-hop. *Run Come Save Me*, in particular, is emblematic of the way in which British rap artists fuse hip-hop with musical and cultural elements from other genres, thereby creating something strategically un-American and distinctively British.

In that context, it is interesting that in interviews Roots Manuva eschews the historical penchant of most British rappers to celebrate and venerate American performers, thereby connecting with the 'source'. Instead, Roots Manuva chooses to pay homage to such diverse and quintessentially English acts as Smiley Culture, Ian Dury and the Blockheads and, somewhat bizarrely, Chas 'n' Dave. Musically, however, the biggest influence on Roots Manuva is the Jamaican sound system culture that he was exposed to while growing up in south London. Indeed, and as several reviewers noted, the backing tracks or 'soundscapes' created by Roots Manuva and over which he delivers his rhymes are as much a product of Kingston, Jamaica as they are of Kingston, London.

In effect, then, *Run Come Save Me* is a musical hybrid; one that draws upon and in many ways reflects the diversity and multiculturalism of contemporary Britain. Like the Scïan Supa Crew album cited earlier,

Run Come Save Me demonstrates the value of Paul Gilroy's and George Lipsitz's interpretations of contemporary popular music, rooted as they are in notions of cultural interchange and the transnational flow of images and information. Nor is Roots Manuva alone in this. The likes of the Prodigy and Massive Attack drew on hip-hop aesthetics, even though neither group could really be described as a rap act. More recently, acts such as So Solid Crew, Audio Bully's, The Streets and Dizzee Rascal have combined hip-hop lyricism with garage beats. Indeed, it is in UK garage and its musical cousin drum 'n' bass that hip-hop's influence is most apparent and most keenly felt. These groups utilise culturally and locally specific references in their efforts to articulate their experiences of what it is to be young, working class and British.

The UK garage scene has also generated considerable controversy in the media, largely because of the way in which some artists have adopted the sort of conspicuous consumption (referred to as 'bling' in garage culture) and violence associated with certain forms of rap music. The focus of such controversy has been the south London collective So Solid Crew. As several critics pointed out, many of the tracks on the group's *They Don't Know* album (2001) were characterised by gangsta-esque violence, misogyny and macho posturing. Moreover, like the gangsta rappers they so obviously copy, So Solid Crew's violence is not restricted to the group's recordings. A 2002 concert at the Astoria in London ended in chaos when gunmen from two rival south London gangs opened fire during the group's set, injuring two men. As the *New Musical Express* and other sections of the music press reported at the time, these shootings were the latest in a number of incidents involving firearms that were linked to London's garage scene. So Solid Crew serves to remind us that not all the cultural formations flowing from the United States to Britain or throughout the Black Atlantic can immediately be seen as progressive.

Notes

1. The term hip-hop encompasses rap music, dance styles such as breakdancing and bodypopping and writing (used instead of the term 'graffiti', which is considered derogatory by many practitioners).
2. Based on the Greek term meaning 'dispersion', diaspora refers to a minority community living in exile. The notion of diaspora involves the displacement of a community of people from an original homeland (which can be notional

or actual) and their transplantation into a new country. The journey from homeland to new location is very often gruelling and is often undertaken in the face of considerable hardships. Although the word has historically been used in relation to the dispersion of Jews and those Black Africans displaced by the transatlantic slave trade, other communities have been transplanted in this way (for example, the Afro-Caribbean community in Britain, or north-African immigrants in France).

3. The name can also be interpreted as 'I Am' or Imperial Asiatic Men.

Bibliography

Bernard, James (1992), 'A newcomer abroad, rap speaks up', *New York Times*, 23 August, Section 2.

Fusco, Coco (1992), 'Pan-American Postnationalism: Another World Order', in Gina Dent (ed.), *Black Popular Culture*, Seattle: Bay Press.

Gilroy, Paul (1993), *The Black Atlantic: Modernity and Double Consciousness*, London and New York: Verso.

Huq, Rupa (1999), 'Living in France: The Parallel Universe of Hexagonal Pop', in Andrew Blake (ed.), *Living Through Pop*, London: Routledge.

Klein, Naomi (2000), *No Logo*, London: Flamingo.

Krims, Adam (2000), *Rap Music and the Poetics of Identity*, Cambridge: Cambridge University Press.

Lipsitz, George (1997), *Dangerous Crossroads: Popular Music, Postmodernism and the Poetics of Place*, London and New York: Verso.

Lull, James (1995), *Media, Communication, Culture: A Global Approach*, Cambridge: Polity Press.

McGregor, Tracii (1998), 'Round the Globe at 100BPM', *Source*, January.

Mitchell, Tony (1996), *Popular Music and Local Identity: Rock, Pop and Rap in Europe and Oceania*, London and New York: Leicester University Press.

Prévos, André (1997), 'The Origins and Evolution of French Rap Music and Hip-Hop Culture in the 1980s and 1990s', in George McKay (ed.), *Yankee Go Home (& Take Me with U): Americanization and Popular Culture*, Sheffield: Sheffield Academic Press.

Stephens, Gregory (1992), 'Interracial Dialogue in Rap Music: Call-and-Response in a Multicultural Style, *New Formations*, 16, 62–80.

LITERARY NARRATIVES

CHAPTER NINE

The Disneyfication of the European Fairy Tale

Jane Darcy

Even our own students, occupying a halfway house between film critics and mass audience, are extremely resistant to critique of Disney film . . . These students consistently cite four easy pardons for their pleasurable participation in Disney film and its apolitical agenda: it's only for children, it's only fantasy, it's only a cartoon, and it's just good business. These four naturalizations create a Disney text exempt from material, historical, and political influences.

Bell et al., *From Mouse to Mermaid* (1995: 4)

Disneyfication as a process could be said to have begun in April 1900, when L. Frank Baum wrote in his introduction to *The Wonderful Wizard of Oz* that 'it aspires to being a modernized fairy tale, in which the wonderment and joy are retained and the heart-aches and nightmares are left out' (Baum 1997: 3–4). He describes the old tales of the Grimm brothers and Hans Andersen as 'fearsome' and claims his tale as setting a new tone for the twentieth century, moving on from the darker mood of the European tales. Although Baum's *Oz* books are very different from Disney fairy tale films, they are alike in seeking to reassure their 'readers' that the modern fairy tale world is full of wonder but ultimately uncomplex and benign. In this sense the Disney fairy tale films, from *Snow White and the Seven Dwarfs* (1937) to *Cinderella* (1950), *Sleeping Beauty* (1959), *The Little Mermaid* (1997) and *Beauty and the Beast* (1999), may take up where Baum left off. Brian Appleyard (1998) has described this minimising of the unpleasant-ness and the complexities of life as the 'super-normal', and Paul Wells, quoting Appleyard, argues that it is a peculiarity of the reception of the Disney film that the audience in general embrace the 'happily ever after' of the 'super-normal' and resist or ignore an intellectual critique of the Disney experience, just as Elizabeth Bell, Lyndon Haas and Laura Sells's students did. Wells goes on: 'It is clear that the framing of "Disney" as a seemingly sinister corporate oppressor, constantly cele-brating, in Giroux's words "deeply anti-democratic social relations", does not, however, seem to sit with the reception of the films' (Wells 2002: 107). Perhaps this is part of what we should understand by 'Disneyfication': not that it is an imposing of a supposedly innocent or saccharine world on the 'reader' but that the reader is complicit in the experience of the text – a willing participant. It is patronising to assume that an audience is a collective 'tabula rasa' upon which the film is inscribed. Readers bring to the visual text, as any other text, their own experiences and reading histories; perhaps they willingly (or wilfully) read the film as personal and emotional and not as a public and political event and are they wrong to do this? The timelessness of the fairy tale is in this sense appropriate for the Disney film; the 'once upon a time' opening is as important as the 'happily ever after' ending in signalling the entry into a world where a different set of standards apply from the world outside the film. In this super-normal or maybe 'ideal' world dreams can still be realised.

Before looking more deeply into how far Disney fairy tale films have either perpetuated or destroyed the old European tradition, we need to examine further what is understood by 'Disneyfication'. One activist definition of the term, in a special edition of *New Internationalist* mag-azine focused on Disney's global reach and called 'The Mousetrap', locates it within the dismal framework of the negative cultural process of standardisation, the homogenisation of (corporate) global culture:

> Centuries of tradition are eroded by the technically dazzling but culturally-biased products of the corporate entertainment industry . . . 'Disneyfication', like economic globalization, tends to ride roughshod over local variety . . . Does this mean that sooner or later we'll all be American? Probably not . . . Cross-fertilization and borrowing from other cultures has invigorated and strength-ened both Western and Third World arts. Think of Gauguin in Tahiti or the jazz-influenced sounds of Ghanaian high-life music.

Great art prospers from contact with the outside world. But corporate culture is different: its guiding principles are efficiency and profit and there is a tendency for those goals to steamroller both diversity and authenticity. (*New Internationalist* 1998)

Note how this begins – 'centuries of tradition' – but, as I explore below, with fairy tales there may not have been any fixed tradition. This relates to a further question about whether there is something as definitive as The European Fairy Tale per se. If, as Jack Zipes has argued, Disney's work marks a continuation rather than a break with this so-called 'tradition', it could be argued that the classic European literary fairy tale collections started the process we now sometimes refer to as Disneyfication.

> Choose one of the Disney fairy tale films based on a classic European fairy tale (see 'Suggestions for further study' for sources). It might be useful firstly to research the history and background of the chosen tale but the aim of the exercise is a close comparison between the Disney film and the literary version of the tale upon which it is based.

The fluid form and history of the fairy tale

But were the European tales so 'fearsome', as L. Frank Baum puts it, and did Disneyfication begin in 1900 with Baum's conscious Americanising of the fairy tale in *The Wonderful Wizard of Oz*? The writers that Baum mentions as examples of the European tales, particularly the Grimm brothers, had taken their tales from an even older and more fearsome oral tradition and had themselves transformed them by degrees into something more suitable for a middle-class family audience. There were seven editions of the Grimms' *Kinder- und Hausmärchen* ('Children's and Household Tales'), and in each subsequent edition the tales became more elaborate, literary and Christian. So what Baum or Disney might see as old is, to those studying the European folk tale, relatively new and already corrupted or simplified or homogenised. If we think of Disneyfication as a process of standardising the tales, erasing their eccentricities and making them suitable for a mass audience then the process could be said to have begun as far back as the late sixteenth century in Europe, with the tales of Charles Perrault. Since then, the staple tales have always been culturally central and popular and, as Paul Wells so rightly says, we should not ignore the impulse towards what he describes as 'a politics of pleasure, where emotional determinacy and agency characterises human ambition and need rather than intellectual or political clarity' (Wells 2002: 109).

There is an underlying sense in much discussion of the genre that the older the tale the more genuine or authentic it is. In the same way that commentators look back to the pre-Disney European tale as somehow representing a more authentic tradition, so, in turn, the tales from the oral tradition are often imagined as pure and uncorrupted originals, told around fires by peasants who led innocent, almost child-like existences. In fact what evidence there is of the oral tradition in Europe suggests a rather different picture. There were and are, for example, not simply peasant prototypes of the tales we now know through the Disney films but a multitude of fairy or 'folk' tales from different national and regional cultures; they were never stable 'texts' but borrowed from each other and were changing all the time. In fact, what most characterises the European tale in its earliest oral phase is diversity. From what we know about the tales they were often very crude and sexually explicit (see the early versions of 'Little Red Riding Hood' in Zipes 1993); they were bawdy and carnivalesque and they were also sometimes used as a vehicle for teaching certain values or even critiquing them. Even after the tales began to appear as literary texts in Italy and France in the late sixteenth and seventeenth centuries most people would still have experienced them as part of an oral tradition of tale-telling. So, for a long time versions varied from one country or region to another and even from one teller to another but the core of the narrative tends to be fairly constant within a tale type, as has been recognised by the Formalist Vladimir Propp (1928), who argued that structural conformity at least is an inherent characteristic of the genre. Propp identified folk tales as having thirty-one basic 'functions' but judged that, far from being the naïve expression of a primitive social group, they embody a simple and unique beauty. Fairy tales may be simple but they are not simplistic. In addition, though versions of the tales were very localised, as European nations increasingly communicated with and colonised the world beyond, there was much cross-fertilisation. Thus, one way and another, the tales were always changing and growing, being adapted for new environments, and cultures and maybe coming closer together. A key question to consider, then, is whether the Disney films are just another variation, a further stage in the developing fairy or folk tale tradition or whether in some way – as many think they do – they violate that tradition.

We know more about the circumstances of literary fairy tales, which began to become the dominant form from the late seventeenth century onwards, than we do about the oral tradition. According to Jack Zipes, the foremost socio-cultural critic of the fairy tale genre, there is little ideological difference between the fairy tales of Perrault, the Grimms and Hans Andersen and the films produced by Walt Disney and, later, the Disney Corporation. In Zipes's reading of the fairy tale 'tradition' all these tales aim to educate and socialise children into bourgeois values, which in turn support a patriarchal framework and naturalise hierarchical social relations. He puts it this way:

> Though the Grimms often show a lower-class boy rising to a higher social station their tales, Perrault's, and Hans Christian Andersen's in fact reinforce the existing structures of power and of gender relations, affecting generations of children throughout Europe and North America. The Disney films based on their tales have continued to reinforce these ideological patterns. (Zipes 2000: 481)

In Zipes's view, whether the context is seventeenth-century France, nineteenth-century Germany or twentieth-century America, the ideological positioning of the text is much the same. There have been writers, film makers and artists who have resisted this model of the fairy tale but they are in the minority. When it comes to a more detailed critique of the genre, however, Zipes is not as inclined to think that the Disney fairy tales are close to the European tradition. For instance, he says of Disney's first full-length animated feature film, *Snow White*, adapted from the Grimms' tale: 'There is no doubt that Disney retained key ideological features that reinforce nineteenth-century patriarchal notions which Disney shared with the Grimms' (Zipes 1994: 89). In the same chapter, though, he suggests that Disney 'cast a spell over this German tale and transformed it into something peculiarly American' (ibid.: 87). Henry Giroux takes a more positive view, saying that Disney succeeded in 'combining high and low culture' and that by doing this he 'opened up new cultural possibilities for artists and audiences alike' (Giroux 1999: 95). Giroux also considers, as Wells does, that it cannot be denied that the films are sites of pleasure, adventure and entertainment. He, however, warns that the animated animals and objects in these films are of the highest artistic standards, but they do not exist in an ideology-free zone. They are tied to larger narratives about freedom, rites of passage, intolerance, choice, greed, and the brutalities of male chauvinism. Enchantment comes at a high price. (ibid.: 96)

The ideology that has underpinned the main literary and visual fairy tales since Perrault's collection of tales *Histoires ou Contes du temps passé* is essentially that of the middle class, which has been the dominant social and political group since the eighteenth century and was in an emergent state earlier than this. Their values and attitudes are represented in the important and influential collections of tales and films and they, rather than the 'folk' or peasantry, become the primary audience for the tales. So the kinds of tales that tend to be selected in the Perrault and Grimm collections and whose tradition Disney has followed have heroes whose resourcefulness and cunning are rewarded and whose direction is definitely upwardly mobile. Classic heroes of this type are *Puss in Boots* and the *Brave Little Tailor*. (Interestingly, Disney made a short feature film of *Puss*, which Zipes has argued is closely autobiographical.) Disney has it in common with the brothers Grimm that he personally achieved fame against the odds, through self-reliance and hard work, and these are not only the values of his class but the values that both he and the Grimms represent favourably in their work, selecting tales for public consumption that lend themselves to their promotion. The strongest critique of this ideological positioning in Disney's work more generally is probably to be found in Ariel Dorfman and Armand Mattelart's key text from 1971, *How to Read Donald Duck: Imperialist Ideology in the Disney Comic*. John Tomlinson describes some of the features of that political critique which may resonate with readings of fairy tales:

> the depiction of Third World nations in terms of racial and cultural stereotypes (and in particular the 'infantilisation' of the people of these countries); the presentation of capitalist class relations as natural, unchangeable and morally justified; . . . the representation of women in stereotypically subordinate terms. (Tomlinson 1991: 42)

On the other hand, it is worth noting that the democratising impulse of much American culture may be confirmed by the observation that Disney is less inclined than the European writers to show royalty in a favourable light; they are often represented in the films as foolish and ineffectual. In addition, Wells interestingly points to the fact that political critiques of Disney have had little impact on their popularity:

> These reactionary, sometimes 'politically incorrect', sometimes culturally inappropriate 'messages' do not become the dominant currency of the films and, instead, a kind of quasi-ideological optimism, innocence and security accrues and endures around the texts even in spite of the post-Dorfman and Mattelart critiques. (Wells 2002: 108–9)

Women in the fairy tale

As a way of developing some of the ideas already raised I will now discuss in more detail the way in which women are represented in the 'classic' fairy tales of a patriarchal culture and some of the interesting critical material that has surrounded the debate. Fairy tale heroines in the 'classic' literary collections are mostly beautiful, pleasant and passive, and win the day (or the prince, who in these cases is often no more than a stock figure) by suffering uncomplainingly, being silent for long periods or by completing some painstaking and repetitive task requiring endless patience. An example of such a heroine is Cinderella, who, of course, suffers in silence when tormented by her sisters. In the Grimms' version of this tale, *Ashiepattle*, we are told that 'her sisters tormented her and poured peas and lentils into the ashes, forcing her to sit there and pick them out again' (Grimm and Grimm 1982: 225). There is also the sister in *The Six Swans* who has the following conditions imposed on her in order to save her brothers: 'You must neither speak nor laugh for six years, and during that time you must make six shirts for us out of starflowers. If you were to speak a single word, all your work would be in vain' (ibid.: 121). Women's silence is a powerful male fantasy. Good women in Disney, as in the classic literary fairy tales, are most often shown in a domestic environment. Snow White is shown cleaning in the opening frame of the film and later she keeps house for the dwarfs. When she arrives at their cottage she exclaims: 'Oh, it's adorable, just like a doll's house. I like it here.' And of its inhabitants she says they must be children, 'and by the look of the table, seven untidy little children'. She then remarks on the dust and cobwebs, saying, 'my, my, my', and is worried that they do not have a mother.

Critically consider gender roles in the two versions, or class structures. How about analysing the ways animals and the natural world are
represented in each version?

The most memorable female characters in the classic collections of
fairy tales, however, are often the older women, the witches, step-
mothers and wicked queens. They are powerful and dangerous, and
almost without exception envious and evil. In a patriarchal tradition
women are pitted against each other but their wicked deeds are paid
for by terrible punishments; their power has finally to be contained
and destroyed. The wicked queen in *Snow White* and Ursula in *The
Little Mermaid* are clear examples of this kind of figure but there are
countless other such women, particularly in the Grimms' tales. A well-
known example of double cruelty by older women occurs in *Hansel
and Gretel*; first the children are cast out by their mother into the
forest to die (the mother often displaced to a stepmother in later versions of the tale), then just when they think they are saved by a kind
old lady who lives in a gingerbread house, we are told:

> But the old woman had only been pretending to be kind, for in
> fact she was an evil witch who lay in wait for children and had
> only built the little bread house to lure them her way. When a
> child fell into her power she would kill it, cook it and eat it, and
> that was a day of feasting for her. Witches have red eyes and can't
> see far, but they have a keen sense of smell like animals and notice
> when people come anywhere near. (Grimm and Grimm 1982: 60)

Feminist critics and writers, in particular Angela Carter, have discovered
many tales, not chosen for the Perrault or Grimm collections, which
illustrate the wisdom, humour and kindness of older women and their
solidarity with daughters and other women generally. Apart from the
broader influence of cultural studies of which in a sense it is a part,
feminist criticism has been the most radical and productive force in
study of the fairy tale in recent years. It is also the case that the Disney
Corporation has to some extent taken on board changing attitudes
to gender and racial identity in more recent animated films, though
how radical and challenging these films really are is an interesting
question.

Snow White and the Seven Dwarfs

How different are the Disney fairy tale films from the European tradition? If we accept that there is a certain broad similarity and continuity of ideology and purpose between the tales of Europe and America, what does the term 'Disneyfication' imply? Is it synonymous with Americanisation or is something more particular implied by the process? Generally speaking the Disney world is one where romantic love and marriage are the focus of life and, as I have already argued, the heroines are essentially obedient, domesticated and passive. This is not so evident in the European literary tales, where marriage tends to act mainly as a plot device for closure. There is no romance or sentiment. For the purposes of illustration in this section I am referring particularly to the tale of *Snow White* but the points could as easily be focused on any other of the Disney adaptations of European tales. Romance is accentuated in Disney's *Snow White*. In the Grimms' version the poisoned apple is accidentally dislodged from Snow White's throat when the coffin is jolted; in Disney's film the prince awakens her with a kiss. Here we have an inter-textual reference to – or, more critically, confusion with – *Sleeping Beauty*. Disney's Snow White is also represented early in the film as dressed in rags, a downtrodden Cinderella-like character. There are many inter-textual references in Disney films; in fact the plot and overall structure is remarkably similar in each film, lending an air of conformity to the portfolio. Disney's Snow White does little to save herself when abandoned in the forest by the huntsman; she is terrified, faints and awakens to find herself surrounded by cute animal helpers. In the Grimms' tale we are told that she gazed around the forest 'trying to think what to do to save herself'. At least here, in the literary version, she is shown taking some initiative. All through the Disney film version Snow White is passive, kept going only by her hope that 'some day my prince will come', as indeed he does in the final frames. She barely knows him, having seen him only once before but she eagerly leaves her loyal friends and companions, the seven dwarfs, to ride off into the sunset with him. Even in the much later, supposedly more 'feminist' film, *Beauty and the Beast*, the action ends with the newly transformed hero, dressed as a prince (a far less attractive character than the beast), dancing with Beauty in a typical romantic scene in a ballroom, reminiscent of a scene from *Cinderella*.

Another common criticism is that morality in the Disney universe is oversimplified. The characters are stereotypes and all moral complexities are reduced to a simple fight between good and evil. For example, in the Grimms' tale of the same name, Snow White is visited by the old woman and tempted with her wares three times (she is not really a witch as in the Disney film). This makes a difference to the meaning of the tale. Firstly, Snow White is foolish enough to allow her in on three occasions, suggesting a measure of culpability on her part. Furthermore, the fact that she is tempted three times has religious connotations. She is first tempted by a comb, which turns out to be poisoned, then by some stays, which the old woman laces so tightly Snow White can't breathe, and finally by the poisoned apple. The nature of the items she is tempted by suggests that she is vain and materialistic and also that she is inclined to satisfy her appetite. In the Disney *Snow White*, the witch visits the cottage only once, with the apple, so we see Snow White much more as a passive victim of evil than as a (partial) participant in it.

There is a similar moral simplification in Disney's *The Little Mermaid*, as A. Waller Hastings has argued. The darkness and pain have been removed from Hans Andersen's tale but so has the mermaid's responsibility for what happens to her. As with Snow White, the mermaid is shown in Andersen's tale as being vain and superficial in wanting to join the human world. She is, however, so determined to have legs that she is willing to lose her voice, suffer agonies as she walks and be banished from her own world and probably the after-world forever. In the Disney film there is no such psychological and social complexity: she wants to leave her own world and become a human in order to win the prince, which she does. In Andersen she fails, but no character representing good ever ultimately fails in the Disney fairy tale world. In Waller Hastings's view, such moral simplification is bad for children because they will grow up thinking the world is designed for the fulfilment of their desires and happiness:

> Disneyfication not only homogenizes individual creations into a simplistic narrative sameness, but eliminates the moral complexities of the original text. The child who reads Andersen's fairy tale has experienced a world in which desires have consequences that may be painful, where wanting something badly enough to suffer for it need not make it happen; the child who views the Disney film experiences a world in which bad things only happen because of bad people, where desire is always fulfilled. (Waller Hastings 1993: 90)

Jack Zipes comments on the rigidity and uniformity of the Disney fairy tale films:

> There is no character development because all characters must be recognisable as types that remain unchanged throughout the film. Good cannot become evil, nor can evil become good. The world is viewed in Manichean terms as a dichotomy, and only the good will inherit the earth. (Zipes 1997: 93)

Jean Baudrillard's observation (1983: 25) that Disneyland provides the image upon which America constructs itself comes to mind here. His model holds good not only for the way that the material world is now Disneyfied and sets standards we aspire to in the 'real world'; I would contend that it is also recognisable in realpolitik, for example in the way the American government in the twenty-first century has launched and handled its 'war on terrorism'. The television images of Osama Bin Laden and Saddam Hussein stand for evil in US global politics, there is an 'axis of evil' (itself recalling President Reagan's construction of the Soviet Union in the late Cold War as 'the evil empire') and, in true opposition, 'those who are not with us are against us'.

But it can also be argued that a Disney film is a fiction, and is its polarisation of good and evil so very different from the fairy tale in many of its other manifestations? The genre is one which is formed around a range of binary oppositions. As we have seen, structuralists like Vladimir Propp would argue that this simplicity is aesthetically satisfying but it has also much more recently often been associated with the process of 'dumbing down'. The related accusation of 'infantilisation' (turning consumers into children) is also important because it embraces the origins of fairy tales, the treatment of characters (the dwarfs, working men all, are even physically reduced), as well as the animation format of Disney film versions themselves. Paul Wells, however, eschews both these readings, suggesting that the process is more akin to Samuel Taylor Coleridge's notion of a 'willing suspension of disbelief':

> For 'readers' perhaps it is more satisfying to enjoy the 'playing out' of the protagonists' progress towards fulfilment; and where it is reassuring to believe that notions of 'goodness', 'right', 'truth' and so on may still exist *even if* there is a full understanding and tacit acceptance of the potentially illusory, contradictory or mis-representative elements of the text in place. (Wells 2002: 111)

Moving on now from moral issues, there is another interesting area where Disneyfication appears to have made its mark on the old tales. Some commentators on the tales maintain that traces of the belief systems of a more mysterious, primitive, even magical world, originating in the oral tradition, have found their way into all the significant collections – Perrault, Grimm, Andersen. The most influential psychoanalytic critic of the genre, Bruno Bettelheim (1976), and one of the most respected critics of its form and meaning, Max Luthi (1947), both in their various ways argue for the aesthetic pleasure to be gained from the tales and for their spiritual and psychological depth. They are, of course, referring mainly to the literary tales rather than the oral tradition but it is implicit in what they say that the spirit of the old oral tales has been captured by the best literary adaptations. Bettelheim, a Freudian, claims that the tales have therapeutic value for children, particularly disturbed children, since they represent in symbolic form the difficulties such children face but also show how those difficulties might be overcome. While Bettelheim's work is now regarded as flawed because of his failure to problematise his sources and the issues he raises, nonetheless he was a great populariser of the notion that the fairy tale gives imaginative expression to the unconscious mind. Luthi, who is more inclined to follow Carl Gustav Jung's notion of the collective unconscious, emphasises the natural magic of the tales. The colour and clarity of a scene like this from the opening of the Grimms' *Snow White* exemplifies what he means:

> Once upon a time in the middle of winter when the snow flakes were falling from the sky like feathers, a queen sat sewing at a window with a frame of black ebony. And as she sewed and looked up at the falling snow, she pricked her finger with her needle, and into the snow there fell three drops of blood. (Grimm and Grimm 1982: 74)

Even though this is, of course, a translation, it is effective in the simplicity of the language, the bold and symbolic use of colour and in establishing a visual picture which frames the story and shows a connection between the indoor and outdoor worlds. This use of colour is continued through the story. The apple the old woman offers to Snow White is red. The dwarfs put Snow White in the glass coffin because, they say, 'this is something we can't bury in the black earth' (ibid.: 80) and later, when the iron shoes are heated up for the wicked queen on a fire, 'then she had to put her feet into the red-hot shoes and dance till she dropped dead' (ibid.: 82). More recently, Wells echoes this reading of the tales when he says that he is moving towards the view that maybe the Disney films are politically naïve rather than politically incorrect. He comments that imagery in the texts appears to be understood in 'a primary, archetypal, rather than culturally specific way' and adds: 'The *spectacle* of archetypal themes and emotions prevails over a cerebral engagement with *ideas*' (Wells 2002: 112).

A further connection between the old tales and the Disney films, though each tradition treats the subject very differently, is the close connection between the human and animal worlds. It is made clear in the Grimms' story that Snow White is a child whom nature recognises as one of her own. When she is running through the woods after the huntsman has released her we are told: 'Then she began to run, and she ran over sharp stones and through the thorns, and the wild animals bounded past her but did not harm her' (Luke 1982: 75). When she is placed in the coffin, an owl, a raven and a dove come to mourn her. This sense of an intimate connection between the human and natural worlds occurs frequently in the European literary tale and is seen by Luthi as central to its form and meaning. No-one in a fairy tale is surprised or terrified when an animal speaks to them, everything is accepted without question. In Luthi's view, 'Folktales strike us as enigmatic because they mix the miraculous with the natural, the near with the far, and the ordinary with the incomprehensible in a completely effortless way' (Luthi 1982: 2).

In your comparative reading of literary and Disney versions, is there an identifiable Disneyfication process at work here or do the versions, as Zipes suggests, display more similarities than differences? Does studying the fairy tale in this way help you to define what 'Disneyfication' may be? You could also consider how reading a film text (especially an animated, musical one) differs from reading a literary text and how effective each is as a medium for representation of the fairy tale. What are the effects of shifting the tale from a European to an American cultural context? Is the Disney film more obviously a commodity (you might research the technical aspects of the film here or the effects of merchandising)? Is there evidence of moral simplification or of 'dumbing down'?

To what extent is all this altered in the Disney films – is depth sacrificed to superficial glamour and spectacle? Mutual respect and supportiveness between humanity and nature is often seen in the European literary tales – not only do animals talk with humans, their physical forms are interchangeable. Humans often change or are changed into animal form. Luthi argues that this gives a sense of unity of being; we are all capable of transformation one into another. In Disney, nature is either represented as alien and dangerous or is reduced to cute prettiness as in the frequent appearances of small musical animals and birds. They are always tame and either sweet and shy, rather like the heroines they befriend, or of the gentle giant variety – all equally harmless and not at all wild. They are alluring, as are the Disney films in general, particularly when accompanied by dazzling technical innovation, music and song. But, bearing in mind the discussion of ideology earlier in this chapter, we have to ask: is this alluring spectacle really so charming and innocent? On the other hand in Baum and Disney, as in the European tradition, the best relationships described are when the human and animal worlds are mutually supportive. There are then rewards for all.

A final point worth consideration is that although Disney took the European fairy tale and Americanised it, it has now been imported back via Euro-Disney, or Disneyland Paris as it became or even Disneyland Paris *Resort* as it is now known. So, *Beauty and the Beast* has now returned to its original home as, apparently, have the Disney family. Roy Disney Jr, speaking in Isigny-sur-Mer on the occasion of the opening of the park, claimed: 'This is a very sentimental place for me, because the roots of my family come right back here to this village . . . it was over nine hundred years ago that Huw d'Isney and his son Robert lived here' (quoted in Smoodin 1994: 8; see also Mills 1993). Around the same time, Michael Eisner, Chief Executive of the Disney Corporation, was asked in an interview how he felt about European left-wing critics of the new theme park. He replied: 'The intellectual, and maybe even the communist, when they bring their children to Euro-Disney, will have a good time' (quoted in Smoodin 1994: 20). Is this Disneyfication *par excellence*, a compelling instance of the way in which, as Zipes has put it, 'as commodity, the fairy tale film sacrificed art to technical invention; innovation to tradition; stimulation of the imagination to consumption for distraction' (1997: 72)?

Sources of suggested tales for study

Andersen, Hans Christian [1837] (1984), *Hans Andersen's Fairy Tales: A Selection*, Oxford: The World's Classics.

Snow White

Snow White (1937), Walt Disney.
Jacob and Wilhelm Grimm, 'Snow White' (1812), in Grimm and Grimm 1982.

Cinderella/Ashiepattle

Cinderella (1950), Walt Disney.
Jacob and Wilhelm Grimm, 'Ashiepattle' (1812), in Grimm and Grimm 1982.
Charles Perrault, 'Cinderella or the Glass Slipper' (1697), from *Histoires ou Contes du Temps Passé*, in Zipes 1989.

Beauty and the Beast

Beauty and the Beast (1999), The Disney Corporation.
Mme le Prince de Beaumont, 'La Belle et la Bête' (1757), in Zipes 1989.
Susan Jeffords, 'The Curse of Masculinity: Disney's "Beauty and the Beast"', in Bell et al. 1995: 161–72.

The Little Mermaid

The Little Mermaid (1997), The Disney Corporation.
Hans Christian Andersen, 'The Little Mermaid' (1837), in Andersen 1984.
Laura Sells, 'Where Do the Mermaids Stand: Voice and Body in "The Little Mermaid"', in Bell et al. 1995: 175–92.

Bibliography

Appleyard, Brian (1998), 'Disney Family Values: the Triumph of Niceness', *The Sunday Times How Disney Makes Magic Supplement*, week 1: Creating Character, p. 8.
Baudrillard, Jean (1983), *Simulations*, New York: Semiotext(e).
Baum, L. Frank [1900] (1997), *The Wonderful Wizard of Oz*, Oxford: The World's Classics.
Bell, Elizabeth, Lynda Haas and Laura Sells (eds) (1995), *From Mouse to Mermaid: The Politics of Film, Gender and Culture*, Bloomington: Indiana University Press.
Bettelheim, Bruno (1976), *The Uses of Enchantment: The Meaning and Importance of Fairy Tales*, London: Thames and Hudson.

Giroux, Henry A. (1999), *The Mouse That Roared: Disney and the End of Innocence*, Lanham, MD: Rowman and Littlefield.

Grimm, Jacob and Wilhelm Grimm (1982), *Selected Tales*, ed. David Luke, London: Penguin.

Luthi, Max [1947] (1982), *The European Folk Tale: Form and Nature*, Philadelphia: Institute for the Study of Human Issues.

Mills, Stephen F. (1993), 'Taking On the Mighty Mouse: Disney and the Americanisation of Western Europe', *Borderlines: Studies in American Culture*, 1:1, 85–107.

New Internationalist (1998), 'Walt's World: A Reader's Guide to Disneyfication', in issue no. 308 (December 1998), entitled *The Mousetrap: Inside Disney's Dream Machine*. http://www.newint.org/issue308/guide.htm

Propp, Vladimir [1928] (1984), *Theory and History of Folklore*, Manchester: Manchester University Press.

Smoodin, Eric (ed.) (1994), *Disney Discourse: Producing the Magic Kingdom*, London: Routledge.

Tomlinson, John (1991), *Cultural Imperialism: A Critical Introduction*, London: Pinter.

Waller Hastings, A. (1993), 'Moral Simplification in Disney's "The Little Mermaid"', *The Lion and the Unicorn*, 17:1, 83–92.

Wells, Paul (2002), *Animation and America*, Edinburgh: Edinburgh University Press.

Zipes, Jack (ed.) (1989), *Beauties, Beasts and Enchantments: Classic French Fairy Tales*, London: Meridien.

Zipes, Jack (1993), *The Trials and Tribulations of Little Red Riding Hood*, London: Routledge.

Zipes, Jack (1994), *Fairy Tale as Myth, Myth as Fairy Tale*, Lexington: University Press of Kentucky.

Zipes, Jack (1997), *Happily Ever After: Fairy Tales, Children, and the Culture Industry*, London: Routledge.

Zipes, Jack (ed.) (2000), *The Oxford Companion to Fairy Tales: The Western Fairy Tale Tradition from Medieval to Modern*, Oxford: Oxford University Press.

CHAPTER TEN

Transatlantic Literature as Critical Resistance to Americanisation

Heidi Slettedahl Macpherson and Will Kaufman

This chapter explores how the concept of Americanisation is central to the reading of transatlantic literature through using two historically situated case studies that offer resisted transatlantic encounters. Transatlantic literature almost by definition (since it belongs neither to one side of the Atlantic nor to the other) includes views from the other side, and is predicated upon an often unequal transatlantic exchange. In its British–American construction, transatlantic literature includes American texts which look towards Britain (or vice versa) and which describe or imagine encounters between individuals that come to represent something larger than personal collisions or rendezvous. Such encounters can take the form of factual travel narratives or memoirs, such as Isabella Bird's *A Lady's Life in the Rocky Mountains* (1879) and Bill Bryson's *Notes from a Small Island* (1995), or fictional texts such as Anne Tyler's *The Accidental Tourist* (1986) and David Lodge's *Changing Places* (1975). In a more complex formulation, transatlantic literature delineates links across and between a variety of nations and continents, linking (say) Chile with England and the US (as in Isabel Allende's *Daughter of Fortune*, 1999), Canada with Poland and the US (as in Eva Hoffman's *Lost in Translation*, 1989), or India with the US by way of unmarked and illegal border crossings (as in Bharati Mukherjee's *Jasmine*, 1989). In these constructions, the transatlantic acts as a space that is contested and undefined, a space in between, a space that is as much imagined as it is real (much like nation-states, whose geographic borders are reinforced by cultural mythology as much as by anything else).

In transatlantic literature the explicit construction of national and literary identities proceeds against a counter-definition that resists it. Our two main case studies here – Mark Twain's *A Connecticut Yankee in King Arthur's Court* (1889) and Jamaica Kincaid's *A Small Place* (1988) – act as nineteenth- and twentieth-century examples of how resistance undermines any easy reading of such encounters. Twain's text taps into the tensions of the historical moment when the rising American empire was set to overtake the declining British empire on the world stage, while Kincaid's text seeks to set American imperialism alongside British imperialism. Kincaid suggests that neither imperial power is absolved from historical wrongs that perpetuate unequal race relations between countries as well as individuals. Toni Morrison has written that definitions 'belong to the definers and not the defined' (Morrison 1988: 190), but as we will show, the resistance of the 'defined' against would-be definers is a powerful counter-force. Overlaying these relations is also the contested and contestable force of Americanisation, and in relation to transatlantic literature, Americanisation is variously constructed. On one hand, it is clear that American imperialism is a powerfully resisted and paradoxically incorporated force; on the other, British imperialism is by no means an innocent and long-forgotten ancestor.

In exploring transatlantic literature and Americanisation, it is imperative to read transatlantically and transnationally, to bear in mind, for example, both Americanness and Britishness (or whichever national identities are being explored), and what those constructions connote. However, as Paul Giles reminds us in his book *Transatlantic Insurrections*, 'to read national literatures in a transnational way is . . . to suggest the various forms of contingency that have entered into the formation of each naturalized inheritance' (Giles 2001: 1). It is this contingency that is emphasised as much as radical rupture. Indeed, it is sometimes difficult even to decide what is American and what is not: Is Bill Bryson's *Notes from a Small Island* an American or a British text? Set in the UK, but focusing on the (carefully crafted) comic persona of a bumbling American abroad, this travel book and memoir was written by a long-term British resident, for the British reading public, with an irony that the average American – or so the truism goes – cannot or will not understand.

It is particularly in relation to the trope of travel that transatlantic literature explores these constructions of national identity. The transatlantic journey and its consequences for narrators, characters, and indeed readers remain central to these texts. As Ernest Hemingway implies in *A Moveable Feast*, transplanting oneself is crucial to writing with a transnational focus: 'Maybe away from Paris I could write about Paris as in Paris I could write about Michigan' (Hemingway 1964: 6). Living the life of an expatriate, Hemingway trawls the *quais* for American books, and more complexly, perhaps, tours the Musée du Luxembourg 'to see the Manets and the Monets and the other Impressionists that [he] had first come to know about in the Art Institute of Chicago' (ibid.: 12–13). Here, then, it is precisely through displacement that the recognition of a national formation can proceed. Hemingway also, however, describes responses that step back from recognition, that indicate a precise refusal to see – for instance, on the part of his travel companion, F. Scott Fitzgerald:

> Scott hated the French, and since almost the only French he met with regularly were waiters whom he did not understand, taxi-drivers, garage employees and landlords, he had many opportunities to insult and abuse them.
>
> He hated the Italians even more than the French and could not talk about them calmly even when he was sober. The English he often hated but he sometimes tolerated them and occasionally looked up to them. I do not know how he felt about the Germans and the Austrians. I do not know whether he had ever met any then or any Swiss. (ibid.: 146)

Fitzgerald may refuse to recognise the contingent nature of national formation, but Hemingway, in delineating it here (and adding the comic twist which makes his travelling companion into a figure of fun, rather than a writer of stature and reputation), suggests that *he*, at least, understands such transatlantic encounters.

Clearly, the transatlantic narrative is defined by the textual recreations of encounters between people and cultures, and the power struggles that ensue in the attempt to impose or resist conceptions of foreignness or hierarchy. Sometimes – if not in Fitzgerald's case – the engagement with such power struggles acts as a transformative experience, but this transformation is not always wholly embraced, and sometimes even backfires, as our first case study reveals.

A Connecticut Yankee in King Arthur's Court: British–American collision

Mark Twain's *A Connecticut Yankee* is a fictional travel narrative in which the American protagonist travels not only through space, but through time as well. The Connecticut Yankee, Hank Morgan, visits upon King Arthur's England all the American ingenuity which, he believes, the benighted peoples of the world cannot but desire. It is important to appreciate the cultural assumptions of nineteenth-century American imperialism, as well as the collision of two Atlantic empires, when interpreting Twain's text. According to a narrative strand with which Twain was dismally familiar, and which, as a leading anti-imperialist, he surely hated, the United States had a 'manifest destiny' to influence if not actually shape the world. John L. O'Sullivan's famous outburst of 1839, in which 'manifest destiny' was first (and so confidently) proclaimed, casts Americanisation in distinctly imperial terms, acknowledging the possibility of resistance but the inevitability of conquest:

> The expansive future is our arena, and for our history. We are entering on its untrodden space, with the truths of God in our minds, beneficent objects in our hearts, and with a clear conscience unsullied by the past. We are the nation of human progress, and who will, what can, set limits to our onward march? Providence is with us, and no earthly power can. (O'Sullivan 1990: 7–8)

The stark opposition between the past, or antiquity, and progress is as fundamental to the earliest premises of manifest destiny as to the latest. US Defense Secretary Donald Rumsfeld's recent division of Europe into 'Old' – against us in Iraq – and 'New' – for us – is only the most recent tapping of the source. In the nineteenth century, American hostility towards its great transatlantic rival, Great Britain, was (according to one popular construction) that of the progressive offspring against the politically geriatric parent. During periods of amity – for instance the great Rapprochement of the 1890s, when Britain and the US finally set aside their hundred-plus years of mutual distrust in order to divide the geo-political spoils (we'll cover our hemisphere, you cover yours) – commentators on both sides of the Atlantic wrote lyrically of the close relationship between the two branches of the great Anglo-Saxon family. In such times Britain and America were less the child and the parent, and more the close cousins. But in moments of intense rivalry – the war of 1812, the expansionist period of the 1840s (when O'Sullivan's 'manifest destiny' most equates with outright territorial conquest), the crisis-ridden 1850s, when Britain and the US challenged each other for control of the Panama isthmus, or in the midst and immediate aftermath of the Civil War – British–American conflict was habitually cast as generational. Hence the future Lord Salisbury's patriarchal contempt for the American upstarts destroying themselves through civil war, too young to instruct the old monarchies in the ways of longevity: 'They have been conductors of a great experiment, ostentatiously set up in the face of all the world, designed to teach the nations wisdom, and to confute the prejudices of old times' (Cecil 1861: 249).

As an early powerful statement of intent, critically consider the extent to which O'Sullivan's (1990) notion of manifest destiny is useful for an understanding of American export literature and culture. You might wish to consider the importance of 'futurity', imperial prowess and resistance, for example.

This generational conflict was in particular a masculine one – a contest of the manly. This was almost inevitable, as the discourse of Anglo-Saxonism was by definition the discourse of strenuous masculinity. 'It is in the deep traits of race that the fortunes of nations are written', wrote Ralph Waldo Emerson in his praise of England, and for him the defining Anglo-Saxon traits were those of men: 'They are of the earth, earthy; and of the sea, as the sea-kinds, attached to it for what it yields them, and not from any sentiment. They are full of coarse strength, rude exercise, butcher's meat and sound sleep' – this indeed is what made England 'the best of actual nations', the master of the sea, the modern powerhouse of wealth and industry, the originator of individual and parliamentary freedoms (Emerson 1981: 455, 457, 513). On the other side of the Atlantic – or so English editorials implied – was a jealous adolescent working through the dangerous hormonal urgencies of manifest destiny. In 1882, England's preeminent literary critic, Matthew Arnold, chided the Americans for their worrying combination of populism and cultural philistinism: 'The United States have created a considerable popular instruction without any serious higher instruction, and will long have to expiate this fault by their intellectual mediocrity, their vulgarity of manners, their superficial spirit, their lack of general intelligence' (Arnold 1974: 4–5).

Such contributions to the transatlantic discourse, in an unstable era of waxing American and waning British imperial influence, could of course prove volatile. British observations upon American braggadocio were common enough fare in the mid-nineteenth century, as journalists in London and Edinburgh derided the vaunting and threats of expansionist organs like the *New York Herald*, which more than once called for the American annexation of Canada and all of Latin America, even at the expense of a war with John Bull. But in at least one important case, the British deprecation stung, and it provides a telling link between the processes of imperial rivalry and the projection of a national literature. In 1887, Arnold – who had denied that American literature even existed (all literature in the English language was by definition *English* literature) – reviewed the memoirs of the recently deceased American president and Civil War hero, Ulysses Grant. The review was double edged, deploring 'an English without charm and without high breeding' while commending an author 'boastful only in circumstances where nothing but high genius or high training, I suppose, can save an American from being boastful' (Arnold 1977a: 145–6). The following year, Arnold's essay 'Civilization in the United States' appeared in the *Nineteenth Century* magazine. Not only was Abraham Lincoln a man without distinction, Arnold claimed, but

> in truth everything is against distinction in America, and against the sense of elevation to be gained through admiring and respecting it. The glorification of 'the average man', who is quite a religion with statesmen and publicists there, is against it . . . [as is] the addiction to 'the funny man', who is a national misfortune. (Arnold 1977b: 360–3)

That very year, America's premier 'funny man' (and, incidentally, the publisher of General Grant's *Memoirs*) was close to finishing a novel that had begun as a simple vision of pure slapstick in a note book entry:

> Dream of being a knight errant in armor in the middle ages. Have the notions and habits of thought of the present day mixed with the necessities of that. No pockets in the armor. No way to manage certain requirements of nature. Can't scratch. Cold in the head – can't blow – can't get at handkerchief, can't use iron sleeve. Iron gets red hot in the sun – leaks in the rain, gets white with frost and freezes me solid in winter. Suffer from lice and

fleas. Make disagreeable clatter when I enter church. Can't dress or undress myself. Always getting struck by lightning. Fall down, can't get up. (Twain 1979, III: 78)

A number of conflicting impulses fed into the writing of Mark Twain's *A Connecticut Yankee at King Arthur's Court* – Twain's resentment for Arnold and, through him, British superciliousness; Twain's own disastrous preoccupation with American business and technology (a preoccupation that was to bankrupt him financially); and his scepticism over the 'beneficent objects' of O'Sullivan's manifest destiny. *A Connecticut Yankee* is one of the nineteenth century's most complex interrogations of Americanisation, fuelled at once by national pride and technological optimism, transatlantic jealousy and desire, anti-imperialism and American self-contempt. It is also, of course, a story of Anglo-Saxon men – American sons and English fathers – doing battle with each other and leaving in their wake a holocaust. Hank Morgan, the Yankee who destroys King Arthur's Camelot is (not for nothing) both an evangelical democrat and an arms manufacturer, the head superintendent at the Colt Arms factory in Hartford, Connecticut. His journey begins with a losing display of machismo ('a misunderstanding conducted with crowbars' that sends him reeling back to sixth-century England) and ends with the massacre of a nation which, in the end, had had enough of the imposition of American 'progress': 'Within the short minutes after we had opened fire, armed resistance was totally annihilated, the campaign was ended, we fifty-four were masters of England! Twenty-five thousand men lay dead around us' (Twain 1987: 36, 404–5). Along this dismal trajectory of manifest destiny gone wrong are many signs, not only of the complexities that marked the generational struggles of British–American rivalry in the nineteenth century, but of subsequent American adventures and resistance to them. Morgan's acknowledgement of Anglo-Saxon 'manliness' ('A man is a man, at bottom. Whole ages of abuse and oppression cannot crush the manhood clear out of him') is undercut by his belief that he can instruct and control the destiny of 'a childlike and innocent lot' through the imposition of American republican principles, a gutter press and technological know-how (ibid.: 279, 53). When it appears that the people are not terribly impressed with the blessings of civilisation that the Yankee's administration brings to them, he resorts to a series of 'shock and awe' effects – blowing up stone towers with lightning rods and blasting powder, shooting bullet holes into the breasts of jousting knights, commandeering an eclipse of the sun. Morgan reverses the

203

generational hierarchy by demeaning the medieval Britons as children; he then racialises them in a manner ironically linking them to the first victims of American manifest destiny: they are, to his mind, 'white Indians' (ibid.: 53). When, in the end, these infantilised aborigines of Old England shock Morgan out of his complacency through their determination to reject the 'beneficent objects' of American progress, he crushes their resistance with his electrified fences and his Gatling guns. Through his own arrogance and his fatal misreading of the resistant determination from those he had presumed to improve, Morgan concludes that in order to save them, he has to destroy them. Few critiques of manifest destiny or Americanisation have been so chilling.

Although Twain's dystopic travel narrative grows out of the transatlantic power struggles of the nineteenth century, its implications have continued to resound. Kurt Vonnegut, for one, reflected upon Twain and *A Connecticut Yankee* in April 1979 – four years after the final failure to impose American democracy in Vietnam, and eight months before Islamic fundamentalists toppled the US-backed Iranian regime and took fifty-three hostages from the American Embassy in Tehran:

> How appalled this entertainer must have been to have his innocent joking about technology and superstition lead him inexorably to such a ghastly end. Suddenly and horrifyingly, what had seemed so clear throughout the book was not clear at all – who was good, who was bad, who was wise, who was foolish. I ask you, Who was most crazed by superstition and bloodlust, the men with the swords or the men with Gatling guns? (Vonnegut 1981: 170–1)

In *A Connecticut Yankee*, the transatlantic encounter is one of destructive collision, and the Americanisation at the heart of it is ultimately resisted – once the awe over the spectacle of magic and power has worn off. Twain offers an extreme illustration of a contest at the heart of what Mary Louise Pratt has termed the 'contact zone', a social space 'where disparate cultures meet, clash, and grapple with each other, often in highly asymmetrical relations of domination and subordination – like colonialism, slavery, or their aftermaths as they are lived out across the globe today' (Pratt 2000: 5). Pratt suggests that a term such as 'contact zone' allows critics to reread moments of historical encounter as ones of 'copresence' as well as 'disjuncture' which allow for 'interactive, improvisational dimensions of cultural encounters' (ibid.: 7). Twain suggests that misreading encounters in the 'contact zone' can lead to horrific and violent conclusions. It is no small irony that the conflict Twain portrays is one between the two imperial powers that would go on to form the 'Special Relationship' of the twentieth century, when military conflict between Britain and the US was for all intents and purposes unthinkable. But in the transatlantic – particularly British–American – context, such a political alliance has not meant the disappearance of the 'contact zone' as a site of conflict and resistance. In our second case study – Jamaica Kincaid's extended essay *A Small Place* – the contact zone takes on a greater, if more subtle, significance, precisely because of the apparent absence of violence. The location is not a battlefield, but rather – from a misguided British–American perspective – a peaceful tourist site.

Jamaica Kincaid's *A Small Place*: British–American Collusion

In *A Small Place*, Kincaid offers an angry memoir of resistance and reclamation that links British colonial rule with contemporary American tourism and uses a vitriolic 'you people' address to explore an Atlantic location – Antigua – which is neither American nor British but impacted on by both. For Kincaid, this Caribbean 'paradise' is a site of violent encounter, with tourists seriously misreading the location, their sight confined to the replication of their own desire. If Mark Twain's fictional travel narrative relies for its effect upon the obtuse cultural blindness of its nineteenth-century protagonist in the contact zone, Kincaid's essay sets out to reveal the same blindness on the part of the twentieth-century tourist.

> From a reading of Pratt (2000), discuss the usefulness of the notion of the 'contact zone', locating your discussion within a reading of a relevant transatlantic literary text.

'If you go to Antigua as a tourist,' Kincaid begins, 'this is what you will see' (1997: 3). Kincaid's opening line is deliberately provocative, because what you will see is defined by its absences, its contrasts. What you will *not* see is the local, inadequate school; the damaged library – except, perhaps as a curiosity, an odd reminder that *these people* have a different way of looking at time, because the sign outside the library says, 'THIS BUILDING WAS DAMAGED IN THE EARTHQUAKE

205

OF 1974. REPAIRS ARE PENDING' (ibid.: 9). As a tourist, you will not see the hospital – at least if you are lucky. You will not see drought (but rather, paradise – who wants rain on holiday?); you will not see the daily (authentic?) lives of those who serve you. What you will see is something else entirely, something that tourist brochures have already prepared you to see:

> You see yourself taking a walk on that beach, you see yourself meeting new people (only they are new in a very limited way, for they are people just like you). You see yourself eating some delicious, locally grown food. You see yourself, you see yourself . . . (ibid.: 13, ellipses in original)

Yet even in this seeing of yourself, you are mistaken, for, as Kincaid goes on to point out, 'a tourist is an ugly human being' (ibid.: 14). Kincaid's tourist is sometimes European, more likely American, and white (always white): the latest in a long line of people with colonial desires and misplaced superiority whose engagement with the contact zone leads to subjugation and destruction – not in the name of manifest destiny or imperial conquest, but in the name of leisure. Like Twain's *A Connecticut Yankee*, which began as an innocent burlesque and gradually darkened into a damning critique of Americanisation, *A Small Place* reveals the logical conclusion of an apparently innocent package tour, through which the tourist is the logical extension of both British colonial rule and American economic might. In this apparently innocent realm, the local 'tradition of service' (as heralded on the official website of Antigua) is the logical extension of slavery. Native and tourist stand in entrenched opposition to each other; what defines them is power, or the lack of it. On the one hand stands the privileged, for whom novelty is an accessible commodity. As Stanley Cohen and Laurie Taylor argue, 'if a sense of routine is a frequent theme in our expression of dissatisfaction with life, then the achievement of novelty is seen as a prerequisite of happiness' (Cohen and Taylor 1992: 68). This happiness – temporary and ultimately unsustainable as it is – can be initiated simply by changing locations. It seems harmless enough – people pack up and go; but in Kincaid's hands, the easy assumption of this privilege leads to a startling instruction as she directs attention to those on the other side of the equation:

> For every native of every place is a potential tourist, and every tourist is a native of somewhere. Every native everywhere lives a

life of overwhelming and crushing banality and boredom and desperation and depression . . . Every native would like to find a way out, every native would like a rest, every native would like a tour. But some natives – most natives in the world – cannot go anywhere . . . They are too poor to escape the reality of their lives; and they are too poor to live properly in the place where they live, which is the very place that you, the tourist, want to go – so when the natives see you, the tourist, they envy you, they envy your ability to leave your own banality and boredom, they envy your ability to turn their own banality and boredom into a source of pleasure for yourself. (Kincaid 1997: 18–19)

A Small Place is, as Salman Rushdie notes, 'a jeremiad of great clarity and force that one might have called torrential were the language not so finely controlled'.[1] Kincaid constructs a persona no less crafted in her anger than Hank Morgan in his ignorance; yet while Morgan feels happy to play games with the English language that he includes in his arsenal against that very language's progenitors, Kincaid – like the Irish novelist James Joyce before her – bemoans the colonialist's language in which her text is written: 'For isn't it odd that the only language I have in which to speak of this crime is the language of the criminal who committed this crime?' (ibid.: 31). For Kincaid as for Twain, English is the language of both the conquered and the conqueror; but in Kincaid's construction, it is the vehicle linking two formerly opposed powers that have joined hands across the Atlantic to subjugate a smaller space. The apparent ease and lack of violence in this particular process of economic subjugation – like the division of the globe into hemispheres of power during Rapprochement or the forging of a 'Special Relationship' – implies that when the 'big boys' stop fighting each other, they can more profitably turn their Gatling guns (or perhaps their cameras or video recorders) against other sites. Kincaid's response is to construct a dawning awareness on the part of an otherwise obtuse tourist: 'You needn't let that slightly funny feeling you have from time to time about exploitation, oppression, domination develop into full-fledged unease, discomfort; you could ruin your holiday' (ibid.: 10). For Kincaid, the creeping Americanisation that defines her homeland and that has both extended and displaced a tradition of British colonialism reinforces the injunction against transatlantic encounters. Such Americanisation takes a variety of forms. It is evident in how financial transactions take place in US dollars and how the gross national product determines local commerce; how 'local' cuisine is flown in from Miami, Florida; how the carnival now includes a 'teen pageant' in which contestants recite American pop lyrics; how 'development' of tourist sites and rows of boutiques selling tourist tat takes precedence over building schools, hospitals, and libraries; and how the Mill Reef Club is an exclusive site run for North Americans, making the beach 'off limits' to the native Antiguans.

In the fourth and final chapter, Kincaid uses the language of glossy brochures to ironic effect:

> Antigua is beautiful. Antigua is too beautiful. Sometimes the beauty of it seems unreal. Sometimes the beauty of it seems as if it were stage sets for a play, for no real sunset could look like that; no real seawater could strike that many shades of blue at once; no real sky could be that shade of blue – another shade of blue, completely different from the shades of blue seen in the sea – and no real cloud could be that white and float just that way in the blue sky; no real day could be that sort of sunny and bright, making everything seem transparent and shallow; and no real night could be that sort of black, making everything seem thick and deep and bottomless. (ibid.: 77)

Herein lies the problem. This tourist site *par excellence* becomes – like Arthur's Camelot – a fatally damaged site, a site of racial and ethnic erasure, where the colour black is connected only to the night, not the (properly subservient and therefore invisible) residents, and where the white tourists recapitulate the positions of their ancestors in ways that mimic positions of power supposedly dismantled in the contemporary world. This transatlantic space harbours a series of specific wrongs left undealt with in both historic and contemporary terms. An anti-travel text, A *Small Place* reenvisions the transatlantic as a place of continuously problematic encounters, and rewrites Americanisation as an extension of British imperialism.

It would wrong to suggest that all narratives of transatlantic travel – whether real, as in Kincaid's essay, or imagined, as in Twain's novel – project Americanisation as an evil that must be resisted, or see the transatlantic as a space of collision and collusion. Some, like Bharati Mukherjee's *Jasmine*, or Eva Hoffman's *Lost in Translation*, show a process of (admittedly contested) assimilation, and explore how Americanisation can be a beneficial force that leads to growth, rerootedness, and celebrated multiplicity. But as our two case studies reveal, it would also be wrong to suggest that what may start out as an innocent journey into the contact zone necessarily remains so.

In reading transatlantic literature – literature that looks beyond its borders to another nation-state or even continent across the Atlantic – what is key is a willingness to explore how literary texts project and define a sense of cultural geography; how they map and remap the space that is criss-crossed and traversed by friendly or hostile forces (and even how friendliness might mask a deadly consequence); and how the contact zone determines both what is incorporated, and what is rejected, by one side of the equation or the other. These texts reflect the attitudes, values, and opinions of the society in which they are produced as much as they attempt to portray – often through a plotted misapprehension – the society to which they refer, and recognising this dual construction is imperative in reading transatlantic literature. The significance of cultural and historical contexts cannot be underplayed: Twain's novel relies on historical situating in order to play out its view of Americanisation, and Kincaid's essay acts as a palimpsest when it overlays American tourism onto a site of British colonial struggle. Americanisation is variously defined by these texts, and variously negotiated – much like the space of the Atlantic itself – and reading such texts requires an awareness of how these factors work together in their constructions of various national and literary identities.

Note

1. This quotation comes from the back cover blurb of the British edition of this text.

Bibliography

Arnold, Matthew [1882] (1974), 'A Word About America', in Matthew Arnold, *Philistinism in England and America*, ed. R. H. Super, Ann Arbor: University of Michigan Press, pp. 1–23.

Arnold, Matthew [1887] (1977a), 'General Grant', in Matthew Arnold, *The Last Word*, ed. R. H. Super, Ann Arbor: University of Michigan Press, pp. 144–79.

Arnold, Matthew [1888] (1977b), 'Civilization in the United States', in Matthew Arnold, *The Last Word*, ed. R. H. Super, Ann Arbor: University of Michigan Press, pp. 350–69.

Cecil, Robert (1861), 'Democracy on Its Trial', *Quarterly Review*, 110, 247–88.

Cohen, Stanley and Laurie Taylor (1992), *Escape Attempts: The Theory and Practice of Resistance to Everyday Life*, 2nd ed., London: Routledge.

Emerson, Ralph Waldo [1856] (1981), *English Traits*, in Carl Bode and Malcolm Cowley (eds), *The Portable Emerson*, New York: Viking Penguin, pp. 395–518.

Giles, Paul (2001), *Transatlantic Insurrections*, Philadelphia: University of Pennsylvania Press.

Hemingway, Ernest (1964), *A Moveable Feast*, New York: Scribners.

Kincaid, Jamaica [1988] (1997), *A Small Place*, London: Vintage.

Morrison, Toni (1988), *Beloved*, London: Picador.

O'Sullivan, John L. [1839] (1990), 'The Great Nation of Futurity', in M. Thomas Inge (ed.), *A Nineteenth-Century American Reader*, Washington: USIA.

Pratt, Mary Louise [1992] (2000), *Imperial Eyes: Travel Writing and Transculturation*, London: Routledge.

Twain, Mark [1889] (1987), *A Connecticut Yankee in King Arthur's Court*, Harmondsworth: Penguin.

Twain, Mark (1979), *Mark Twain's Notebooks and Journals*, ed. Robert P. Browning et al., 3 vols, Berkeley: University of California Press.

Vonnegut, Kurt (1981), *Palm Sunday*, London: Jonathan Cape.

MASS MEDIA

CHAPTER ELEVEN

Global Media and Resonant Americanisation

Paul Grainge

> Time Life International was started in 1945 because the U.S. was literally the only power in the world capable of restoring some of the continuities of civilization . . . It is this towering uniqueness of power and influence [of the US] that is . . . the factual premise – the existential premise that Time Inc. should do things in the international world.
>
> Henry Luce, 1965

In February 1941, media mogul Henry Luce wrote an editorial in *Life* magazine that was to become a key, if not defining, moment in the modern discourse of Americanisation. Responding to the lack of national purpose that Luce saw deriving from the continuation of isolationist policies in the inter-war years, 'The American Century' proposed a more expansive role for the United States in world affairs. Luce believed that Americans had been unable 'to accommodate themselves spiritually and physically to the fact of power' (cited in Hogan 1999: 11–29). The remedy, he argued, was for American people to 'accept wholeheartedly our duty and our opportunity as the most vital nation in the world and to exert upon the world the full impact of our influence for such purposes as we see fit and by means we see fit'. The United States had been exporting its political ideals, economic systems, scientific knowledge and cultural products around the world for decades prior to Luce's missionary statement. However, Luce was perhaps the first person to realise the significance of the media in supporting the projection of American power in the postwar diplomatic and economic order.

In the emerging climate of the Cold War, and in a period when the American media was achieving worldwide dominance, the sponsorship of liberal capitalist values – especially the linkage of freedom with free trade and communication – became the ideological bedrock of Time Inc. magazines in both domestic and foreign markets. Luce believed that overseas editions of *Time* and *Life* were a tool of especial influence, offering 'something that the leading people all over the world can read: one common ground of what is going on in the world' (cited in Prendergast 1986: 81). With assumptions of common ground rooted in ideas of economic and cultural modernisation, news content in *Time*, *Life* and *Fortune* was powerfully geared towards a liberal order shaped by the United States. In ideological terms, the magazines were bound in the climate of 'capacious Americanisation' that Peter J. Taylor associates with the early postwar period (Taylor 1999: 3–16). As one *Time* imitator, *Der Spiegel*, wrote in 1961:

> No man has more incisively shaped the image of America as seen by the rest of the world, and the Americans' image of the world, than Henry R. Luce . . . Luceforic printed products are the intellectual supplement of Coca-Cola, Marilyn Monroe and dollar diplomacy. (Cited in Swanberg 1972: 181)

In Taylor's argument, 'capacious Americanisation' describes the moment of high hegemony that the United States experienced between 1945 and 1971: a period when American economic and political dominance was at its peak, the United States was relatively secure in a position of world leadership, and the projection of American civil society had become the basis and ideal of the future for many non-Americans. Taylor draws upon the world-systems analysis of cultural influence developed by Immanuel Wallerstein (1979). This provides a model of global development where particular states are given a historically specific location in the system of world capitalism. Wallerstein suggests that, since the sixteenth century, this system has had different centres at different times. While states (rather than abstract market forces) have always been the handmaidens of world capitalism, the location of particular states within the system has changed. Replacing Britain, which itself replaced the Netherlands, the United States emerged in the twentieth century as the core society around which particular values were attached and subsequently spread. Explaining how the economic and cultural power of hegemonic states defines the 'prime modernity' of a particular period, Taylor suggests that 'Americanisation is the name given to a process of emulation and adaptation under the condition of consumer modernity' (Taylor 1999: 6). The spread of mass production, mass consumption and mass mediation – the hallmarks of consumer modernity – are intimately bound with the force and projection of America in the last century. This does not guarantee that the United States can perpetuate its key position in the world system, however, or has even done so in the last three decades. Indeed, within Taylor's periodising model of hegemonic influence, 'capacious Americanisation' gave way in the 1970s to what he calls 'resonant Americanisation.'

The 'resonance' of Americanisation suggests a transition less in the degree of US influence around the world than in the ideological context of transmission. It describes a situation where American culture is ubiquitous but has also, at some level, lost its hegemonic legitimacy. The reception and local adaptation of American products, commodities and values is a complex issue that can be addressed in manifold periods and places, and with differing conclusions regarding issues of accommodation, emulation, resistance and fear. Resonant Americanisation does not seek to harden the experience of America in foreign contexts in either positive or negative terms. Rather, it attempts to locate the influence of the United States within a historically broad, and resolutely global, perspective.

Carl Strikwerda suggests that the 'globalisation debate has enormous implications for the study of the United States' (Strikwerda 2000: 333). Put simply, an increasing sense of global inter-connectivity has challenged ideas of American exceptionalism. This has implications for Americanisation theory, shifting the discussion of national influence and power from coercive models of imperial domination (the imposition of a unified 'them' on a vulnerable, but equally unified, 'us') to the more complex nature of global relationships that go beyond the bounded limits of national territory and ideology. According to Jonathan Friedman, globalisation is not another, more intense, form of Americanisation, as some might argue, but is instead suggestive of 'changing conditions of world hegemony' (Friedman 2000: 139–46). By this he means the relative decline of Western and US hegemony. The United States is, of course, a major architect of what is often called neo-liberal globalisation. This describes a powerful ideological formation where the well-being of democracy and culture is associated with the maintenance and extension of free-market principles. The US has been at the heart of the impetus towards deregulation and free international trade; it has been a major proponent and beneficiary of the global restructuring of the media; and it has generally marked the global economy with a heavy American input and accent. It would be wrong to suggest that globalisation somehow diminishes American influence and power. If 'global processes materialise in national territories', as Saskia Sassen suggests, the United States is a key site of economic, military, legal, cultural and ideological force (Sassen 1996: xi). However, it would also be wrong to conflate globalisation with American influence and power. In a global moment characterised by the destabilising of organisations, institutions and values that have relied for their authority on a once-apparent stability and fixedness – including the idea of the nation-state – the United States is no longer a unified or radiating site of cultural influence. Americanisation theory is obliged to account for this development.

In the remainder of this chapter, I want to use *Time Atlantic* – the international edition of *Time* serving Europe, Africa and the Middle East – to suggest particular transitions that have shaped the mode and discourse of American influence within international news media. In the postwar period, *Time* magazine played an important role in the dissemination of American values and liberal ideologies. As such, one might ask what effect the increasingly global organisation and operation of the parent company, Time Warner, has had on *Time*'s more recent profile and news identity. How, in particular, can *Time Atlantic* be related to the globalisation of media forms, firms, flows and effects? Dominic Strinati has made attempts to 'trace out the links between Americanisation, the dominant international role of American money and culture, and the increasingly transnational character of culture and information' (Strinati 1992: 50). Strinati seeks to establish a meaningful framework for Americanisation critique, exploring the changing structures of American global power. While rejecting postmodern theories of transnationalism that subscribe to a fragmented global order with no discernible centre, he does acknowledge that the 'isolated splendour of American global hegemony is coming to be challenged not only by Europe and Japan, but by an admittedly embryonic set of cosmopolitan and cross-national relations' (ibid.: 50). I want to examine *Time Atlantic* in this context. In developing the issue of resonant Americanisation, we might pose the following question: how, if at all, has *Time Atlantic* been challenged, changed or forced to refine itself in the context of the global, and what implications might this have for the Lucean discourse of American world influence?

> Luce's essay 'The American Century' is a key document in studying the discourse of Americanisation in the twentieth century. Use the reprinted version in Hogan (1999) to consider:
> 1. Who you think Luce is addressing
> 2. What the defining aspects of the 'American Century' seem to be according to Luce
> 3. How concepts such as freedom and destiny are used in the essay.

Time Atlantic: 'global reach and local touch'

Time Inc.'s status as a global media player came to the fore in 1989 when, facing a hostile takeover bid from Paramount, the company merged with Warner Brothers in a $14 billion deal. This became the most widely discussed merger in a period where global media consolidation was becoming the quintessence of corporate survival. Since the late 1980s, there has been a spate of mergers and acquisitions that has seen the emergence of several colossal vertically integrated media conglomerates, including the News Corporation, Disney, Bertelsmann, Viacom, and Time Warner. Media commentators have described the 1990s as 'an all-out rush to claim global turf' and Time Warner swiftly established itself as the biggest of all media titans (see Herman and McChesney 1997: 53). Despite incurring heavy financial losses after the merger in January 2000 with America Online, the conglomerate remains a formidable corporate force. With stakes in publishing, cable, music, film, video, television, professional sports teams, retail outlets, studios, cinemas and theme parks, Time Warner has relentlessly pursued its commitment to ever-deepening global media expansion.

In 1990, Steve Ross, then head of Time Warner, explained that 'the new reality of international media is driven more by market opportunity than national identity' (cited in Morley and Robins 1995: 11). In the same year, Time Warner launched a new motto: 'The world is our audience'. During the 1990s, Time Warner developed a vision of global connectivity that figured the restructuring of national media industries, and the development of a global media market, in terms of a new and borderless world order. Describing a process of 'bringing the world closer together,' Ross said:

It is up to us, the producers and distributors of ideas, to facilitate this movement and to participate in it with an acute awareness of our responsibilities as citizens of one world . . . We can help to see to it that all peoples of all races, religions, and nationalities have equality and respect. (Cited in Morley and Robins 1995: 11)

This illustrates the celebratory rhetoric that frequently emanates from global media industries and their corporate executives. Typically, the exponential growth of free trade and communication is set in terms of *consumer* freedom and the democratic spread of information. While the globalisation of media firms has brought with it changes in strategic operation, it has also become a matter of discourse, meaning the values and attitudes that are used to justify and legitimate dominant interests in the new global economy.

As the largest international edition of Time Warner's flagship publication, *Time Atlantic* was especially subject to the structural and discursive changes of the 1990s. *Time Atlantic* has distilled the body of the parent magazine for international audiences ever since the first issue appeared in July 1946. Since the 1990s, however, there have been significant changes in the way the magazine has been produced and marketed. In a time when international sales are becoming a crucial source of income for American media corporations, new sensitivities have developed towards the local markets in which cultural products circulate and are made to compete. *Time Atlantic* is a useful index of what might called the 'local–global nexus,' meaning in this case a dual orientation in the magazine towards regional (national, European) identities and transnational political, cultural, and economic developments.

There is, of course, nothing new about international media operations and regional marketing. The media history of *Time Atlantic* is linked to the growth of Time Life International, the corporate body responsible for co-ordinating all of the company's foreign activities in the postwar period. European headquarters were established in London in 1953 and in Paris in 1960. This reflected charged efforts, in the words of *Life* publisher Andrew Heiskell, to make 'the maximum effort to establish as many beachheads as possible' (cited in Prendergast 1986: 82). This not only involved corporate diversification into broadcast television and book-publishing; it also meant expanding Time Inc.'s international magazine base. During the 1950s and 1960s, renewed editorial efforts were given to international and foreign-language editions of the company's flagship magazines, including *Time Atlantic*, *Time Pacific*, *Time Canada*, *Time Latin America*, *Life International*,

Life en Español, and *Life Asia*. By 1968, Time Life International was responsible for ten per cent of total corporate revenues. Foreign media markets were rarely free of difficulty, however. Confronting issues of censorship, erratic delivery and uneven audience figures, the decision was taken in 1968 to disband Time Life International. This did not mean sacrificing international interests but restructuring operations on the basis that Time Inc. was 'a "world" corporation rather than a U.S. corporation with an export division' (cited in Prendergast 1986: 100). This was part of a more general drive in the 1960s towards multinational corporate organisation that involved utilising factors of production, distribution and marketing on a global basis.

Until 1996, *Time Atlantic* was produced in New York City. With transnational media corporations becoming ever more sensitive to the relation between global organisation and local marketing and presence – what the European editor of *Time Atlantic*, Chris Redman, described as 'having global reach and local touch' (Redman 1996: 5) – the production of *Time Atlantic* moved entirely to London in the 1990s. While the magazine had been printed in Europe since the 1940s, and European stories had been edited from offices in London and Paris for much of the postwar period, never before had an entire staff of writers, designers, photo editors, researchers and production experts worked outside of New York. One of the 'fruits of decentralisation', according to Redman, was the development of a magazine 'that is global yet attuned to our regional readers' (ibid.). This marked a discreet change of emphasis. In editorial terms, *Time Atlantic* was no longer the journalistic offspring of an American parent but more of an expatriate relative, regionally embedded and savvy of local quirks and concerns. The magazine was less a media 'beachhead,' deepening the penetration of American corporate presence and national values, than a knowledgeable and curious beachcomber of Atlantic shores.

Describing a redefinition of the relationship and power balance between the traditional mass-media industries and their consumers, J. Michael Jaffe and Gabriel Weimann suggest: 'Mass media domination based on ideological imperialism is shifting in favour of an information market dominance based on cultural recruitment and segmentation' (Jaffe and Weimann 2000: 306). They point to a transition in the configuration of media power that is useful in theorising a change in the international profile of *Time Atlantic*. While Luce's missionary effort to spread the powerhouse of American values may once have shaped *Time*'s identity abroad, this has given way to more focused, and regionally inflected, niche marketing. The special-projects editor of

Time Atlantic, James Geary, explains that decentralisation in 1996 saw the convergence of commercial and editorial imperatives: the desire to make the international editions of the magazine more profitable and at the same time more relevant to regional audiences (Geary 2001). Since the transition of operations to London in 1996, *Time Atlantic* has placed greater emphasis on its European coverage and news orientation, although not without also recognising how its American style becomes a differentiating hook in a highly competitive marketplace of magazine weeklies and general-interest news products. According to its own advertising, *Time Atlantic* provides European readers with 'the most thorough and thoughtful coverage of international news and a different perspective on the news events in their own communities' (*Time* 1992: 6). For Geary, this difference in perspective is linked to the fact that *Time* is 'in Europe but not of Europe'. By March 2001, under the new editorial helm of Ann and Donald Morrison, *Time* made its regional focus explicit by launching itself boldly as 'Europe's newsmagazine'.

In 2001, *Time Atlantic* was the biggest selling international edition of the parent magazine (and of any international news magazine) with a circulation base of 627,000. Published in American English throughout Europe, Africa and the Middle East, the highest subscription rates for *Time Atlantic* are in the British Isles (120,000), Germany (95,000) and France (95,000). Accounting for people reading (rather than buying) copies of the magazine, the estimated weekly audience is 2.1 million. This compares with *Time Asia* with an audience of 1.9 million, *Time Latin America* (audience 350,000) and *Time South Pacific* (audience 614,000). The international editions of the magazine have similar demographic profiles to the domestic edition, focusing upon high-income, college-educated professionals. However, they tend more towards elite audiences within media, business, government and academia. According to Belinda Baker (2001), marketing director for *Time Atlantic*, the magazine's target audience is made up of affluent world travellers, leaders and opinion makers. Taken from a ranging set of details about the magazine's readership (produced by *Time* for the attention of advertisers), fifty-seven per cent of subscribers come from business and industry, seventy-five per cent are male, sixty-nine per cent frequently or occasionally drink champagne, fifty-seven per cent spend hotel nights on business, and seventy-three per cent travelled abroad in the last year. While the domestic issue is likely to advertise automobiles and life insurance, appealing to its substantial middle-class readership, *Time Atlantic* contains more ads for first-class air travel, mobile phones, Rolex watches and other designer apparel, suggesting from the outset a market interest in a wealthy professional and business stratum.

A demographic sense of *Time*'s international readership is significant on a number of levels. Not least, it points towards the magazine's particular interpretation of local–global concerns, specifically the way that regional issues are framed with an affluent global readership in mind. *Time Atlantic*'s internationalism is effectively geared towards brokering local (specifically European) identities through transnational frameworks that support what Jonathan Friedman calls the 'cosmopolitan-capitalist experience of the world' (Friedman 2001: 143). Heralding the launch of a 'refreshed' magazine in 2001, Ann and Donald Morrison explained that 'the definition of news is changing in this globalised, post-cold war world, when political divides are being replaced with concerns about prosperity, its pursuit and consequences' (Morrison and Morrison 2001: 4). In this context, the United States is no longer a determining focus of news content in *Time Atlantic*, at least not as it was once figured along the said political divide. I would nevertheless argue that America is still given an anchoring power within the magazine's filtering of neo-liberal concerns. It is here that we return to issues of resonant Americanisation.

Critics have argued that transnational corporate interests have increasingly disassembled the imperatives of national ideology. This does not mean to say, however, that national interests and identities have been renounced. Clearly, multinational media conglomerates have strong national affiliations in terms of their business origins and organisation. In this context, one might argue that *Time* magazine has a vested interest in the fashioning of American international power, especially in terms of legitimating transnational systems (legal, economic, political, cultural) that are based on US models and that may ease or benefit the global operations of Time Warner. The question of 'Europe' as a market and geopolitical entity is a case in point. John Dunning (1993: 166–89) suggests that the completion of the internal European market in 1992 has revitalised US direct investment in the region across the board of manufacturing, financial, construction and consumer industries. In the sphere of communications, Time Warner has taken various steps to enlarge and preserve its stake in the region. This has involved direct resistance to attempts by the European Union in 1992 to create a continental policy that would establish trade barriers to American media products, especially imported television programming. However, it can also be observed in such developments as the geographical relocation of *Time Atlantic* to London and, more discreetly, in the interpretive frameworks proffered by the magazine. Of course, *Time Atlantic* is no simple mouthpiece for Time Warner; one cannot assume that any particular chain of media ownership will guarantee a determined ideological position. The magazine does invest in a certain idea of Europe, however, that constructs the region through a framework that engages key neo-liberal assumptions about the linked benefits of cross-border flexibility, multicultural pluralism, and cultural/capital flow.

The 'new Europe' has become a staple subject for *Time Atlantic* special issues. While certain issues have dealt with the promise and pitfalls of reinventing nationhood in postnational times ('The New France', 15 July, 1991; 'Renewed Britannia', 27 October 1997; 'The New Reign in Spain', 17 November 1997), other issues have addressed the specificity of European identity as it reaches a turning point 'fraught with dangers yet tantalisingly rich in promise' ('The New Europe', 9 December 1991). Perhaps the most prospective intervention that *Time Atlantic* has made in the discourse of European identity has come in a number of winter special issues. These include 'Europe: 50 Remarkable Years' (1996), 'Visions of Europe' (1998) and 'Fast Forward Europe' (2000). There is not space here to unpack the focus and concern of each issue. In general terms, however, the details and difficulties of European integration are set, in each issue, within a framework where a realigned sense of geopolitical, economic and cultural identity is seen to generate a new and promissory regional strength.

Amidst the range of commissioned essays that detail the nuances of European life in the post-Cold War milieu, the cut and thrust of *Time*'s coverage is staked on the potential of pan-European regionalism. This has implications for the United States, and the American multinationals that operate in Europe. In a concluding *Time* essay in 'Europe: 50 Remarkable Years', Jacques Attali, former President of the European Bank for Reconstruction and Development, considers whether or not a strong Europe would be in the best interests of the US. His short answer is yes. He writes: 'It is my belief that America's real interest is in the further elaboration of a powerful European Union' (Attali 1996: 143). Not only would this relieve America of the sole burden of overseeing world affairs, it would give Europe a defining role, through the euro, of 'integrating a significant part of the planet into the world economy'. Only with a strong Europe, Attali believes, could the three powerful continents of North America, Europe and Asia 'have the means to set up the real agenda for the 21st century: communications and information networks, the battle against the criminal economy, the reduction of atmospheric pollution, and promotion of freedom and culture through a diversity of languages and ideas'.

Attali does not speak for *Time* but neither are his views entirely removed from the paradigmatic neo-liberalism that underpins the magazine in discursive terms. Rhetorically, both Attali and *Time* invest in a discourse that posits a new world order defined by global free markets, the liberating potential of new technologies, and that looks implicitly towards the United States in shaping transnational relations. If, as Attali suggests, 'a renewed United States of Europe awaits the appearance of its Jeffersons, Washingtons and Hamiltons', a renewed global order is, according to former *Time* managing editor Walter Isaacson, rooted in the diffusion of American-led free-market democracy. Describing the ascendance of American values in the late twentieth century – encompassing democracy, individual liberty and free markets – Isaacson writes: 'To the degree that America remains an avatar of freedom, the Global Century about to dawn will be, in Luce's terminology, another American Century' (Issacson 1998: 103). In discursive terms, the United States becomes (and in this sense remains) a developmental model in terms of both the pedigree of its political vision and the basis of its liberal capitalist value system (see Grainge 2002).

Dominic Strinati (1992) suggests that while the political economy of Americanisation is undisputed in the global media system – meaning the dominant role of American capital and finance in the industries that produce popular and media culture – analysing discursive processes and consumptive practices can generate more ambiguous conclusions about the process and experience of 'Americanisation'. In this chapter, I have argued that *Time Atlantic*, once framed by Henry Luce as a tool of national influence, is no longer defined in any simple sense by the sponsorship of American values. In its negotiation of the local–global nexus, *Time Atlantic* figures a discourse of America, but in relation to postnational configurations that have increasingly seen the emergence of global elites, agendas and commercial imperatives. Luceforic printed products may once have been the intellectual supplement of Coca-Cola and Marilyn Monroe but, in the global media market, *Time* is no longer the missionary agent of America's 'towering uniqueness of power'. If 'resonant Americanisation' describes a conjuncture where the ubiquity of US forms and cultural products in the world is matched with the need to renew or reconfigure the hegemonic basis of American power, *Time Atlantic* suggests particular transitions in the mode and marketing of US media/discourse abroad.

Examine a recent copy of *Time* magazine and consider the extent to which it may or may not convey an 'Americanised' perspective on news events. What narrative or visual elements contribute to the magazine's discursive identity? Consider what might be revealed by examining *Time* issues from different historical periods.

Bibliography

Attali, Jacques (1996), 'For a New Political Order,' *Time* winter special issue.

Baker, Belinda (2001), personal interview with author, 23 March.

Dunning, John (1993), *The Globalization of Business*, London: Routledge.

Friedman, Jonathan (2000), 'Americans Again, or the New Age of Imperial Reason', *Theory, Culture & Society*, 17:1, 139–46.

Geary, James (2001), personal interview with author, 23 March.

Grainge, Paul (2002), 'Remembering the American Century: Media Memory and the *Time* 100 List', *International Journal of Cultural Studies*, 5:2, 201–19.

Herman, Edward and Robert McChesney (eds) (1997), *The Global Media: The New Missionaries of Corporate Capitalism*, London: Cassell.

Hogan, Michael J. (ed.) (1999), *The Ambiguous Legacy: U.S. Foreign Relations in the American Century*, Cambridge: Cambridge University Press.

Issacson, Walter (1998), 'Luce's Values – Then and Now', *Time*, 9 March.

Jaffe, J. Michael and Gabriel Weimann (2000), 'New Lords of the Global Village?', in Reinhold Wagnleitner and Elaine Tyler May (eds), *Here, There and Everywhere: The Foreign Politics of American Popular Culture*, Hanover, NH: University Press of New England, pp. 288–308.

Morley, David and Kevin Robins (1995), *Spaces of Identity: Global Media, Electronic Landscapes and Cultural Boundaries*, London: Routledge.

Morrison, Ann and Donald Morrison (2001), 'Time for a Change', *Time*, 2 April.

Prendergast, Curtis (1986), *The World of Time Inc.*, New York: Atheneum.

Redman, Chris (1996), 'Europe, 50 Remarkable Years,' *Time*, winter special issue.

Sassen, Saskia (1996), *Losing Control? Sovereignty in the Age of Globalization*, New York: Columbia University Press.

Strikwerda, Carl (2000), 'From World-Systems to Globalization: Theories of Transnational Change and the Place of the United States,' *American Studies* 41:2/3, 333–48.

Strinati, Dominic (1992), 'The Taste of America: Americanization and Popular Culture in Britain', in Dominic Strinati and Stephen Wagg (eds), *Come On*

Down: Popular Media and Culture in Post-War Britain, London: Routledge, pp. 47–79.

Swanberg, W. A. (1972), *Luce and His Empire*, New York: Charles Scribner's Sons.

Taylor, Peter J. (1999), 'Locating the American Century: A World Systems Analysis', in David Slater and Peter J. Taylor (eds), *The American Century: Consensus and Coercion in the Projection of American Power*, Oxford: Blackwell, pp. 3–16.

Time (1992), 21 September.

Wallerstein, Immanuel (1979), *The Capitalist World Economy*, Cambridge: Cambridge University Press.

Further reading

Written in a time when theories of media imperialism held sway but still useful for its historical breadth and detail, a classic critique of American media power in the twentieth century is Jeremy Tunstall, *The Media Are American: Anglo-American Media in the World* (London: Constable, 1977). A more contemporary account, written from the vantage point of political economy and maintaining an imperialist thesis, is Edward S. Herman and Robert W. McChesney, *The Global Media: the New Missionaries of Corporate Capitalism* (London: Cassell, 1997). A nuanced analysis of how cultural identities are being reshaped in the period of global media consolidation, focusing specifically on Europe, can be found in David Morley and Kevin Robins, *Spaces of Identity: Global Media, Electronic Landscapes and Cultural Boundaries* (London: Routledge, 1995). For ranging essays on American power in the climate of globalisation, see both David Slater and Peter J. Taylor (eds), *The American Century: Consensus and Coercion in the Projection of American Power* (Oxford: Blackwell, 1999) and a special issue of the journal *American Studies* 41:2/3 (Summer/Fall 2000), which focuses on the subject of 'Globalisation, Transnationalism and the End of the American Century'. For a cultural and material analysis of *Time* magazine in the 1990s, see Paul Grainge, 'Remembering the American Century: Media Memory and the *Time* 100 List', *International Journal of Cultural Studies* 5:2, 201–19.

CHAPTER TWELVE

9/11 Multiplied by 24/7: Some Reflections on the Teaching of September 11th

Alasdair Spark

What I want to discuss in this chapter is not so much the meaning of 9/11 as how study of the event can reveal the forms and the limits of America's appeal to British citizens. To do so, I will draw upon my experiences in the teaching of several student workshops on September 11th conducted at various institutions in the UK (including my own) during the period from September 2002 to January 2004.[1] Part of the project of American Studies is to examine how American culture has been exported globally (which is to say, how it has been received locally), and part of this consists of studying how the spectacle of America is relayed to the corners of the world – in material items and patterns of consumer culture, but perhaps most of all in television. It is too formulaic to count this simply in the reception of American-made dramas, thrillers, game shows and the like, and the cultural imperialism they allegedly sustain. Instead, we have to recognise that in the globalised situation following the end of the Cold War, our consumption of the spectacle of America has become not just more complex, but also more complicit. This is why 9/11 offers such a valuable moment for study – because it problematises so well both the loyalties and the doubts which are inherently part of the transatlantic exchange.

Where were you when? Remembering 9/11

It seems obvious to mention, but it was immediately noticeable that students recognised the term '9/11' at once, even though it employs the American style of dating (not 11/9). In fact, this deviation from the normal encapsulated the event and rendered it distinctive for British students; with little prompting, students expressed the view that '9/11' (and after) spoke closely to their personal relationship to America. For the American Studies tutor, therefore, 9/11 offers a very significant opportunity to explore Americanisation and the so-called 'special relationship' with students, not least by the examination of a subject with which they clearly feel engaged.

This was immediately evident in my discussion with the student groups about how and when they first learnt about the events of Tuesday, 11 September and the attacks on the World Trade Center towers and the Pentagon. All vividly recalled their shock and surprise and had strong memories of where and when they learnt of the attack – intriguingly for this generation some reported that the news first came from text messages from friends on mobile phones. Most seemed ready primed to place the event in their own lives in terms of their knowledge of similar events – almost all mentioned similarities to what they had heard about reactions to the news of the deaths of President Kennedy and John Lennon, and in the context of their own lives, to what they had already experienced in the death of Princess Diana in Paris in 1997. This meant that for almost all 9/11 was recognised as a television event – real knowledge came when it was first seen on TV. Since it took place in the early afternoon in the UK, only a very few reported seeing the attacks live as an interruption to normal programming; for most, the first act was to seek out a TV set, and so the memories are of images on TV, repeated time and time again over the forthcoming days. Many recalled spending all of the rest of that day and night watching reports from New York, and many noted similarities with the intense 'rolling' reporting of Princess Diana's death and funeral and the suspension of ordinary life, and, no less, ordinary television, which resulted. To understand the experience of 9/11, therefore, it is not just the '9/11-ness' of the events that needs study, but also its '24/7-ness', the constant reporting and thus its domineering place as the correlative for every other issue – a state which continues in the USA, but has come to be questioned in Europe. The experience of viewing the attacks on television might therefore be best described as the first part of an experience in which 9/11 is multiplied by

24/7 – in other words, an intensified and totalising state in which everything, everyone, everywhere, is made part of, or defined by its relationship to, this event. In effect, the television coverage was the first iteration of the Bush doctrine of preemption (you are either with us or against us) which now defines American foreign policy.

Perhaps most of all, discussing the TV images (and repeating them to student groups via extracts from various documentaries) provides a powerful opportunity to discuss the event in terms of the 'media spectacle'. This term was coined in the 1960s by the French cultural critic Guy Debord, who argued that the place of the spectacle in society was being intensified by the novel technology which conveyed it to audiences, most especially the development of television and global satellite relay. It was not just that existing spectacles would be covered by the new media; these technological changes meant events would be created solely to be viewed as spectacles by global audiences. An early example would be the moon landing in July 1969, an event driven by Cold War geopolitics, but only really rendered meaningful by being televised. A recent example would be Janet Jackson's revealing performance at the half-time show of the 2004 Superbowl – at time of writing, the most searched item on the Internet ever.

The term 'media spectacle' has increasingly been applied to how events are being experienced and, moreover, manufactured for our experiencing in the contemporary world. Since Debord's *Society of the Spectacle* (1967) 'spectacle/the spectacular' have become terms applied to contemporary celebrity, sport, music, movies, war, and politics. America is often seen as the prime, even the extreme, site for such, and so the experiences of the USA are often seen as Americanising influences globally, and as precursors or harbingers for other nations – the Kennedy assassination, the Gulf War, the O. J. Simpson trial, the Monica Lewinsky scandal and the 2000 US Presidential election have all been cited. Drawing directly on the work of Karl Marx, Henri Lefebre and the Frankfurt school, Debord's analysis is highly politicised and focuses in part on the capacity of the spectacle to appropriate the most intimate and revolutionary human impulses and desires. Debord with fellow activists became known as 'situationists' for their attempts to create situations which subverted the spectacle. Academic theorists and critics have tended to view media spectacles in less totalised ways, as sites where contests over identity and status

---

are carried out. See Marilyn Garber, Jann Matlock and Rebecca Walkowitz (eds), *Media Spectacles* (1993); Ien Ang, *Living Room Wars* (1995); Paul Thaler, *The Spectacle: Media and the Making of the O. J. Simpson Story* (1997); and Douglas Kellner, *Media Spectacle* (2003). Alternative strands of Debord's influence can be seen in the critiques and strategies of the anti-corporate movements, and in Naomi Klein's *No Logo* (1999).

How did it happen for you? 9/11 as a live media spectacle

The most significant ideas about the spectacle since Guy Debord have been those of another French critic, Jean Baudrillard, particularly with reference to the 1991 Gulf War. Bringing Baudrillard together with the attack of 9/11 provokes spirited classroom discussion. His provocative statement that the Gulf War 'did not happen' has often been (mis)quoted, not always affirmatively. When this phrase is presented to students, many at first treat it as arrogant and absurd – of course it happened, people died. However, given further exposition of Baudrillard's argument that the Gulf War *did not take place* in the sense that for western audiences the war only existed on television, and thus only as a detached, simulation of the event, then the relevance becomes clear. For 18–21-year-old students the Gulf War is of course a childhood memory, but most easily recognised the truth of Baudrillard's claim in half-remembered images of grainy pictures relayed from the nose cameras of 'smart' bombs, and in the experience of viewing the coverage of other wars since. Given this awareness, it was worth enquiring with the student groups whether they generally felt sceptical about the images they consume from television and were cynical and distrustful of the media. Most agreed that they usually were, but they accepted that images of 9/11 seemed to circumvent this. When asked to consider why this was so, the explanation was universal: these images were trusted because they were live.

Introducing such ideas (and of course the above bowdlerises Baudrillard), it is fruitful to ask how they can be applied to 9/11. Among the questions I asked were:

- Did 9/11 'happen' for you beyond watching TV?

- Do you think 9/11 fulfils or disqualifies Baudrillard's arguments about media spectacles?

What was most noticeable about the responses gained in the workshops was that students in fact did report a heightened sense of involvement, evidently as a result of the intense 24/7 reporting of the event and their own round-the-clock viewing. Many again made comparisons with the death of Princess Diana when expressing how much the scenes shown on TV of the devastation in New York had moved them, and motivated them to individual action. This was particularly evident when talking to the more recent groups of students who back in 2001 were part of a school community, and who often reported organising memorial ceremonies, or collective acts of writing to the American embassy or to officials in New York City. Most also mentioned their sense of partici- pation in moments of public mourning in the UK, ranging from the memorial service in St Paul's Cathedral – again, viewed on TV – to the playing of the US anthem at the Trooping of the Colour and to more local moments of sadness among family and friends. Generally there- fore, 9/11 seemed to serve as a moment in which the British relation- ship with America was experienced starkly and affirmatively. Only a few recalled that they had felt much doubt and concern during 9/11 about the relationship, though, as I will discuss in the final section, this feeling has shifted for many since.

To facilitate discussion at this point, I found it fruitful to refresh memories by showing various images of 9/11; for instance, the opening from the HBO documentary *In Memoriam* contains a sequence which presents a digest of the attacks, as do various programmes presented by CNN. Reactions were interesting: the now very familiar image of American Airlines Flight 11 hitting the North Tower and then United Airlines Flight 175 crashing into the South still produced gasps; the scenes of the buildings' collapse still stunned the viewers into silence. Asked to comment on the images, students often made statements to the effect that they wanted to look away, but could not, and that the images were 'magnetic'. When questioned further about their reaction to these images of 9/11, one issue repeatedly surfaced – their similarity to spectacular images of the destruction of the urban skyline that had already been seen in movies such as *Die Hard*, *True Lies*, *Deep Impact* and *Armaggedon*.[2] However, asked why they thought that popular movies had anticipated and made entertaining such devastation, few answers were forthcoming. This repeated gap led me to introduce the students to Damien Hirst's notorious description in 2002 of the attack on New York as 'visually stunning' and 'wicked, but a work of art' (he later withdrew the comment).[3] Many students' first reaction to this was that it was tasteless publicity-seeking, but most came to admit that they did find in the images exactly the fascination, power and structure which Hirst had claimed.

Such reactions suggest the importance of thinking of 9/11 as a *terrorist spectacle*. It was worth questioning whether the primary aim of the attacks on the twin towers was, in fact, to cause their destruction. By this, I mean to ask if the purpose of the attacks was not instead to dominate American (and world) television with terrifying images, and in that sense to feed Baudrillard's sense of the Gulf War back upon itself and so upon its consumers. As such, 9/11 was the terrorist equivalent of the moon landing: an event which existed not for its own sake – to destroy the buildings and kill large numbers of Americans – but for its facility in providing a terrifying live and infinitely repeatable spectacle. After all, the term 'terrorist spectacular' was coined during the 1970s to fit novel circumstances like the Munich Olympics massacre in 1972. If today the experience of war for the developed world exists largely in TV images, then commanding the images wins the war – a lesson learned negatively in Vietnam, positively in the first Gulf War and elaborated upon with considerable sophistication by government and military alike in the second. The strike on 9/11 revealed that this lesson had also been learned elsewhere. Practised in flight simulators and dress rehearsals, this attack on America and in America fed back upon the very media systems themselves that produced the images in order to create a TV spectacular without precedent or equivalent. Baudrillard's comments on 9/11 in an article called 'The Spirit of Terrorism' confirm this: 'To a system whose surplus of power does not allow any challengers, the terrorists respond[ed] with a definitive act also impossible to duplicate' (Baudrillard 2001: 135). William Merrin put it well when he wrote of the comparisons between the Gulf War and 9/11:

> September 11 was [like the Gulf War] a single, devastating strike from the air, carried on the screens of the globe, allowing no response from the victims and, in its spectacle, making even the eventual US military reaction – bombing the rubble of Afghanistan – an inadequate response that can do nothing to erase those images. (Merrin 2002)

I would argue that the truth of the events of 9/11 as a post-Baudrillardian spectacular is most of all revealed by the precise timing of the attacks – towards the close of network breakfast programmes such as *Today* and *Good Morning America*, all of which are broadcast live from studios in New York City. If attacked only an hour later, the death toll might have been in the order of ten times the 2,700 or so the two towers claimed. The seventeen-minute interval between the first and second impact guaranteed that live cameras would be turned from inside the breakfast TV studios to outside, so that images we have of the second attack are multiple, while the first was caught on tape only by accident. The success of this strategy can be measured by the fact that the coverage was almost instantaneous (the first reports came in two minutes after the first impact) and then became total. Normal programmes and commercials were suspended for several days on the CBS, ABC, and NBC networks; MTV, the Home Shopping Network, and other like channels in effect declared themselves inappropriate and went off air, displaying placards telling their viewers to tune to a news station; 24-hour news coverage was provided not just by CNN and Fox News, but by all three networks.

These mediatisations of 9/11 can easily be illustrated by visiting one of the websites devoted to preserving the live TV footage of the attacks carried on the different networks. Probably the most comprehensive is www.tvarchive.org, which carries streaming video recording the attacks as they unfolded live not just on the major US networks, but on others from around the world.

What's missing from this picture? Live TV and the repetition of 9/11

Live also meant uncensored, and it seems that al-Qaeda were well aware that censorship of the live image was impossible – in this sense, 9/11 was exactly a response to the manufactured, manipulated and controlled images of the Gulf War, and one that preyed on the seductive spectacularity of the images which the attack generated for the US media. However, it is striking that some 9/11 images were not carried live, or if they were, were not replayed later. Asking students which images these were at first produced confusion, until I realised that British TV had only briefly carried them – the images were, of course, those of trapped people jumping and falling from the top storeys of the World Trade Center towers. Recently these images have become the subject of considerable analysis because of their peculiar power, particularly to ascertain the identity of those falling.[4] Upon playing such images to student groups (they are shown in the HBO documentary), more often than not for the first time, their reaction was shock and terror. An interrogation of the particular terror held by these images and why, despite being so memorable, they were omitted from the many repetitions and memorialisations of the event, was aided by first playing an extract from a documentary which deliberately chooses to leave them out – the Naudet brothers' *9/11*. The Naudets were mid-way through filming a documentary about recruits to the New York Fire Department when 9/11 occurred, and they were the source of the footage of the first plane crashing into the North Tower. Both their video crews sped to the buildings with the Fire Department and shot images in the mezzanine and foyer. However, their documentary deliberately includes only the crashing sounds, not images, of falling people hitting the foyer roof, ostensibly for reasons of good taste. Following this, I would then show the uncensored footage from the HBO documentary and I asked students the following questions:

- What do you think this absence in the compilations speaks to?
- Does the sound or image of people falling remind you of any other disaster?
- If these images were too terrible to repeat, why?

The replies students gave most often repeated notions of good taste, arguing that the images were too horrible to show or view. In that sense, they might suggest an interesting self-limiting aspect to the spectacle, or a counter-spectacular tendency within it – on this, more later. When asked to consider the question of equivalents or antecedents, students usually found little to offer. Nothing in their experience seemed to match the terror contained in these images, with their implied message: what would I do? However, *without fail*, in every session someone would hesitatingly offer that, even though it sounded silly, well, it did remind them of the scenes at the close of the 1998 movie *Titanic*, as passengers jump from the upending ship, and one in particular hits the propellers with a hollow clang. This was a fascinating and revealing comparison to make, one which, unforced, reveals what I would argue is the real reason for the frequent censorship of the images of falling people, and thus their taboo power as a spectacle. Just like the passengers left stranded on the *Titanic*, these images present a quite precise terror, one of being beyond rescue, thus providing a revelation about the inability of state authority to adequately protect its people or provide for their escape.

Despite the efforts to expunge it, this terror continues to lurk on the margins of images of 9/11. I showed students an image taken from 'Here Is New York', a project which seeks to express the meaning of 9/11 via what the organisers call the democracy of photographs. (George 2002: 186) A few of the images in their gallery (and book, published in 2002) were taken by professional photographers, but the majority come from members of the public who took an image of this immense event happening in their city. The pictures vary in quality and subject, but one stands out: an image of the North Tower; the gash in the side of the building where Flight 11 crashed through is clear, but there is little flame or smoke. I give a copy to students and ask them to look carefully. After a few minutes, someone sees it – a tiny blur, a woman standing on the edge of the ripped curtain wall, peering down, trying to decide what remains of her future.

'We've got TV.' Counter-spectacles to 9/11

The *Titanic* disaster is also often seen as a *fin de siècle* moment, the first puncturing of Edwardian certainties about progress, soon to be confirmed in the Great War. Such a comparison is moot for an America which celebrated the end of the Cold War and the end of history that resulted, but has now replaced it with the 'War on Terror', a title with which Fox News captions its daily bulletins.

If we consider the attacks on 9/11 as having begun a new war of images, it is fruitful to ask what American 'counter-spectacles' might exist, and so whether William Merrin's claim that no reply to the attack could suffice, that no meaningful retaliatory image was possible, really holds true. To assist, I asked the groups the following questions:

- Have you seen anything that you would argue constitutes a counter-spectacle to the 9/11 attacks?
- If so, how powerful and effective did you find these, and why?

Among the items students nominated as effective and moving were the anniversary spectacle of the laser beams shining upwards in the outline of the footprint of the towers, various spectacles of remembrance, such as the funerals of New York Fire Department members, the candle-lit vigils and displays of photographs of the missing, anniversary ceremonies, and the various competing designs for replacement buildings (the winning design by Daniel Libeskind has now been selected). In regard to the question of replacement buildings, I showed the student groups a counter-image which made its way across the Internet not long after the attacks. It shows five replacement towers, each identical in design to the originals, but each of different height, with the centre tower the tallest. The caption reads 'The New World Trade Center'. After a few seconds' puzzlement at the apparent bombast, most saw what the image maker intended – a giant fist, with the middle finger raised in the familiar American gesture of contempt.

The other type of counter-spectacle most often nominated was constituted by the various commemorative documentaries such as those already viewed; most agreed that they mobilised feeling. Other forms of television also provide opportunities to discuss spectacle, and to illustrate this I showed the student groups an example: *America: A Tribute to Heroes*, the fund-raising telethon which was broadcast live on all the major networks on 21 September 2001. This two-hour prime-time event provided an unprecedented lineup of performers including Stevie Wonder, Bruce Springsteen, Tom Petty, Celine Dion, Wyclef Jean, Limp Bizkit, Paul Simon, Billy Joel and Neil Young, plus, introducing them and working the phones, movie stars such as George Clooney, Tom Hanks, Halle Berry, Jack Nicholson, Goldie Hawn, Julia Roberts, Jim Carrey, Brad Pitt, Jennifer Lopez – the list goes on. Without much prompting, students recognised this as an attempt to reply to the spectacular power of the images of 9/11. The clip which proved most provocative for discussion was the climax of the event, in which Clint Eastwood offered a solo summation of American grief and resolve, which then segued into a rendition of 'America the Beautiful' led by the country and western singer Willie Nelson and sung (with varying knowledge of the words) by the assembled celebrities. Interestingly, student reaction to this was universally negative. Partly this was in response to the anthem, which was seen by British students as an 'over the top' display of patriotism all too typical of Americans. Partly it also appeared to come from a desire to separate celebrity and politics, which expressed a similar sense of British cultural superiority over America. This was most remarked upon in response to Eastwood's speech, which many saw as striking a false note because it was too reminiscent of acting roles such as Dirty Harry.

To contrast this, I next showed students a rather different musical performance. It consisted of an ultra-low-budget music video shown on the UK Black Entertainment Network in late 2002. The performers are identified only as 'Various' and the song as 'Medley' but it consists of an ensemble reggae version of 'The Best That You Can Do' (a.k.a. 'Arthur's Theme' from the 1981 movie of the same name), with substituted lyrics that include 'How could they go and attack my New York City? . . . The best that we can do is pray for love.' Despite much effort I have been unable to trace the performers. Presumably because of the low production values, the strangeness of the adapted song, and the unrecognised performers, almost universally the groups regarded this video as a spoof – but given the event in question, this was inconceivable. Lacking a context for the images, students could find no purchase in it as a counter-spectacle. Indeed, it seemed unusual that Black people could sing patriotically about the United States. In fact, the video is perhaps the most interesting counter-spectacle response to 9/11 I have found, coming as it appears to do from the immigrant Jamaican community in New York, offering a strong expression of the very particular patriotism of the newly arrived immigrant.

Finally, in this discussion of counter-spectacles, I showed student groups a short report aired on CNN Headline News on 7 December 2001, following the American invasion of Afghanistan and the conquest of Kabul. In it, Jason Bellini (on loan from MTV) wanders around Kabul looking for satellite dishes; he finds several dishes, appropriately enough home made from flattened Coke cans, and interviews the owners, who have also invested in decoders and TV sets – all banned by the Taliban. Bellini discovered an enthusiasm for TV. An old man says that if he had $200 he would get a TV and sit all day watching it, while an Afghan boy tells him: 'During the Taliban we had lots of time to play with toys. Now we've got TV. We've got freedom.'[5]

This provided the most controversial element of the workshop, with students disagreeing vigorously about its meaning – not least in the context of their own relationship to TV and Americanisation after 9/11. Among the points that student groups repeatedly raised in their responses to this CNN report were these:

- Was the abandonment of a traditional lifestyle in favour of American consumerism wrong? Or is this patronising, imagining a pastoral, non-Americanised state which we would not accept ourselves (particularly for women)?
- Does the arrival of satellite dishes mean that America will win,

not by force but by the power of TV, and the appeal of consumer capitalism it promotes?

As students all agreed, these questions are just as valid when asked of British–American relations.

'No firmer friend'? The special relationship after 9/11

Several American commentators have used the same phrase to sum up the meaning of 9/11: that America's 'holiday from History' was over. It is a neat phrase, certainly redolent of viewing 9/11 as a *Titanic*-tinged event, but the meaning is surely double edged. The term was used by commentators on the right such as George Will who saw 9/11 as a call to dispense with the frivolities of the 1990s (Monicagate et al.), and in response the US defence budget is now at its highest ever ($379 billion), bigger than the budgets of all the other members of NATO put together. For the right, the hope is that al-Qaeda (like General Yamamoto after Pearl Harbor) has awakened a sleeping giant. In contrast, liberal commentators such as Susan Sontag have argued that the imperial giant never sleeps. Sontag thought it was the American people who were asleep, failing to recognise that 9/11 was not an attack on civilisation, but on 'the world's self-proclaimed sole superpower, undertaken as a consequence of specific American alliances and actions' (Sontag 2001: 32). Thus, her hope is that after 9/11 Americans will wake up and realise that their government's actions abroad, especially in the Middle East, have consequences back home.

This divide has been mirrored in the UK, but with the added dimension of the British relationship to America. As President Bush's 2002 declaration of war against the 'axis of evil' made clear, if other nations do not stand with America, then they will be counted as standing against. Generally, 9/11 was seen by students to have problematised the 'special relationship'. Students noted that British sympathy for America on 9/11 emerged as an instinctive response to the images from New York, but it was noticeable that whenever I showed a clip of an American news report on Tony Blair's visit to Washington, DC in November 2001, during which President Bush declared that America had 'no firmer friend' than Blair and Britain, it was met with groans. Much of the negativity centres on President Bush. Very few said they had regarded the President with respect before 9/11, and events since have not changed this view. Frequently mentioned was the 2000 election and the criticisms made by Michael Moore, the documentary director and author of the UK bestseller *Stupid White Men*, which accuses Bush of stealing the presidency on behalf of big business. While the students I talked to did not necessarily share them at the time, they did recognise anti-American reactions to 9/11; such views were commonly summed up in terms of payback, that Americans 'got what they deserved' or had 'asked for it'. While few had read the strong criticisms of America made in the press by the likes of Arundhati Roy, several recalled moments such as the edition of the BBC's political discussion programme *Question Time* held two days after 9/11, and the hostile attitude of some of the audience to the American ambassador. Prompted by this, I would ask the groups the following questions:

- What do you now feel about 9/11? Looking back, do you think your feelings then were an overreaction?
- How have subsequent events (Afghanistan, Iraq) affected your perceptions of 9/11?

While they remained a minority in all the groups, a significant number of students did now feel that they had overreacted to the event, often saying that they felt they had been too swayed by the power of the images. Generally, the relationship between the US and the UK was recognised as having grown tense since 9/11 and many felt that America had squandered their sympathy. Elements of the war on terror such as the detentions at Guantanamo Bay and indiscriminate bombing in Afghanistan were often mentioned. Unsurprisingly perhaps, holding a revised view of the significance of 9/11 appeared most closely related to the 2003 war in Iraq, and accusations of American aggression, the flouting of the United Nations and, postwar, the failure to find any weapons of mass destruction. In effect, something perceived as founded on a false rationale – Iraq as a legitimate locale for President Bush's war on terror – has made problematic much of the sympathy generated by 9/11. In addition, scepticism has reestablished itself and many students seemed to feel a willingness to consider conspiratorial explanations for 9/11 and after, such as Gore Vidal's passionate fantasy that the events of 9/11 were stage-managed as the pretext for a coup by big business. Ironically, but revealingly, many again had been made aware of these issues via American critics such as Moore.

Concluding impressions

These workshops proved revealing of the British–American relationship as perceived and experienced by British students. As consumers of America since birth, students recognised that for all practical purposes they assemble their lives using many American or Americanised ingredients, and that therefore their loyalties and tastes are significantly directed towards the United States. Hence, as an attack on the familiar, 9/11 struck home, much more so than events with a far greater death toll elsewhere have done, or could do. What most affected them were the images, particularly the images of people forced to jump to their deaths, incidents which echoed the movie *Titanic*, but also perhaps a perception of *Titanic* as the transforming cultural moment of a generation. Of course, the fact that it was relentlessly televised made a difference, but it could not have been otherwise: unlike the Afghans interviewed by Jason Bellini, having viewed the spectacle of America via television for years, British viewers were already complicit. So, are we all American now, as some claimed in the aftermath? Intriguingly the evidence of the attempts at counter spectacle suggest not. Students understood attempts such as the *Tribute to Heroes* telethon, but they distinctly found that the anthem and the Clint Eastwood monologue only confirmed their differences with and from America. Equally, while they possessed the vocabulary to see the 'finger' of the 'New World Trade Center', they did not – perhaps could not – possess the local cultural specifics to appreciate that the reggae song was genuine. Finally, the most significant reply to 9/11, the invasion of Iraq, significantly cut into loyalties and raised doubts and fears, not least about the consequences of too close an alliance with America. In sum, 9/11 does present evidence of the exchanges, resonances, and hybridities which have become the preferred terms employed by recent models of Americanisation, but it also reveals the limits of these, not least in the conjunction between American cultural power and American strategic power.

Notes

1. The AMATAS project was funded by HEFCE as a Further Development in Teaching and Learning Project in American Studies. Apart from sessions at University College Winchester, this account is drawn from visits to

Liverpool John Moores University (2003), Falmouth College of Art (2003) and University College Chichester (2003 & 2004.) These were with Year 1 groups in American studies and media studies, which had the effect of moving backwards in memory from a constituency that was working before entering higher education in 2001 to students who were in the sixth form in 2001. I do not pretend that the responses from these students have been located in their institutional background or that they are generally representative. My aim is simply to provide an account of my own experiences teaching this issue and offer it as a think-piece to provoke ideas about how teaching can be organised around 9/11 and so facilitate wider student learning about their own relationship with the United States. I should point out that my own experience of 9/11 and the several months after took place in the United States. Any of the teaching materials mentioned can be provided for interested colleagues upon request.

2. In a curious recognition of this relationship, in 2002 the Pentagon held a widely publicised symposium in which movie directors were invited to meet with intelligence officers to speculate on possible future attacks.
3. For details, see http://news.bbc.co.uk/2/hi/entertainment/2268307.stm
4. See for instance Junod (2003).
5. A transcript can be found here: http://edition.cnn.com/TRANSCRIPTS/0112/07/nr.00.html

Bibliography

George, Alice Rose, Gilles Peress, Michael Shulan and Charles Traub (2002), *Here is New York*, Zurich: Scalo.

Baudrillard, Jean (1995), *The Gulf War Did Not Take Place*, Bloomington: Indiana University Press.

Baudrillard, Jean (2001), 'L'esprit du terrorisme', in *Le Monde*, 3 November; translated by Kathy Ackerman as 'The Spirit of Terrorism', in *Telos*, 121 (Fall), 134–42.

Debord, Guy [1967] (1994), *The Society of the Spectacle*, New York: Zone.

Garber, Marilyn, Jann Matlock and Rebecca Walkowitz (eds) (1993), *Media Spectacles*, New York and London: Routledge.

Junod, Tom (2003), 'The Falling Man', *Esquire*, September, http://www.esquire.com/features/articles/2003/030903_mfe_falling_1.html

Kellner, Douglas (2003), *Media Spectacle*, London: Routledge.

Merrin, William (2002), letter to the *Guardian*, 11 September, http://www.guardian.co.uk/september11/oneyearon/story/0,12361,790055,00.html

Moore, Michael (2002), *Stupid White Men*, London: Penguin.

Sontag, Susan (2001), 'A Mature Democracy', *New Yorker*, 24 September.

Roy, Arundhati (2001), 'The Algebra of Infinite Justice', *Guardian* Saturday Review, 29 September, www.guardian.co.uk/saturday_review/story/0,,559756,00.html

Visual sources

9/11 (2002), Goldfish Pictures.
America: A Tribute to Heroes (2001), Warner Brothers.
In Memoriam: New York City 9/11/01 (2002), Home Box Office.

VISUAL AND
MATERIAL CULTURE

CHAPTER THIRTEEN

National Icons, Social Fabrics:
The Transatlantic Trajectories of the Quilt

Janet Floyd

Introduction: the quilt as an American thing

The quilt[1] may seem, on first consideration, an obscure example through which to examine debates about Americanisation. Americanisation has been used, after all, as a term to evoke the relentless movements and homogenising results of modernisation or globalisation. It is mass cultural forms, Hollywood and youth culture especially, that often provide the organising examples within a debate about Americanisation that explores inter-cultural encounters ranging from complex negotiation to resistance. Craft objects such as quilts, rich in local and regional reference, are plainly – or so the argument goes – highly vulnerable to, if not already overwhelmed by, the world of mass production. In this essay, however, I want to argue that the quilt, profoundly associated with past tradition as it is, provides an illustration of some of the disjointed histories of Americanisation.

The quilt is, after all, perceived as a very 'American' thing, though it was brought to America from Europe.

> In this chapter I am tracing the multiple histories of a thing perceived as American within and outside the US, but the same histories and debates might fruitfully be pursued with reference to other material

objects, for example those with strong but shifting associations with tradition, such as the Navaho rug, or those with strong associations with mass production: Barbie would make an interesting comparison not only with respect to transatlantic trajectories but also with respect to her participation in mainstream feminist debates. On both of these see Attfield 1996; for the latter see Rand 1995 and Rogers 1999.

In America and elsewhere the history of the quilt is often folded within a history of the 'frontier', of the mass migration into the United States – of Americanisation in the sense of immigrant assimilation into the dominant values of the United States. But, in its life as an American thing, the quilt has also accrued other meanings, of which the most powerful has been its identity, within feminism, as a symbolic expression of women's lives, expression and creativity. Indeed in the back-migration to Europe of quilting in the 1970s and 1980s, it was this American feminist reading of quilts that decisively shaped the British understanding of quilts and quilting. The quilt, then, might provide a tale – or perhaps two tales – of Americanisation. But within these two tales – of the adoption of the quilt as American on the one hand, and the exporting of it back to Europe with its meaning recast, on the other – lie other sub-texts. It is with examining the overlapping stories through which we can understand this American object – and thus the opaque processes that characterise Americanisation – that I am concerned here.

Quilting may be traditional but, unlike many craft forms, it has not become a marginal activity. Indeed, a useful starting point for any discussion of quilts must be to observe their many appearances within American culture at the turn of the twenty-first century, and also to reflect on reasons for the unusually elevated status of the quilt by comparison with other forms of craft work. Quilts are recreated, reproduced and consumed in spaces both public and intimate, in cultural forms both highbrow and popular, in an unceasing procession of exhibitions, in fiction, in popular film, in innumerable books picturing quilts of the past, in countless instructional texts on quilt-making, in antique dealers' shops and department stores, in the output of so-called cottage industries and in museum catalogues. The widespread fascination with quilts that these appearances suggest goes far beyond that accorded to other craft forms – to hand-thrown pottery, for example, or wood-carving – or to such other popular (and equally collectable) stitched textile forms as samplers, rag rugs, woven blankets and coverlets. Nor is the quilt simply the preferred popular example of a traditional craft artefact. It has, throughout its history in America, been popular as an object for domestic display, the stuff of magazine articles and stories written for women assumed to be homemakers. For all its obvious association with the world of the private life, the quilt has become that unusual thing, a domestic object of great significance 'outside'.

While quilts are often understood to express the value and vibrancy of local and communal networks, within which most quilts are produced, the quilt is also described as a national icon in America. Elaine Showalter has argued that the quilt has replaced the 'melting pot' as a symbol of national identity, that it is a powerful metaphor for evoking a disparate but appealing national social fabric (Showalter 1991: 169). Cheryl Torsney and Judy Elsley write that it is 'the blazon of the national consciousness as well as the balm to our collective guilt over national tragedies', by which one assumes they refer to the 'Names' quilt made to commemorate victims of the HIV virus (Torsney and Elsley 1994: 1). Other nations have made the same association between quilt and the national community: the Welsh quilt has been understood as the sign of a distinctive national identity and as a demonstration of the possibility of the survival of nationality, while depopulated or economically vulnerable regions within and outside the United States have used the presence of a quilting tradition to assert the vitality of regional rural culture. But it is in America that the connection between quilt and nation is reasserted and received most enthusiastically.

Quilting seems most likely to have originated in the Middle or perhaps Far East, thousands of years ago, in the production of warm clothing. But in America it has been continually associated with a process of Americanisation in the sense of assimilation into American values, long imagined as generated by, and developed to its highest expression in, an Anglo-American experience of westward expansion. The quilt, and specifically the patchwork quilt, with its use of fabric recycled from old garments and cloths, has acted as a wonderfully accessible metaphor for the 'frontier' myth of a new American life stitched together from materials with different and disparate origins. Susan Arpad's explanation is a common one: 'For many women living in the rural midwest between 1850 and 1920, their worlds must have appeared fragmented, disordered, lonely, bleak, filled with dirt, flies, dung and mud . . . [quilting] created order out of chaos, giving meaning to lives that, for many women, must have been experienced as . . . chaotic' (Arpad 1988: 24, 15). The very creation of a quilt can be understood as a lesson in the Protestant values at the heart of the Anglo-American project: austerity, self-sufficient frugality, hard work, the careful husbandry of every resource. And indeed, long after the 'pioneer' period, Bets Ramsay and Merikay Waldvogel, writing about Tennessee quilting in the late 1980s, assert that 'the Puritan and pioneer habits still apply' to women quilt makers in rural areas (Ramsay and Waldvogel 1986: 3): they are still bent on making the best of whatever can be gleaned, still willingly struggling to transform the scraps of the old life into a magnificent (though thrifty) new whole.

Figure 5 Log cabin quilt, c. 1860.
Reproduced by kind permission of the American Museum in Britain, Bath.

At a more general level still, quilts seem to encode cultural cohesion. As Jane Schneider and Annette Weiner have argued, cloth itself has, in the weaving together of its threads, the ability to evoke the ties of the social fabric. It also has the quality of fragility: we know that it will wear out, that it will have to be mended and finally thrown away (Schneider and Weiner 1989: 5–6). This contradictory significance is recalled in the quilts that became popular during the crisis of the Depression, when, on the one hand, the revival of regular, geometric patterns evoked a tradition of adhering to social norms in the face of change, while, on the other, the use of washed-out pastel colours recalled a faded, threadbare tradition of make do and mend (Peck 1990: 102; Weissman and Lavitt 1987: 67).

The novel and film *How to Make an American Quilt* (Otto 1991; Moorhouse 1995) appeared at a point when understandings of the quilt in America were well established within the mainstream. They tackle ideas of tradition and explore the meaning of quilts for women. What emotional and ideological work is performed by the quilt in this novel and this film? Do you see problems with the claims made for the quilt here and elsewhere?

Becoming American

If much of the American discussion of quilt-making characteristically situates quilts in a shared past experience of 'frontier' America, the quilt as a form has something much more interesting to demonstrate about the disparate processes by which a thing may become 'American'. It tells the rather opaque history of the contact zone rather than the grand narrative of the 'frontier'. It exemplifies the changes, haphazard and difficult to grasp, that occur in the context of international migrations as least as effectively as it provides a metaphor for the national mythology of the individual immigrant striving to achieve the usual miracle of self-transformation. So, for example, even the apparently transparent process of Americanisation where we see a certain patchwork pattern called by one name in the British isles and then renamed in the United States raises problematic questions as to what shift in behaviour or experience, tradition or ideology is taking place. Is the change of pattern name from 'Rocky Road to Dublin' to 'Rocky Road to California' simply insignificant, merely a nod to a different landscape, or even, to all intents and purposes, no change of view in any sense of that world? Certainly some western historians have argued that, in the context of rural domestic and communal life, a change of space that may be highly significant to men is not especially significant

Figure 6 *Rocky Road to California*, 1886.
Reproduced by kind permission of the American Museum in Britain, Bath.

to women who, during this period, spent their lives in and around the domestic space. Or might the journey to Dublin and the journey to California have very different connotations to the Irish migrant stitching the pattern?

A different and equally challenging example that shows the quilt caught in the complex process of Americanisation lies in the way in which the immigrant may import remembered motifs from the former home into established American patterns covertly, as suggested in discussions of the African American quilt (Benberry 1992: 5–6). In this example, we are faced with the question of whether 'old' African motifs have been Americanised in the sense of being subsumed within an American object, or whether the quilt expresses a dual identity for the quilter, or indeed if a rebellious African identity is encoded in the quilt that enfolds the white American mistress of the house. Certainly, for some scholars of the African American quilt, the African tradition of quilting suggests complex origins for this American 'icon'.

In a third and final example suggestive of the multiple sites of immigrant Americanisation, we see the Amish (who had no quilting tradition of their own until migrating from Europe to the United States, but whose quilts have come to seem perhaps the most distinctive and the most highly valued of American quilts) making quilted coverlets in America as a result of contact with neighbours. Meanwhile, Arlette Klaric has suggested that 'pattern names such as Indian hatchet and the familiar sawtooth design suggest borrowings from Native American art traditions' (Klaric 1990: 64).

In essence, then, examining the relationships between migrants and quilting demonstrates the sheer difficulty of attributing national identity to any object. Migration to America was, in any case, part of a great shift of populations in a range of movements in the nineteenth century. Likewise quilts were imbricated in movements of international trade in which America did not necessarily take a central or even pivotal role. The American quilts stitched for the wealthy American colonists of the late eighteenth century, for instance, were much like those made for the elite in Britain. They were broad pieces of cloth on which embroidered or printed pieces of cloth were sewn. The fashion for this practice, which is called appliqué, began in England and it arose from the craze for the 'chintz' fabrics imported into Britain by the East India Company from Bengal. These fabrics, printed with trees, birds and flowers, were expensive; so much so that they became a bedrock of the company's trading empire. Consequently, those who were able to buy them preserved them carefully, and, as they became worn, cut out their patterns to attach as appliqué to quilts. Eventually, as demand grew, British firms manufactured their own chintzes specifically for use in appliqué. As the fashion spread to the United States, the fabrics were exported and sewed into American quilts. They were 'English' and 'Indian' as well as 'American' quilts.

Figure 7 Medallion quilt, c. 1832, with a chintz border.
Reproduced by kind permission of the American Museum in Britain, Bath.

Reinventing the tradition:
quilts as American women's things

By the 1970s, quilting had itself become a regional, rural activity laden with traditional and retrospective associations. But, if the quilt had been dwindling in importance, it was explosively revived in a famous exhibition of quilts at the Whitney Museum of Modern Art in 1971 (which went on to tour all over the world) called 'Abstract Design in American Quilts'. Not only were quilts restored to public notice in this high-cultural context; at the same time, they appeared in the different context of a grassroots revival of craft skills. It was the fashion for this latter kind of activity, no doubt, that generated 10,000 entries for a quilt competition in *Good Housekeeping* in 1976.

The impact on quilt-making was twofold. It was very quickly taken up and lauded as a feminist art form by the burgeoning feminist movement, who saw in quilts an alternative tradition of female creativity. The plain strips of fabric in Amish quilts, for example, could be perceived as the forerunners of abstract act and the abstract expressionism of painters such as Mark Rothko. In another overlapping argument for the importance of quilts as women's work, the quilt could be seen as a metaphor for women's lives – lives which could be perceived as a patchwork of separate elements pieced together – and for a perceived talent for collaborative expression quite foreign to dominant (male) models of self-expression, which privileged an individualism charged by rivalry. Cecilia Macheski, for example, writes of the ways in which 'the repetition and variation of patterns might be taken as evidence of the intricate, deliberate and often subversive networks women created as they told one another stories' (Macheski 1994: 1).

The association between quilts and the discussion of women's social position was not new, but it took a new form in 1970s America. In American quilting fictions of the nineteenth and early twentieth century, we find scenes of rural (rather than frontier) quilting bees where women met together to assemble and finish a quilt that celebrated the rich tradition of domestic skill handed down through women. Such fictions also explored the cruelties as well as the comforts of female communities, particularly their ability to suppress as well as to nurture the individual impulse. Stories of quilting are often concerned with a response to death and loss, as one would expect in stories about a craft form which was often produced to recognise the rituals of birth, marriage and death. There is often an association between quilting and old women in these quilting fictions, and a sense that the tradition of quilting together is itself coming close to death.[2]

When we look at the feminist discussion of the 1970s and 1980s, however, we see quilting brought to bear on a very different conception of womanhood. First there was the association with the frontier. In this context, quilts could be associated with an active independent and productive life that was identifiably feminine, but far from the seclusions of suburbia and the robotic routines of housewifery. Arlette Klaric, writing of contemporary American quilts, reviews the femininity encoded in frontier women's quilts enthusiastically: '[Quilts were used] to line wagons for protection against the elements, as packing material for fragile items, and to shield the exposed sides of the wagons from Indian arrows. They functioned as burial cloths for the dead laid to rest along the trail. In the primitive log cabin and sod dwellings that first sheltered settlers, quilts were hung on the walls and over windows and doors to please the eyes and spirit as well as to warm the body' (Klaric 1990: 3). At the same time quilting, it was argued, was a form that, in its use of the silent language or secret codes of textile patterns, transcended boundaries of region, class and ethnicity (Showalter 1986: 223; Wass 1995: 7). Joan Mulholland looks at quilts in this light when she annotates her essay 'Patchwork: The Evolution of a Women's Genre' with the following: 'On a personal note, writing this article, about the secret language of women, has felt at times like a betrayal, but it is meant to be an affirmation of women's ability to find a way of speaking when there is little scope for them to do so, and it is a salute to their skills' (Mulholland 1996: 68). In America, the quilt has remained charged with an ideal of a separate, exclusive femininity that is creative and collaborative whilst still being based in the domestic realm.

Back-migrating to Europe

Britain saw a revival in quilting in the 1970s as well, and there is an apparently complete consensus as to its origins in the American revival. Hardly an account exists of the dramatic rise in the profile of quilting in Britain in the 1970s and the subsequent takeup of quilting as a woman's art that does not take Jonathan Holstein's exhibition in New York in 1971 as its starting point. It is clear that the worldwide tour of a version of that exhibit, 'American Pieced Quilts', which came to Bristol and Manchester in 1975, generated an audience for further exhibitions of American quilts: in 1976 the American Museum in Britain took its quilts exhibit to the Commonwealth Institute in London, and other English cities and towns followed suit, mounting smaller exhibits of American quilts. Beyond this flurry of exhibitions, though, British would-be quilters turned to America for guidance. A British quilters' guild was set up in 1979, following an American model, and those involved invited Michael James and Beth and Geoffrey Gutcheon, well-established American art quilters, to run workshops inducting English practitioners into quilt art. Meanwhile, Ron Simpson, an independent Canadian collector, took a collection of quilts, 'Patchwork Quilt, Working Women Artists' to thirty-five venues between 1975 and 1981, giving talks and slide shows. His account of that project, 'The Patchwork Quilt: A Feminist Perspective', seems to have made no bones about the superior range of North American quilts or the ideological context that made it possible: while North America allowed a 'scope of personal freedom' from 'rules and regulations', Britain has a 'more static, insular population' (even though most of the quilts he discussed were not in fact North American) (Aberystwyth Arts Centre 1988: 24–5). The assumption that British quilting had died out leaving a vacuum which American quilts triumphantly filled was commonplace. Holstein himself, writing a biography of his exhibition, describes a visit to England in which British traditions of quilting were nowhere in evidence: 'There were so few, in fact, that I began to think that the whole thing might indeed have been an American invention' (Holstein 1991: 74).

This sense that the American intervention revealing the potential of quilts was decisive for British quilting, and that there was a void as far as an indigenous tradition was concerned, is made evident in catalogues of the period. So, for example, the writer of the catalogue for the exhibit of American quilts that took place in Wisbech, Cambridgeshire in 1977, while making the point that 'neither patchwork nor quilting was invented in America', goes on to describe quilting solely in the context of pioneering: 'the American quilting tradition begins with the landing of the Pilgrims in New England in the Autumn of 1620, and the harsh realities of Winter in the New World' (Wisbech Society 1977). A bibliography of 'books consulted' is given at the back of the pamphlet which includes only the work of the English curators of the American Museum in Britain. Those publications that existed in Britain at the time (some of them newly in print) which explained the native traditions are ignored.

Even after a decade of subsequent British quilting activity, the Crafts Council catalogue for the 1993 exhibition Contemporary American

Quilts revisits the issue of a mighty American tradition as opposed to a British void. The catalogue includes a lengthy interview with the American quilter Penny McMorris, in which McMorris considers some of the distortions of the 'usual story' of quilts in America, in particular the mythologies surrounding quilting as a female pursuit. Interestingly, it is Michelle Walker, the English quilter who writes the introduction within which the interview is set, who goes back to the by now well-trodden history of American quilting beginning with the pioneers in America, and then cites the Whitney exhibition in 1971 as the starting point of British quilting.

What we seem to have, then, is a process of Americanisation in which British quilters collude in, if not insist upon, the primacy of American tradition and work in the field. They are emphatically incurious about the British and European origins of quilting; even if they agree that quilts were taken by European migrants to America, they have no interest in describing them. It may be possible to argue that this is supine cultural behaviour in the face of aggressive American self-advertisement, but there is perhaps an alternative possibility. It is noticeable that British quilters often stress the high seriousness of their work and, unlike their American colleagues, set work that is useful or centred on the domestic space in a less than flattering light. At the same time, they regularly emphasise that quilting's centre and tradition is 'somewhere else' (that is, in America) and that they are, therefore, in a position to construct themselves and their work much as they please, to continually start over. So some British quilters use – replicate – characteristically American quilt patterns but apparently judge that they give those patterns and their work different significance by renaming them: for example, the British quilter Susan Hagley, discussing her 2000 work 'Meandering No 5', points out that the traditional name for this characteristically American pattern is 'Drunkard's Path', but makes no further reference to the relationship between that pattern and the pattern she has given to her work (Denton 2001: 30–1) The British quilter Dinah Prentice, having appeared in *Take 4*, a publication showcasing four British quilters which to some extent situates quilts in an American feminist tradition, remarks three years later that she intends to 're-mean' herself 'through changes in medium and image'. On interviewing Prentice, Celia Eddy wrote that

> On reflection she came to feel that the dominant sensibility of *Take 4* was modernist and she wanted to incorporate post-modernist feeling in her work. This has resulted in work which is

much less polemically 'feminist' in tone and intention and which invites a much freer and more discursive involvement on the part of the viewer. (Eddy 2001)

It seems, ironically, that the form which for Americans represents, if not a shared history, then certainly the ideal of collaboration across boundaries, has been transmuted, in a new tradition of quilting in Britain, into a form without history, a past in which tradition or indeed any preceding interpretation is seen to have a potentially constraining force.

By the late 1980s, however, another quite different response to the American intervention had occurred. In the face of burgeoning activity in the field, the British Quilt Study Group was set up. Part of its project had to do with asserting, once again, the high seriousness of a certain register of quilting. But equally important was its crusading emphasis on an indigenous and discrete British tradition. Where American and British writing on American quilting has placed movement and accommodation to change at its heart, some British experts have gone to considerable pains to construct the development of British quilting as highly localised, independent and merely interrupted somewhat by the arrival of American quilts in the exhibitions of the 1970s onwards. The background to this vision of British quilting enjoys a longer historical sweep than that of nineteenth-century migration: quilting is traced back to the ancient world, back through the use of quilting as clothing, back within the history of sewing. The American story is consequently of peripheral importance.

At the same time, the growing tendency in this writing of British tradition has been to locate quilting not in the world of domestic collaboration but in practices of employment (men's and women's) and within pre- and post-industrial practices of textile use. Janet Rae, for example, locates quilting practices within different and shifting class requirements over time, foregrounding the use of stitch for employment and as a means of training. Her description of Elizabeth Fry pacifying the maddened female prisoners of Newgate through introducing patchwork could hardly be more different from the American scene of the sewing bee (Rae 1987: 10).

By the late 1990s Dorothy Osler, who served as the first 'heritage officer' of the Quilters' Guild of Great Britain, and others had constructed a northern quilting tradition in which the quilt reflected a regional 'character': '[North Country quilts] have a strength of purpose, a strong aesthetic quality and an honesty and integrity which perhaps reflect the social and cultural circumstances in which they were made' (Osler 2000: 5). Meanwhile the journal of the British Quilt Study Group, bent on focusing in its first number on North Country 'strippy' quilts (that is, quilts made of long strips of cloth) chooses to assert a difficult point that an 'essentially . . . British quilt type' nevertheless has parallels with the American bars quilts (British Quilt Study Group 1999: 9). In apparently writing back to a perceived Americanisation of quilts as a form in Britain, this writing of 'quilts that are uniquely British' has produced a national tradition characterised by a stronger denial of influence even than that allowed in the American tradition. Osler tells the story of a strippy quilt made by one Hannah Peart of Swinhope, Allendale (Northumberland), a centre of North Country quilting, before she migrated. That this quilt has remained in the possession of her great-granddaughter is surely, for Osler, gratifying evidence of a strong local tradition. What is significant is that Peart made the strippy quilt before she migrated, not that she lived the rest of her life in New York state and that the quilt was returned by an American descendant (British Quilt Study Group 1999: 17).

Conclusion

Quilts have long held the power to attract explanations that place them at the heart of national and regional culture. Their reputation demonstrates the impulse to use material objects to mirror and justify the past, but it also shows how different kinds of tradition and different points of departure from tradition can be constructed through things. The Americanisation of the European quilt from the nineteenth century evinces a determination to narrow the quilt's significance to one dominant idea, but its feminisation demonstrates the possibility of turning its meaning to different and potentially radical ends. The process of revival of the quilt in Britain through a powerful American intervention demonstrates a similar point: that the introduction of the American object may drain local activity of its meaning, but that it can also act as a powerful prompt to complex strands of response and resistance. For most people on both sides of the Atlantic, the quilt probably maintains its meaning as an American thing, but agreeing that this is the case tells us little about the endless possibilities for reconstruction and retelling that make them interesting to us.

Notes

1. A quilt in its simplest form consists of two pieces of cloth, a top and a backing, separated by a layer of padding. The whole is held together with decorative patterns of stitching. Sometimes blocks of pattern or motifs from patterned fabrics are sewn onto the top in a process called appliqué, though this process is also sometimes referred to as quilting. Finally there is the process referred to as 'piecing' and 'patchwork', in which pieces of cloth are sewn together edge to edge to make a design. All three processes are called 'quilting' in the popular and scholarly (as opposed to the specialist) writing on quilts. Images of quilts are easily accessible on the internet, but http://www.womenfolk.com/historyofquilts/qhlinks.htm and http://www.britishquilthistory.co.uk are particularly comprehensive sources.
2. See the collections edited by Benberry and Crab (1993) and Macheski (1994). Mary Wilkins Freeman's 'An Honest Soul' (1885) and Susan Glaspell's short play *Trifles* (1916) are especially famous and widely anthologised.

Bibliography

Aberystwyth Arts Centre (1988), *Quilts Traditional and Contemporary: An Exhibition Organised by Aberystwyth Arts Centre*, Aberystwyth: Aberystwyth Arts Centre.

Arpad, Susan S. (1988), 'Pretty Much to Suit Ourselves: MidWestern Women Naming Experience through Domestic Arts', in M. F. Motz and P. Browne (eds), *Middle-class Women and Domestic Material Culture 1840–1940*, Bowling Green, OH: Bowling Green State University Popular Press, pp. 11–26.

Attfield, Judy (1996), 'Barbie and Action Man: Adult Toys for Girls and Boys', in Pat Kirkham (ed.), *The Gendered Object*, Manchester: Manchester University Press, pp. 80–9.

Benberry, Cuesta (1992), *Always There: The African American Presence in Quilts*, Louisville, KY: Kentucky Quilts Project.

Benberry, Cuesta Ray and Carol Phinney Crab (eds) (1993), *A Patchwork of Pieces: An Anthology of Quilt Stories 1845–1940*, Paducah, KY: American Quilter's Society.

British Quilt Study Group (1999), *Quilt Studies* 1.

Crafts Council (1993), *Contemporary American Quilts*, London: Crafts Council.

Denton, Susan (ed.) (2001), *Quilt Art: Moving On*, Callington: Quilt Art.

Eddy, Celia (2001), 'Dinah Prentice "re-meaning" herself', http://www.quilt.co.uk

Holstein, Jonathan (1991), *Abstract Design in American Quilts: A Biography of an Exhibition*, Louisville, KY: Kentucky Quilt Project.

Klaric, Arlette (1990), 'Contemporary American Quilts: Art/Icons/Relics', in *Contemporary Quilts USA*, Boston: Boston University Art Gallery, pp. 1–19.

Macheski, Cecilia (ed.) (1994), *Quilt Stories*, Lexington: University of Kentucky Press.

Moorhouse, Jocelyn (dir.) (1995), *How to Make an American Quilt*, Universal Pictures.

Mulholland, Joan (1996), 'Patchwork: The Evolution of a Women's Genre', *Journal of American Culture*, 19:4, 57–69.

Osler, Dorothy (2000), *North Country Quilts: Legend and Living Tradition*, Barnard Castle: The Bowes Museum.

Otto, Whitney (1991), *How to Make an American Quilt*, New York: Random House.

Peck, Amelia (1990), *American Quilts and Coverlets in the Metropolitan Museum of Art*, New York: Metropolitan Museum of Art/Dutton Studio Books.

Rae, Janet (1987), *The Quilts of the British Isles*, London: Constable.

Ramsay, Bets and Merikay Waldvogel (1986), *The Quilts of Tennessee: Images of Domestic Life*, Nashville: Rutledge Hill Press.

Rand, Erica (1995), *Barbie's Queer Accessories*, Durham, NC: Duke University Press.

Rogers, Mary F. (1999), *Barbie Culture*, Thousand Oaks, CA and London: Sage.

Schneider, Jane and Annette B. Weiner (1989), *Cloth and Human Experience*, Washington: Smithsonian Institution.

Showalter, Elaine (1986), 'Piecing and Writing', in N. K. Miller (ed.), *The Poetics of Gender*, New York: Columbia University Press, pp. 222–47.

Showalter, Elaine (1991), *Sister's Choice: Traditions and Change in American Women's Writing*, New York: Oxford University Press.

Torsney, Cheryl and Judy Elsley (eds) (1994), *Quilt Culture: Tracing the Pattern*, Columbus: University of Missouri Press.

Wass, Janice Tauer (ed.) (1995), *Connecting Stitches: Quilts in Illinois Life*, Springfield: Illinois State Museum.

Weissman, Judith Reiter and Wendy Lavitt (1987), *Labors of Love: America's Textiles and Needlework, 1650–1930*, London: Studio Vista.

Wisbech Society (1977), *American Patchwork Quilts*, Wisbech: Wisbech Society.

CHAPTER FOURTEEN

Portraying the Black Atlantic: Americanisation and the National Museum

Carol Smith

Americanisation and the national museum

This chapter examines two very different processes of 'Americanisation' embedded in the ideological nation-building carried out by the respective National Portrait Galleries (NPGs) of Britain and the USA. The foundation of the American gallery in 1968 involved the deliberate Americanising of one of the national institutions of the British Empire. Its rationale, and aim of promulgating national consensus at a time of political unrest, adapted for US purposes the project founded in London more than a century earlier. More recently, the subsequent export of curatorial ideas and exhibitions to Britain constitutes a different, and arguably more benign, form of Americanisation. I will show that these two forms of cultural influence are intimately bound up with, and must be understood alongside, the shifting relationships between 'race'/ethnicity and national identity on both sides of the Atlantic.

Brian Wallis encapsulates the complex and dynamic process by which the visual interacts with the production of the nation:

> Visual representations are a key element in symbolizing and sustaining national communal bonds. Such representations are not just reactive . . . they are also purposefully creative and they can

generate new social and political formations. Through the engineered overproduction of others and through controlling the way in which images are viewed or by determining which are preserved, cultural representations can also be used to produce a certain view of a nation's history. (Wallis 1994: 266)

In the British and American NPGs, the processes of 'engineered overproduction of others' and control of 'the way in which images are viewed' have historically primarily been brought to bear on visualising the nation in terms of 'race'. Both galleries were founded in the service of white-centered constructions of citizenship and nationhood, with a subsequent omission of the images and histories of non-whites, and to some extent they remain caught within the imperialist narrative of their foundation. However, in their more recent responses to multicultural and transnational narratives of identity formation, these institutions, their collections and their audiences have acknowledged their existence in the Black Atlantic, as much as the imperial Atlantic of the 'special relationship'.

It might seem a strange critical move to positively analyse national institutions such as museums and galleries through the Black Atlantic frame, since Paul Gilroy states that 'different national paradigms for thinking about cultural history fail when confronted by the intercultural and transnational formation that I call the Black Atlantic' (Gilroy 1993: x; see also Gilroy 2000). Alan Rice echoes this call to move beyond national institutions in his engagement with radical narratives of the Black Atlantic by citing the failure of museums and 'other arbiters of national cultures (both European and African) to narrativize or memorialize the history of the middle passage' (Rice 2003: 202). Clearly it remains important to open up these alternative spaces and methodologies, but I would argue that it is also important to engage with nation-building institutions such as the portrait galleries, since they have the potential to reverse practices of exclusion, and are by no means immune to the influence of 'Gilroyan' inter-cultural and transnational formations. They can be the sites of inclusion that critics such as Lola Young have argued for (Young 2002). Moreover the study of these institutions shows that the project of visualising the nation has always been conflicted and tenuous, and thereby can offer ways of recovering an inclusive national narrative. Gilroy argues that we should want to 'desire to transcend both the structures of the nation state and the constraints of ethnicity and national particularity . . . [that] . . . these desires are relevant to political organising and cultural criticism' (Gilroy 2003: 19). To mark the historical changes in the ways that race and ethnicity have configured national narratives can be a first step towards such transcendence.

Such work has been begun by critics working on and in national museums and public spaces. Young, Sandell Savage and Eilean Hooper-Greenhill have shown the way for national institutions and academies to collect, and to display, their collections in ways that engage with the critical debates surrounding the racially non-white or so-called marginal cultures of Britain and America. Hooper-Greenhill has pointed out that the way in which any museum/gallery collects and curates its holdings should be read as a cultural and political act:

> The ways in which objects are selected, put together, and written or spoken about have political effects. These effects are not those of the object per se: it is the use made of these objects and their interpretive frameworks that can open up or close down historical, social and cultural possibilities. By making marginal cultures visible, and by legitimating difference, museum pedagogy can become critical pedagogy. (Hooper-Greenhill 2000: 148)

Hooper-Greenhill's sense of these 'historical, social and cultural possibilities' reflects the synthetic approach of work in cultural studies, and in particular Lauren Berlant's discussion of the formation of American citizenship through such activities as visiting Washington, DC and especially the Mall (Berlant 1997). Three recent collections demonstrate an ongoing engagement with these possibilities. As is clear from their titles, *Exhibiting Cultures: The Poetics and Politics of Cultural Display*, *Exhibiting Dilemmas: Issues of Representation at the Smithsonian* and *Displays and Cultural Encounter: Representing 'Otherness'* all seek to take back inside the gallery and the museum the critiques and ideas articulated in work on the cultural politics of identity, such as Berlant's.

However, it would be wrong to suggest that the multicultural turn among curators is solely due to outside influence. The work of Sidney Kaplan for example is rightly acknowledged as pioneering the critique and displacement of white-centred 'interpretative frameworks'. Kaplan's critique exposed the historical trajectory whereby the contributions of African Americans were at first represented then subsequently largely ignored by museums in their construction of the national narrative. Kaplan's response through public lectures, publishing, and curating exhibitions in national institutions can be seen in the exhibition and notes for 'The Portrayal of the Negro in American Painting' and the illustrated lecture 'The Black Soldier of the Civil War in Literature and Art' (Kaplan 1991). In both of these works a diverse range of pictorial sources (oil paintings, photographs and newspapers) are employed to show how the image of the African American has always been (albeit sometimes negatively) integral to the constructed narrative of American history. His work thus is an exemplary method of how institutions can be made to review and redisplay their works and we will return to his exhibition and catalogue for the NPG in Washington, *The Black Presence in the Era of the American Revolution, 1770–1800*, below.

Vivien Green Fryd and Kirk Savage have continued this type of work in their examinations of the deployment of types of ethnicity in government-commissioned public art work (Fryd 1992; Savage 1997). Fryd convincingly argues that the work commissioned to decorate the Capitol after the 1812 war represents a conscious desire to create an image of Americanness to unify public consensus in the face of political and sectional divisions. She shows how European models of architecture and sculpture were Americanised through the stereotypical depiction of subjugated Native Americans. These images were used to justify and reinforce an imperialist self-image of (white) public consensus, which was further protected by the exclusion of any images of slavery or of free educated Black people. As Fryd explains, 'Jefferson Davies, secretary of war in charge of the Capitol extension between 1835 and 1857, especially wanted no references in the national legislative building to the slave system that he supported and that caused such sectional turmoil and disagreement' (Fryd 1992: 5). All of this critical work demonstrates how 'Americanisation' deliberately included, excluded, or appropriated certain racial groups to ensure that the nation being built was understood as racially white.

The Americanisation of national portrayal

The foundations of the galleries in London (1856) and Washington (1968) have been carefully researched by Marcia Pointon, Margaret Chisum and Brandon Taylor. Both have their genesis in a longer tradition of aristocratic patronage and collection of family paintings, but the idea of a *national* portrait gallery was shaped once and for all by the particular impulses behind its foundation in mid-nineteenth century Britain: an investment in the narrative of civilisation, an interest in the ideological legitimation of the imperial nation, and the importance of the public dissemination of both. The institution has remained geographically and conceptually unique to Britain and its former colonies. There are at present only four national portrait galleries worldwide (London, Edinburgh (1882), Dublin (1884) and Washington), though the Portrait Gallery of Canada is being founded.[1]

As an example and contribution to the moulding of Britishness, Pointon points to the importance of the ideological knotting together of the biographies of great individuals, the power of rationality, and the subsequent political effect of the method of display. This gave a specifically national dimension to 'the evolution of human civilization embodied in a classified sequence of historical (predominantly masculine) portraits, scientifically identified and researched [which] was understood to be publicly gratifying, reassuring and encouraging' (Pointon 1993: 238). She situates the American gallery as a conscious attempt to emulate such effects, stating that its foundation 'is very much in the tradition of the nineteenth-century galleries in terms of its founders' aspirations and the politics of its establishment' (ibid.: 228). This suggests an understanding of Americanisation as a process of adapting and imitating European models, as with the decoration of the Capitol.

In both Britain and the USA, the NPG was conceived in terms of a cultural strategy overdetermined by a political project. The London and Washington galleries are cultural responses to internal political and social unrest and to a perceived external rivalry or threat: for Britain in 1856 waning aristocratic power and France; for America in 1968 continued civil-rights protests, the assassinations of Robert Kennedy and Martin Luther King Jr and the anti-Vietnam war protests at home, and the Cold War abroad. A more detailed examination of the foundations will demonstrate how they operated according to the exclusive nationalism criticised by Paul Gilroy and others.

NPG London

The foundation of the London National Portrait Gallery is a nation-building exercise with a profoundly anti-French flavour. In his plea for the establishment for such a gallery in the House of Lords on 4 March 1856 Philip Henry Stanhope located its inspiration in France:

Many acres of such spoiled canvas [battle and court paintings] presented themselves upon the walls of Versailles: but their Lordships would also recollect the great pleasure, and as it were refreshment, with which they passed these tawdry battle pieces and Court pageants into a gallery of much smaller dimensions, and much less gorgeous decorations, containing excellent contemporary portraits of celebrities of French history. He thought few Englishmen could be at Versailles without wishing that in our own country, while the errors of the larger galleries should be avoided, some attempt should be made not only to emulate, but to extend the example set in the smaller one. (Quoted in Saumarez Smith 1997: 9)

Stanhope's speech encapsulates the network of art history, the meanings of public display, and the particularity of national history which are deployed in the service of recognising Englishness as the ideological core of the nation. Englishness defines each field. In the realms of art history portraiture is preferred over battle or court scenes, reflecting the progressive Whig history of the period with its emphasis on the importance of great individuals (read white men) to British history. Englishness is by implication all that is rational, of the correct size and put to proper use, in contrast to the oversized and overblown French decorations and room dimensions.

Thus nation-building here is sustained through external projection against the French and the desire for social mastery at home and through the Empire. Brandon Taylor has in *Art for the Nation* recently situated the foundation of the NPG within the larger social and political controlling impetus behind the founding of all of the national galleries in Victorian London. He details how the NPG's deliberate policy of selecting portraits based on the identity of the sitter rather than the aesthetics of the image was central to the sense of Englishness which was being exported thoughout the globe – and shown in London to inculcate national cohesion in an increasingly economically mobile urban population. The London display gave a view of national history that was historicising and evolutionary, and that gave a sense of national character and progress whose implications for the present age were supposed to be clear: that English (and by extension British) history consisted of the actions of eminent men; that their eminence derived from their actions; and that such a history was largely impermeable to 'foreign' traditions (Taylor 1999: 99).

This synergy between national history and curatorial policy was enshrined in the phrasing of the rules which the trustees have had before them at every meeting since 1857. Rule 1 states:

The rule which the Trustees desire to lay down to themselves, in either making purchases or receiving presents is to look to the celebrity of the person represented rather than to the merit of the artist. They will attempt to estimate that celebrity without any bias to political or religious party. Not will they consider great faults and errors, even though admitted on all sides, as any sufficient ground for excluding any portrait which may be valuable, as illustrating the civil, ecclesiastical, or literary history of the country. (Saumarez Smith 1997: 12)

As has been written elsewhere (Smith 1999), until recent modernisation of the permanent galleries, this resulted in a representation of the history of Britain as being made exclusively by white males. The small number of women represented mostly derived their claim through family connections (e.g. royalty) or as tokenised, exemplary symbols of the feminine contribution to history (e.g. Florence Nightingale). The even fewer portraits featuring non-whites were concentrated in the Victorian rooms and the non-whites are never the sole named subjects but are always represented in relationship to the main (hence 'British') white focus.

Thus the NPG London perpetuated a selectively racialised (and gendered) embodiment of the nation-state. Its focus on the paintings of individual white men meant that the way these men acted en masse, in elective groups or through class affiliation, was submerged within a larger national narrative. It is the history of white invention, exploration and war – the evolutionary history described by Taylor above. What is relegated to the margins is the history of the class and race of all of the peoples (the enslaved as well as the slavers) of the Black Atlantic that contributed to this narrative and generated the capital which paid for the painting and housing of the portraits (see Gilroy 1993; Rice 2003; Wood 2000.)

NPG Washington

Given its royalism, its exclusive ethnic particularity, its embrace of aristocracy and rejection of Frenchness, the London NPG seems a surprising model for an American institution of the late 1960s. Why did the self-proclaimed land of the free look to such an imperialist and exclusive institution as a central part of its nation-building? The answers to this question lie in two different narratives of foundation, cohering around two forms of Americanisation.

One of these, which we might call the 'official narrative', is offered by Margaret Chisum, the NPG's own research historian, who traces the history of the gallery back to the foundation of the nation itself and to Charles Wilson Peale's collection of American heroes of the Revolution shown in his National History Museum in Philadelphia in 1788. In a detailed essay she traces the chance the Smithsonian Institution had to purchase this collection in 1847, through the many attempts to set up the NPG, to the opening on 7 October 1968. She emphasises continuity of purpose, the contributions of the directors of the Smithsonian complex and the size and aesthetic superiority of the portraits in the resulting collection. By focusing on the early date of the Peale collection and the foundation of the Smithsonian (1846) – 'When the Smithsonian was founded, there was no such thing as a national portrait gallery in the English-speaking world' (Chisum 2001: 14) – she provides an American and independent origin for the NPG Washington, which implicitly rejects any sense of imitating the British model.

Chisum does subsequently acknowledge the influence of the example of the NPG in London, emphasising the work of translation necessary to Americanise European models. She relates how in 1886 Robert C. Winthrope, President of the Massachusetts Historical Society, was inspired by a visit to the London gallery to call for

> the establishment of a National Portrait Gallery in Washington where the history of our country should be illustrated by a series of likenesses of those who have been eminent in its civil or military service or in scientific or literary labors from our earliest colonial period or certainly from our constitutional era. (ibid.: 14)

Notice the echoes of the NPG London's foundation. Winthrope's language and definition of who should be included reiterate the London trustees' Rule 1. We can see an echo of Philip Henry Stanhope's trip to Versailles, except there is no anti-English sentiment to parallel Stanhope's anti-French. Nevertheless, in each case it is clear to see one nation-building project defining itself in comparison to another, constructing a similar but significantly different incarnation of the institution. Here the difference is marked in the discourse of politics – the reference to the constitution implying the uniqueness of American democracy.

Chisum's careful narrative concerns itself with a long and integrated history of portraiture and American history, situating its institutionalisation in the actual founding of the gallery as just another date in the long history. This narrative is organised in terms of art history, via the dates of the purchase of John Singleton Copely's self-portrait, and the start of collecting photographs in 1976, and thus presents the gallery's relationship to other galleries as one of apprenticeship and exchange. The institution of an NPG can be 'borrowed' and imported as long as at the same time it is Americanised.

As stated above, Marcia Pointon has written about the importance of understanding the relationship between the galleries in terms of the political moment and aims of their founders. In her discussion of the American gallery Pointon covers similar ground to Chisum but focuses on the opening of the Washington gallery and the first exhibition, 'This New Man: a Discourse in Portraits'.[2] She describes how 'in the year of the Chicago riots and the uprising of young women and young men demanding new forms of participation in government, the American establishment chose to assert the myth of the white American man' (Pointon 1994: 64). Where Chisum makes nothing of the political context at the time of the foundation of NPG Washington and stresses only the aesthetics of the portraits, Pointon convincingly outlines how the deployment of highly regarded forms of art such as portraiture was central to political and cultural propaganda campaigns against so-called subversive forces at home and abroad. She claims that when Hubert Humphrey was taking up the cause of the founding of the NPG gallery in 1960 'it was effectively as a weapon in the cold war' (ibid.: 59). It is worthwhile examining Humphrey's statement in detail for the way in which he aligns the process of museum foundation, cultural propaganda and nation-building:

> Washington must have a cultural status at least equal to its position as the political, military and economic centre of the free world. It lacks such a commanding status at this time. In fact, the *New York Times* recently compared Washington unfavorably with the provincial city of Tiflis, USSR [now Tbilisi, the capital of Georgia]. A National Portrait Gallery will make a major contribution to our national life, will foster patriotism and educate the coming generations in the high ideals which distinguish us as a nation. (Cited ibid.: 60)

The figures chosen to 'foster patriotism and educate' were, overwhelmingly, white men. As we can see from the catalogue to the exhibition, of the 161 portraits chosen there were only eleven women (all white) and five men of non-white ethnicity. Of the latter three were Native Americans (Joseph Brant, Osceola and Sitting Bull) and two African Americans (George Washington Carver and Frederick Douglass).

Humphrey's reference to invidious comparison between Washington and the Soviet provinces highlights a further international dimension. In the process of Americanisation delineated by Pointon, the US adaptation of the NPG is a matter of utilising the British institution as a civilising force to tame the unruly at home and abroad even if this also meant importing the racialised and gendered ideologies associated with such a historical institution.

Washington's partial selection of Americans in terms of race/ethnicity was contested at the time. Margaret Mead, invited as one of the opening speakers to the symposium on the exhibition, was reported in the *New Yorker* to have remarked: 'This is a black city. There's something wrong with this audience. Some people are not here' (ibid.: 51).

What was wrong with the institution, Mead implied, was that it had been only partially Americanised. It had not acknowledged (like many other national institutions in politics and education at the time) the importance of groups such as African Americans to the American nation. We might pause to ask whether what Mead describes as omissions are in fact structural elements of a process of white centering. As noted above, the work of Vivien Green Fryd has demonstrated that the non-representation of African Americans was often coupled with the deployment of representations of Native Americans to represent all other ethnicities and hence to naturalise the process of American imperialism and displace the history of slavery. In any case, there was a response to voices such as Mead's from the NPGs on both sides of the Atlantic.

We will now compare some of these responses, with particular reference to the depiction of one resonant transatlantic figure, Olaudah Equiano, whose life and autobiography have been central to theories of the Black Atlantic.[3]

PORTRAYING EQUIANO

Two images of Equiano were used in the exhibitions discussed below. The first is the frontispiece from *The Interesting Narrative*, which can be found on the websites of both galleries (http://www.npg.org.uk; http://www.npg.si.edu). This is a black-and-white engraving by D. Orme after W. Denton and shows a three-quarter-length portrait of a well dressed Black man holding a book – presumably the Bible. It is reproduced in several versions in the Penguin edition of *The Interesting Narrative* (Equiano 1995) and in both catalogues (King et al. 1997; Kaplan and Kaplan 1973). The second is a three-quarter-length oil painting again of a well-dressed Black man who looks directly at the viewer (this is reproduced on the cover of the Penguin *The Interesting Narrative* and the catalogues of the exhibitions). This second image hangs in The Royal Albert Memorial Museum in Exeter and is labelled 'A Negro Man called Olaudah Equiano'. However, Reyahn King and Vincent Carretta have argued conclusively that this portrait is not actually Equiano. While this attribution of the sitter has been agreed in art history, the portrait still circulates as Equiano outside these arenas. Why do you think this is? Is it a legitimate response to the scarcity of such positive representations of Black men from this period, or a capitulation to the fame of Equiano himself?

Portraying Equiano for the nation

The first attempt to break up this white particularity can be seen in the exhibition 'The Black Presence in the Era of the American Revolution 1770–1800' in the National Portrait Gallery in Washington, curated by Sidney Kaplan and Emma Nogrady Kaplan in 1973. The exhibition was commissioned as part of the bicentennial celebrations culminating in 1976. The exhibition, as with Sidney Kaplan's other work discussed above, can be read as a careful and meticulous address to the major racial problematic of that declaration and the Black human slaves who were so conspicuously deprived of human status. In the foreword to the book of the exhibition, the then Director of the NPG, Marvin Sadik, revealed the cultural and political context of the 1970s with its accent on civil rights and contested narratives of Black identity was central to the setting up of the exhibition, albeit in a displaced manner. He stated:

[This exhibition] presented by a museum called the National Portrait Gallery, is by its very nature a precarious – and worthwhile – enterprise. Among the many hundreds of portraits painted during this period, the faces of Afro-Americans are very rare. For this reason, the authentic few that have survived are all the more

271

crucial to the construction of a true iconography of the Revolution. (Sadik in Kaplan and Kaplan 1973: viii)

Sadik's statement both acknowledged the importance of historical context and the shift in racial attitudes – a shift thrown into relief by the discontinuity between his own use of the term 'Afro-American' here and the frequent use of 'nigger' in the artefacts included in the exhibition. Yet he sidestepped any detailed engagement with this history of slavery by focusing instead on the material production of the images – portraits are lost rather then never painted at all and only Afro-Americans have a race/ethnicity. So even though Kaplan's exhibition was temporary and could be recuperated by the gallery director as a simple matter of reclaiming a stable and universal truth in the larger context of the founding of the gallery it did contest the default whiteness that the gallery had so far promulgated.

Kaplan organised the exhibition into seven sections defined both by historical chronology and type of intervention: Homage to Liberty, Preludes to the Declaration, Bearers of Arms: Patriot and Tory, The Black Clergy, The Emergence of Gifts and Powers, Against the Odds and The Incomplete Revolution. Those who served with the white heroes of the Revolution such as Agrippa Hull or founded such institutions as the African Methodist Church (Richard Allan), and who were therefore thought to be respectable and perhaps acceptable to white America both in the eighteenth century and in the 1970s, predominate.

Olaudah Equiano appears in the fifth section, 'The Emergence of Gifts and Powers', along with that other star of the Black Atlantic, Phillis Wheatley, a combination which is repeated thirty years later in their pairing in Paul Gilroy's *Between Camps*. Both are represented by the frontispiece to their published writings. The section on Wheatley is entitled solely by her name. The section on Equiano has a subtitle, 'The Image of Africa', an identity underscored by the choice of illustration, which is an engraving after the frontispiece but with the significant addition of the descriptor of him as 'A Native African From the Coast Of Guinea'.

The majority of the figures in the exhibition came from or were descendants of African slaves yet Equiano is the only one to have this articulated as being so central to his identity. The section on him largely consists of quotations from his *Narrative* dealing with his early life in Africa and West Indian slavery, and little space is given to what was the longest period of his life, spent in freedom in England. Is this because to fully admit such a hybrid and transnational identity, one embedded in the institution of slavery, would not have fitted into the founding of the new American nation which the exhibition was commemorating?

Not necessarily. Such a partial inclusion might better be explained by reference to Kaplan's introduction to the section on Equiano where after lamenting the destruction of history and languages of Africa by slavers he states that there can be found 'only a few black voices, furnishing images of a real Africa and real Africans' (Kaplan and Kaplan 1973: 193). Equiano functions within the exhibition as the authentic link to Africa – an important inclusion especially for those African American viewers in the 1970s. He is deployed to define the Atlantic for Blacks and whites but only as a negative history of the middle passage and slavery and not of the longer and culturally diverse history of exchange defined by Gilroy. The partial nature of such a narrative is dependent on the singularity of his description as 'The image of Africa' rather than as an African/British sailor who latterly served 'freely' as a sailor on slaving ships – 'freely' in the sense of economic compulsion rather than the physical control of slavery. Kaplan's strategic placing of Equiano is understandable given the 1970s context, yet it does by implication reaffirm the white-centredness of mainstream American identity. Multiracial narratives are added to the national record only in such ways that they do not disturb the unitary nature of American identity formation. Thus the Kaplan exhibition is on the one hand a contestation of prevailing gaps in the public staging of American identity in such institutions as the NPG. Yet it is also an example of how such contestations are bounded by the ideological and exclusively national narratives such institutions were founded to perpetuate.

'Faces of the Century' (NPG London, 1999) included images of non-white ethnicity chosen by such celebrities as David Bowie, David Puttnam, and Helena Kennedy, while Black British figures such as Trevor Phillips were among those asked to choose their important images of the twentieth century. Race/ethnicity was also one element of 'Below Stairs: 400 Years of Servants' Portraits' (NPG London, 2004), as it is in Dr Caroline Bressey's temporary photographic exhibition and her leaflet 'Diversity: Images of Black and Asian People in the National Portrait Gallery'.

We can see a parallel strategic deployment of Equiano's image in the NPG London exhibition 'Ignatius Sancho: An African Man of Letters'

(1997). This temporary exhibition was an unusual one for the gallery, whose permanent display was at that time overwhelmingly white. As noted above, the impetus for recent attention to debates concerning diversity and the representation of a multiracial England in the gallery in London partly comes from America and its highly publicised arguments over multiculturalism. This could be seen then as a positive intervention of Americanisation.

The exhibition strongly contextualised Ignatius Sancho[4] within eighteenth-century Britain, in doing so offering a corrective to the omission or the decorative/symbolic images of blackness in portraits such as those of Louise De Keroualle (NPG 479) and Queen Victoria (NPG 4969). As with the American NPG exhibition the care in the curation of the exhibition deserves praise – especially as it might be said to offer a corrective to the white-centredness of the gallery's historical collections. The gallery has been especially successful in recent years in using temporary exhibitions and photography to break the normative whiteness of the permanent collection, not least as part of a conscious effort to find new audiences (see Hargreaves 1997).

The introduction to the Sancho exhibition catalogue by Caryl Phillips stresses the importance of figures such as Equiano and Sancho for the long-term history of successful assimilation of Africans in Britain. Britain is held up as 'the earliest model of vigorous interaction between those of the African diaspora and those of European origin' (Phillips 1997: 13). So here, as with the Kaplan exhibition, the history of race/ethnicity in the African/European frame is represented as a positive part of the larger history of Britain. The larger narrative is not disturbed, nor is the permanent collection of the gallery. The images and essays in the catalogue focus on literary London as a positive space of interaction of Blacks and Europeans, while Sancho and Equiano are valorised as exemplifying the best attributes of Englishness via their work ethic. It is Equiano's buying his own freedom and then assimilating into the mercantile bent of the age as explorer and shopkeeper which is highlighted here. The history of slavery is particularised to the West Indies and the Americas, rather than Britain itself. Thus here in distinction to being an 'Image of Africa' (NPG Washington), Equiano is a literary and wealthy Englishman who by dint of hard work gains his freedom and public acclaim. The London exhibition can be read to have borrowed the attention to the deployment of non-white ethnicities from Washington. However, the employment of this curatorial Americanisation is tempered by a combative and contrasting nationalist narrative. America is figured as the site of slavery and the rupture of history; Britain as a positive site of identity formation for Equiano and Sancho, one which Americans need to copy: 'It is no wonder that in order to understand the roots of their own African diasporan traditions Americans have begun to look at Britain' (ibid.: 13).

Britain's involvement in slavery is thus represented as an economically necessary evil, which was eradicated, historically of course well in advance of the USA. In sum, the Sancho exhibition realises its aim of pluralising British identity, but also to some extent undercuts the rethinking of the nation necessary to fully acknowledge the historical Black Atlantic.

Both galleries now do make efforts to represent diversity but as the case of Equiano has shown, they tend to do so through a deployment of these images in partial ways to keep the overall national narrative in place. A rethinking of the 'national' and a major rehanging of the permanent collections is therefore ultimately necessary. The preoccupation with a transatlantic other signalled by the prominence of Americanisation can only foreclose this project.

In Exeter the Equiano portrait is hung in the World Cultures Room – 'world' here meaning Africa, Asia and the Pacific. It is the only portrait in the room; the rest of the exhibits are material objects from these cultures. It hangs above a display case in which there are iron manacles and is flanked by two captions, one explaining the Atlantic slave trade, the other East Africa and two cases of masks. The attempts at an informed curatorship are evident, and a caption in the room draws further attention to such issues, but no attempt is made to rename the portrait or to make strategic links to the kinds of narratives of contemporary colonialism. How would you display the Equiano portrait? What critical/historic information would a viewer need?

Examine the websites of both galleries (http://www.npg.org.uk; http://www.npg.si.edu). What other comparable Black Atlantic figures have the galleries collected (e.g. Frederick Douglass, Phillis Wheatley, Harriet Tubman and Paul Robeson) and how are they described? Who would you add?

Notes

1. The Portrait Gallery of Canada will open after 2006. According to the paper given by Lily Koltun at the *Faciality: Philosophies of the Face* conference (NPG London, November 2003) this new gallery will be consciously more democratic and challenging of both artefacts and sitters.
2. At the conference *Americans: Facing Portraiture* (NPG London, October 2002), Chisum presented a paper on the history of the American gallery which pointedly dismissed Pointon's version.
3. Olaudah Equiano (1745?–1791). Born in Africa, kidnapped into slavery, shipped to the Caribbean and worked as a slave in the triangular slave trade. Bought his freedom through his own work in 1766 and subsequently worked on transatlantic slave ships, took part in an Arctic expedition and trading voyages to Turkey. Settled in Britain and worked on the proposed resettlement of Blacks to Sierra Leone and for the abolition of the slave trade. He gained popularity and wealth through the publication of the various editions of his autobiography *The Interesting Narrative of the Life of Olaudah Equiano, or Gustavus Vassa, The African. Written by Him.*
4. Sancho was born on a transatlantic slaveship, arrived in Britain aged two and became a servant in the Duke of Montagu's household. He left service and opened a grocer's shop in Mayfair while becoming part of the literary and musical establishment of his time. His portrait was painted by Gainsborough in 1768.

Bibliography

Berlant, Lauren (1997), *The Queen of America Goes to Washington City*, Durham, NC: Duke University Press.

Chisum, Margaret C. S. (2001), 'The National Portrait Gallery', in Carolyn Kinder Carr and Ellen G. Mile (eds), *A Brush with History*, Washington: Smithsonian Institution Press, pp. 12–21.

Equiano, Olaudah (1995), *The Interesting Narrative and other writings*, ed. Vincent Carretta, London: Penguin.

Fryd, Vivien Green (1992), *Art and Empire: The Politics of Ethnicity in the U.S. Capitol, 1815–1860*, London: Yale University Press.

Gilroy, Paul (1993), *The Black Atlantic*, London: Verso.

Gilroy, Paul (2000), *Between Camps*, London: Allan Lane.

Hallam, Elizabeth and Brian V. Street (2000), *Cultural Encounters: Representing Otherness*, London: Routledge.

Hargreaves, Roger (1997), 'Developing new audiences at the National Portrait Gallery, London', in Amy Henderson and Adrienne L. Kaeppler (eds), *Exhibiting Dilemmas: Issues of Representation at the Smithsonian*, Washington: Smithsonian Institution Press, pp. 183–202.

Hooper-Greenhill, Eilean (1997), ed. *Cultural Diversity: Developing Museum Audiences*, London: Leicester University Press.

Hooper-Greenhill, Eilean (2000), *Museums and the Interpretation of Visual Culture*, London: Routledge.

Kaplan, Sidney and Emma Nogrady Kaplan (1973), *The Black Presence in the Era of the Revolution, 1770–1800*, Greenwich, CT: New York Graphic Society.

Kaplan, Sidney (1991), 'The Black Soldier of the Civil War in Literature and Art', in Sidney Kaplan, *American Studies in Black and White*, ed. Allan D. Austin, Amherst: University of Massachusetts Press, pp. 101–23.

Karp, Ivan and Steven D. Lavine (1991), *Exhibiting Cultures: The Poetics and Politics of Cultural Display*, Washington: Smithsonian Institution Press.

King, Reyahn (1997), 'Ignatius Sancho and Portraits of the Black Elite', in King et al. (1997), pp. 15–42.

King, Reyahn, Sukhdev Sandhu, James Walvin and Jane Gridham (1997), *Ignatius Sancho: An African Man of Letters*, London: National Portrait Gallery.

Phillips, Caryl (1997), Foreword in King et al. (1997), pp. 9–14.

Pointon, Marcia (1993), *Hanging the Head*, London: Yale University Press.

Pointon, Marcia (1994), '*1968* and All That: The Founding of the National Portrait Gallery, Washington D.C.', in Marcia Pointon (ed.), *Art Apart*, Manchester: Manchester University Press, pp. 50–68.

Rice, Alan (2003), *Radical Narratives of the Black Atlantic*, London: Continuum.

Saumarez Smith, Charles (1997), *The National Portrait Gallery*, London: National Portrait Gallery.

Savage, Kirk (1997), *Standing Soldiers, Kneeling Slaves*, Princeton: Princeton University Press.

Smith, Carol (1999), 'This Sporting Nation', *Soundings* 13, 94–112.

Taylor, Brandon (1999), *Art for the Nation*, Manchester: Manchester University Press.

Townsend, B. J. (1968), *This New Man: A Discourse in Portraits*, Washington: Smithsonian Institution Press.

Wallis, Brian (1994), 'Selling Nations: International Exhibitions and Cultural Diplomacy', in Daniel J. Sherman and Irit Rogoff (eds), *Museum Culture: Histories, Discourses, Spectacles*, London: Routledge, pp. 265–300.

Wood, Marcus (2000), *Blind Memory*, Manchester: Manchester University Press.

Young, Lola (2002), 'Rethinking Heritage: Cultural Policy and Inclusion', in Richard Sandell (ed.), *Museums, Society, Inequality*, London: Routledge, pp. 203–12.

CHAPTER FIFTEEN

Biff! Bang! Pow! The Transatlantic Pop Aesthetic, 1956–66

Simon Philo (with Neil Campbell)

Peter Blake's *Some of the Sources of Pop* (2000) is a retrospective, genre-defining painting and some would say typically nostalgic. This piece would seem to confirm several long-established misconceptions about Pop art and particularly its status as an art form that pays endless homage to American things. Whilst there are 'British' ingredients here in these sixteen silk-screened windows – the mod shirt and tie, the pre-decimalisation price tag – it is of course 'America', its pop culture icons, symbols and products, that dominates our field of vision. British Pop, particularly the so-called 'down-town', subjective variety practised by the likes of Blake through the first half of the 1960s, was often perceived as uncritical of largely American-led social and cultural change, and so rather celebratory in temper and tone (see Seago 1995). It was viewed by many observers as aggressively pro-American, accused of staking out a position that angered and disappointed those who saw American culture as rather shallow and worthless. Pop art, some critics felt, was about as appealing a prospect as enduring an hour's worth of that great American pop cultural import of the period, rock'n'roll!

Pop art, then, was seen by its many detractors as an uncritical celebration of western consumerism – as a 'fan's note' to a way of life largely driven by the United States. It is, after all, the Stars and Stripes that sit proud almost in the centre of Blake's piece! From this perspective, it would appear that Pop art stood as yet another example of 'Americani-sation' – the world of art succumbing, as so many other cultural arenas have done, to a US dominance that shifts into overdrive after the Second World War. If not literally 'made in America', since Pop art first sur-faced in Britain, then certainly made of, out of, or from America.

Yet this is not the full story. For Pop and responses to it can be made to 'fit into' contrasting reactions to American presence and influence on the world stage. Pop art can, therefore, be viewed as yet another example of cultural imperialism. And indeed, many, as we'll see, treated it in this way – negatively, as a real threat to something indigenous and somehow more authentic. But it can also offer us a good example of the way in which American culture or, more specifically, versions of that culture, can be actively appropriated or 'used' by non-residents in conscious and sometimes highly critical and, by implication or extension, even political ways.

The postwar context and the Independent Group

Performing on stage in Dublin in 2001, the Scottish comedian and actor Billy Connolly told his audience that he remembered the 1940s and the 1950s as a time when 'The world was beige and the music was crap. It was like being stuck in the fucking Eurovision Song Contest in a school uniform.' Connolly's typically colourful assessment of the state of the nation in the immediate postwar years is confirmed by a more sober Anthony Sampson in his 1962 study *The Anatomy of Britain*, when he described the UK in this period as a kind of living museum (see Sampson 1962).

Richard Morrison, writing in 2003, added that

unquestionably the country was much worse off, materially, than it is now. One in three homes had no bath; one in twenty didn't have piped water. Bomb craters still scarred industrial towns, even the heart of London. Food was rationed. Television sets had penetrated just 4 per cent of homes . . . In 1953, few families could boast a fridge, car or washing machine . . . Britain fifty years ago seems to have been an insufferably dull, petty, lazy, snobby, slow, insular, unambitious, blinkered and smug place. (Morrison 2003: T2, T3)

279

Yet, if Britain was a dull, drab, pinched place yet to emerge into full postscarcity – food rationing did not end until 1954 – there were some, principally but not exclusively the young, who wanted to transform their immediate environment, to add colour to it, by embracing the exciting cultural alternatives offered by the United States.

Indeed Morrison writes that

> the impression everywhere in June 1953 was of an exhausted, inert and skint country trapped in outmoded attitudes . . . But a dam was about to burst. British culture was turned upside down in the 1950s as for the first time, the masses defined the cutting edge. Popular TV formats devised in that decade – the soap opera, game show, cop drama – proved so durable that they still dominate the ratings today. Disrespect was in the air. The quintessential fictional heroes of the mid-Fifties were anti-establishment anti-heroes . . . And, in the most far-reaching change of all, a new species of humanity was about to be created. It was the teenager. For the first time in history the unruly tastes of children would take precedence over their parents' wishes. The generation gap was born. And it had a soundtrack to match. Even as London was preparing for the Coronation, a truck driver in Tennessee was slipping into a mobile recording studio to cut a record as a birthday present for his mum. Within three years Elvis Presley would be the most famous former truck driver on the planet – and the rock and roll era would have begun. (ibid.: T2, T3)

'For the majority of British teenagers during the 1950s', as John Walker has pointed out, 'America was the promised land and the source of entertaining movies and dynamic rock music' (Walker 1998: 210). In fact, this reaction of British youth to the thrill and promise of American culture predates both rock'n'roll and the Second World War. Young audiences in the prewar years often found that Hollywood movies offered them pleasurable alternatives to the confines and restrictions of British cultural life.

The English poet Philip Larkin wrote of the potentially oppositional significance of another, less mainstream, American cultural 'import' in his life during the 1930s. 'For the generations that came to adolescence between the wars', he wrote,

> jazz was that unique private excitement that youth seems to demand. In another age it might have been drink or drugs, religion

or poetry . . . In the Thirties it was a fugitive minority, a record heard by chance from a foreign station, a chorus between two vocals, one man in an otherwise dull band . . . Sitting with a friend in his bedroom . . . we took it in turns to wind the portable HMV, and those white and coloured Americans, Bubber Miley, Frank Teschmacher, J. C. Higginbotham, spoke immediately to our understanding. Their rips, slurs and distortions were something we understood perfectly. This was something we had found ourselves, that wasn't taught at school (what a prerequisite that is of nearly everything worthwhile!), and having found it, we made it bear all the enthusiasm usually directed at more established arts. (Larkin 1970: 1–3)

For Larkin and his friends, then, an appreciation of jazz was bound up with both pleasure and resistance – in fact, resistance was to be found in the pleasures to be had from collecting and listening to this music.

Writing of the same period but about the ways in which its popular music and dance provided opportunities for young British women to challenge notions of acceptable behaviour, Mica Nava writes that 'America operated psychically . . . as an imaginary somewhere else; as a refuge and a fantasy of a better future, as a means of breaking away from the constraints of class and parental conventions of deference, denial and despair' (Nava 1999: 76). However, within the Establishment – and among the British intellectual elite of all political persuasions – there was open hostility to what was interpreted as cultural imperialism:

The overwhelming majority of British intellectuals in the 1950s were hostile to what they interpreted as the Americanisation of their society. Hollywood movies, commercial television, glossy magazines and consumer goods were interpreted as symptoms of cultural degeneration and material greed. (Whiteley 1987: 45)

Raymond Williams – echoing George Orwell's famous description of the UK as 'Airstrip One' – declared Britain to be 'culturally an American colony', and saw US popular culture as particularly destructive and detrimental to the nation's good health. This was a view memorably shared by Richard Hoggart in his late-1950s study *The Uses of Literacy*, which contrasted what he saw as the 'full, rich' working-class life of the interwar years with the 'thin', 'pallid', 'insipid' and evidently Americanised life being increasingly, enthusiastically, and so disturbingly led by 1950s teens with their 'American slouch' and their love of 'the mechanical record-player' with discs which 'almost all are American' producing 'the "hollow-cosmos" effect which echo chamber recording gives'. All in all, this milk bar world of popular cultural forms was 'to a large extent . . . a myth-world compounded of a few simple elements which they take to be those of American life' (Hoggart 1962: 248).[1]

Similarly in the British art establishment the Second World War had arguably (and maybe understandably) intensified a definable 'Britishness' – or more specifically perhaps 'Englishness' – in much of the officially sanctioned work of the period. However, what was also becoming clear was that it was New York – and not Paris – that was taking centre stage in the art world and this westward-shifting axis of influence was something that many British fine-arts students, if not their sometimes backwards-looking, Euro-fixated tutors, came to recognise. Founded in 1950, London's Institute of Contemporary Art (ICA) appeared to acknowledge what those young students already knew, in 'act[ing] as the "gateway to Europe"' for American art. And, as Anne Massey notes, it was 'the ICA [that] showed the work of [the Abstract Expressionist] Jackson Pollock for the first time in London [and] American speakers were also welcomed . . . often introduced via the American embassy in Grosvenor Square' (Massey 1995: 68). It was through the ICA that those artists we might now identify as Pop's pioneers came to the fore. This was a group of painters, architects, critics and theorists who met at the institute and called themselves the Independent Group (IG), gathering formally for the first time in 1952.

By the time of their second series of meetings over the winter of 1954–5, the IG's desire to exchange enthusiasm for contemporary technology, design and the mass media had narrowed somewhat to a mutual fascination with specifically American popular culture, a shared interest fuelled by one of their number's return from a rare trip to the States with a trunkful of popular magazines – *Life*, *Mad*, *McCalls* and the *Saturday Evening Post* – and records. Americana was, then, at the very heart of their discussions and the work that a number of them subsequently produced had those magazines integrated within the IG's art itself. As Lawrence Alloway observed,

we discovered that we had in common a vernacular culture that persisted beyond any special interests or skills . . . that any of us might possess. The area of contact was mass-produced urban culture: movies, advertising, science fiction, Pop Music. We felt none of the dislike of commercial culture standard among most intellectuals, but accepted it as fact, discussed it in detail, and consumed it enthusiastically . . . These interests put us in opposition both to the supporters of indigenous folk art and anti-American opinion in Britain. (In Lippard 1966: 31–2)

With the first stirrings of what becomes known as Pop art, the IG, then, were challenging the conventional view of what we might call 'the arts pyramid' – which traditionally placed fine art at its narrow summit and mass culture at its wide, gloopy base. What Dick Hebdige has termed their 'symbolic defection to the forbidden glossy continent' of America constituted some kind of revolutionary act – considered simultaneously alarming and downright disloyal by Britain's 'cultural police'. We should not lose sight, Hebdige warns,

> of the radical nature of Pop art's original proposal: *that popular culture and mass produced imagery are worthy of consideration in their own right, and, in addition, provide a rich, iconographical resource to be tapped by those working within the fine arts.* (Hebdige 1988: 121)

For, as art critic Robert Hughes points out in *The Shock of the New*, 'the imagery of American capital was an equaliser, an escape from class: and 'good' culture in England was inextricably bound up with social ranking, the property of the genteel and the paternal' (Hughes 1991: 342).

Scottish artist Eduardo Paolozzi might be considered a pioneer of the Pop pioneers, as his late-1940s and early-1950s collages actually predate the formation of the Independent Group, of which he was a prominent member. Paolozzi made his collages from books, postcards, advertisements and popular magazines. Some critics have argued that in these works the artist offers little or nothing in the way of critique or commentary, but merely 'gathers and presents' in a neutral fashion. Others see the possibility that Paolozzi is deploying images and objects as 'signs of freedom asserted against the economic and cultural constraints, as dreams, implicitly subversive' (Hebdige 1988: 128). Such views would seem to connect with Alex Seago's definition of the use of collage itself as a medium that 'invites the transgression and violation of boundaries of taste, genre and class' (Seago 1995: 105).

Paolozzi declared pieces like *Real Gold* (1950) to be anti-art and his work from this period is rooted in both a 'feeling' for American popular culture and a theoretical, intellectual response to the presence of such a culture in his own life. He is grappling to come to terms with Americanisation in the post-war British context.

Figure 8 Eduardo Paolozzi, *Real Gold*.

Examine *Real Gold* and/or Paolozzi's other collages to see how the form of the work can be related to arguments about relations between America and other cultures, to 'Americanising' cultural exchanges. Why is the collage form a useful technique through which to suggest these debates? Consult Blake (2000) for some ideas.

The ICA apparently embraced 'America', but it was its high culture – and principally the fine art of Abstract Expressionists such as Pollock – not its popular culture. Artists like Paolozzi, though, were producing work that came out of a more open-minded relationship to the everyday world. Whilst the Institute paid lip service to broadening art's appeal in the UK, Paolozzi's outward-looking art was demonstrably about the 'here and now'. It seemed accessible and relevant. The IG, then, attempted to come to terms with the new mass-media age at a time when virtually every other cultural critic in Britain remained virulently opposed to popular culture. For the likes of Paolozzi, America operated with potentially transgressive power, derived principally – as we've already seen – from placing it deliberately and unapologetically up against the 'official' culture.

'American magazines', Paolozzi observed,

represented a catalogue of an exotic society, bountiful and generous, where the event of selling tinned pears was transformed into multi-coloured dreams, where sensuality and virility combined to form, in our view, an art far more subtle and fulfilling than the orthodox choice of either the Tate gallery or the Royal Academy. (Cited in Walker 1998: 13)

'We goggled at the graphics and the colour-work in adverts for appliances that were almost inconceivable in power-short Britain,' confirmed influential IG member Peter Reyner Banham,

and food ads so luscious you wanted to eat them. Remember we had spent our teenage years surviving the horrors and deprivations of a six-year war. For us, the fruits of peace had to be tangible, preferably edible. Those ads may look yucky now, to the over-fed eyes of today, but to us they looked like Paradise Regained – or at least a paper promise of it. (Cited in Massey 1995: 84)

We might agree then with David Brauer when he sees British Pop art developing 'from a relationship with American culture analogous to standing outside the toy shop with one's nose pressed against the glass' (Brauer 2001: 55). And it is clear that any longing, or envy even, is mixed with a desire to 'use' US popular culture as some kind of 'weapon' (Walker 1998: 18), to strategically deploy the American dream, as perceived in Britain via the mass media, 'to name what seemed to be wrong with English culture' and to critique its source as well (Robert Kudielka, cited in Walker 1998: 13).

Autumn 1956's 'This is Tomorrow' exhibition showcased – although not exclusively – the work and thought of the IG. Twenty thousand visitors to this month-long show purchased 1,500 catalogues, which featured a reproduction on the cover of Richard Hamilton's collage *Just What Was It That Made Yesterday's Homes So Different, So Appealing?* and a list of 'hates' and 'loves' reminiscent of Vivienne Westwood and Malcolm McLaren's punk manifesto twenty years later. On the 'hate' list were 'the English way of life . . . beauty of refinement . . . church'. On the list of 'loves', rather curiously, 'Eartha Kitt' and 'deep penetration'!

In Hamilton's now-famous collage, the artist himself professed to want to present an inventory of popular culture, but this is frequently seen as problematic, for it is difficult to discern with any degree of certainty exactly what his position on this culture is (see Figure 9).

Hamilton, however, was adamant that he was in no way setting out to mock; that he intended his work to be witty but affectionate. Yet, I think this piece does communicate the slightly arch, detached, possibly even ironic perspective of the knowing consumer. In 1957 Hamilton offered this definition of Pop: 'Popular (designed for a mass audience); Transient (short-term solution); Expendable (easily forgotten); Low Cost; Mass Produced; Young (aimed at Youth); Witty; Sexy; Gimmicky; Glamorous; Big Business' (cited in Livingstone 1990: 36).

As Pop art's chroniclers have pointed out, the IG – notwithstanding its 'happy embrace of America' (Green 1998: 88) – was still engaged in an intellectual enquiry; and so could never quite give itself over and up as completely as our next batch of artists perhaps did. For, where Hamilton remains 'cool', Pop's second wave – led by Peter Blake – was 'hot'. Artists like Blake put themselves – sometimes literally, as we'll see – in the picture, in the midst of all this cultural stuff, signifying that they could enjoy popular culture without feeling the need to intellectualise, without any traces of anxiety, without seeing and living it as a guilty pleasure.

286

Figure 9 Richard Hamilton, *Just What Was It That Made Yesterday's Homes So Different, So Appealing?* 1992/1956 original

Peter Blake and the Young Contemporaries

We might see British Pop art as part of a larger cultural revolt against the parochialism of the post-war years, and it is no coincidence that Pop art flowers in the years between the Suez Crisis – the 'first crack' in the British Establishment's façade – and the Profumo affair. These were two national traumas that dealt hammer blows to the conservative (with both a small and big C) old order. 'Like [its contemporary rock'n'roll] music', it was 'a form of aggression against the established order, and like pop music it used sex, humour and even banality as a means of disruption' (Hewison 1986: 45–6). Set alongside events like Suez though, it was apparent that Britain was changing fast in some ways. The late 1950s and early 1960s were economic boom years – wages rose, there was virtually full employment and the country was

287

awash with affordable consumer goods. And the young in particular had more expendable income and leisure time than ever before.

Peter Blake, the son of a Dartford factory worker, had attended lectures by Eduardo Paolozzi and Richard Hamilton at the ICA and it was, arguably, in discussing his work and its relationship to 'pop music' that Lawrence Alloway came up with the term 'Pop art' (Rudd 2003: 12, 30). Blake was fascinated by American popular culture and immersed himself in it, but not uncritically, and was clearly interested in all aspects of 'street-level' Americana – fashion, film stars, music. He was a 'user' of these artefacts and experiences in a way that Hamilton or even Paolozzi could or would never allow themselves to be. Indeed, Blake once commented that the generation of the IG 'were Fine Artists researching into popular culture like sociologists' whereas his relationship to it was experiential and intimate – 'Pop culture was the life I actually led' (in Seago 1995: 175).

As you might expect of a man who shared a flat fee of just £200 for producing the Beatles' *Sgt Pepper* album art work, Blake was both a 'fan' and an enthusiastic and unapologetic consumer of pop culture and music in particular. But although Blake enjoyed American popular culture he resented the idea that Pop art *was* American. Indeed in 1962 he was angered by reviews of his work in New York that implied it was a pale imitation of American art and refused to exhibit there again until 2002 (Rudd 2003: 32). So although Blake employs a mixture of home-grown and American pop cultural materials in early works like *On the Balcony* (1955–7) and *Toy Shop* (1962), American subjects became increasingly significant in Blake's work between 1959 and 1964, where he paints rock'n'roll performers, such as Bo Diddley (1963) and the Beach Boys (1964), and film actresses such as Marilyn Monroe, Kim Novak and Tuesday Weld. Through these works, like many young working-class Britons at this time, Blake sought to compose a fugitive identity through his use of American cultural materials without, in any sense, abandoning his Britishness. And nowhere is this seen more clearly than in *Self Portrait with Badges* (see Figure 10).

In this piece, Blake wears his American trophies with pride, distinctly dressed in American iconic objects: baseball boots, jeans and denim jacket and clutching an Elvis Presley fan comic in his hand. He is, however, noticeably standing solemnly in a very dark, damp-looking English landscape as if to contrast quite dramatically (and ambiguously) the two cultures. Self-portraiture is often about staking an identity and here Blake, once described as a 'Chelsea pensioner of the pop revolution', sporting his medals, is most definitely and playfully defining his as one moving between and across cultures and traditions.

Figure 10 Peter Blake, *Self Portrait with Badges*.

On the evidence presented in this image, what relationship does the artist appear to have with America/n culture? And is his work here simply a celebration of all American things? Give your reasons.

Richard Pells has noted of the political significance of British youth's immersion in American popular culture that

> the young did not gravitate to American culture simply because it offered useful lessons in how to dress and act. Many wore T-shirts and blue jeans, chewed gum and drank Coca-Cola, as a gesture of rebellion against both the older generation and all forms of authority... To be absorbed with mass culture was also a way for the young to assert their freedom from adult supervision. (Pells 1997: 240–1)

Blake's American garb, and the bold contrast it strikes with the rather drab, dingy suburban surrounds of the English garden with its broken fence, shows him 'parading' his 'provocative affiliations' to an alternative culture, to a 'Coke' culture as opposed to a 'wine' culture, as one critic would have it (Whiteley 1987: 6). Here Blake is both literally and symbolically striking a pose and, if the UK's brand of Pop art was about anything, then it was surely about the attitude, the stance, the 'pose'.

In 1961 the 'Young Contemporaries' show, which is often seen as the beginning of the High Pop era, saw the emergence of Peter Phillips, David Hockney, Derek Boshier, Joe Tilson, and the expat American R. B. Kitaj. Whilst all of these artists were grouped together as Pop, this undeniably media-friendly tag tended to obscure some big, often fundamental, differences between them. In this respect, Pop art cannot be said to have had a prescriptive programme or agenda. It did not constitute a 'consciously integrated art movement' so much as a group of artists 'whose work [was] related to certain central themes' (Finch 1969: 10). Yet even here some further qualification is necessary. For, whilst these were artists linked by their use of and reference to the mass media and popular culture, they were often separated by the uses to which they put such reference points. Phillips, for example, had collected Superman and Captain Marvel comics as a boy and seemed to embrace pop culture without apology, without any apparent trace of embarrassment or guilt. He described his art in this period as coming out of 'an emotional response to various things that young guys would like'. His work is pacey and racy, using collage form and juxtaposition to engage the viewer with his meditations on the popular, meditations that were often ambiguous and indeterminate. It is urban, subjective and anti-intellectual: 'I've never been analytical about American things. I like American things, but I also like Japanese things, I like French things . . . ' (in Walker 1998: 99). However, artists like Phillips and Blake helped 'blow away the grey and brown cobwebs of the Fifties with playful and culturally relevant work' and in doing so they transformed 'their youth and their appropriation of "America" into future-threat' (Hebdige 1988: 130). Out of ambiguity and juxtaposition their work continued to raise different questions about the nature, extent and power of American influence on other cultures, and, through the very structures of their work, to engage the viewer in a dialogue.

Some Pop artists, Hockney for example, quickly sought to distance themselves from the label; for others, such as Phillips, Tilson and Boshier, the tag was less of a problem. But while Boshier was happy to be labelled 'Pop', his 'take' on America in this work, such as 1962's *England's Glory*, is somewhat open to debate. Boshier was adamant that he didn't employ 'America' in his work simply because he was in love with it or the idea of it. He was rare among Pop's so-called 'second wave' in actively seeking to critique Americanisation. In Ken Russell's 1962 documentary 'Pop Goes the Easel', Boshier says 'I'm interested in the whole setup of American influence in this country. The infiltration of the American way of life . . . I think the Englishman probably starts with America at the breakfast table . . . with the cornflakes' (in Brauer 2001: 66). His work is more forthright, more politically charged. Boshier had read works by Marshall McLuhan, Vance Packard and J. K. Galbraith in the 1950s and was rather more politically engaged with debates about the so-called 'affluent society', wanting to use his art to 'explore the phenomena of American power and the process of Americanisation' more overtly (see Walker 1998: 92). Thus in works from 1961, such as *Situation in Cuba* interrogating US foreign policy, or *Pepsi-Culture* – in which the Union flag is cornered by two Pepsi bottle tops – suggesting debates over cultural imperialism, Boshier's works of this period have a definite political perspective.

Whilst Blake's *Some Sources of Pop Art* features a small Union flag being overwhelmed by a Stars and Stripes, it could hardly be construed as an attack on the suffocating presence and effect of American culture in British lives. In contrast, Boshier's dissenting *England's Glory* refuted the straightforward celebration and instead insisted on interrogation.

In fact, this work offered a pretty explicit condemnation of cultural imperialism, from its bitterly ironic title to the image itself of the tattered and torn symbol of UK naval power being swallowed up by the invading forces of America symbolised by the flag.

Conclusion

It is often suggested that British Pop 'yearned for America', but even if this is closer to the truth than knowledge of Derek Boshier's work should allow, is it really accurate to argue (and assume) that it did so simply and uncritically? It is a fallacy to view UK Pop as devoid of political import, particularly when making lazy contrasts with the seemingly ever-ironic, highly self-conscious American version. Even if we accept that celebration *is* the defining and dominant mode, it is worth arguing that this in itself should be considered tantamount to adopting some kind of 'political' stance, since it represented an attack on the cultural status quo if nothing else! What we see in much British Pop art is a version of 'America' being deployed deliberately, selectively, and self-consciously, suggesting that whilst 'Americanisation [could] indeed [be] cultural imperialism it was also [for certain individuals and groups] a mode of resistance' (Sinfield 1989: 156).

Note

1. Hoggart's *The Uses of Literacy* and the work of the Independent Group are also discussed in Chapter 6.

Bibliography

Blake, Peter (2000), *About Collage*, London: Tate Gallery Publishing.
Brauer, David, Jim Edwards, Christopher Finch and Walter Hopps (2001), *Pop Art: US/UK Connections, 1956–66*, Houston: Menil Collection.
Green, Jonathon (1998), *Days in the Life: Voices from the English Underground 1961–1971*, London: Pimlico.
Finch, Christopher (1969), *Image as Language: Aspects of British Art 1950–1968*, London: Pelican.
Hebdige, Dick (1988), *Hiding in the Light: On Images and Things*, London: Routledge/Comedia.

Hewison, Robert (1986), *Too Much: Art and Society in the Sixties*, London: Methuen.

Hoggart, Richard [1957] (1962), *The Uses of Literacy*, Harmondsworth: Pelican.

Hughes, Robert (1991), *The Shock of the New: Art and the Century of Change*, rev. ed., London: Thames and Hudson.

Larkin, Philip (1970), *All What Jazz*, London: Faber and Faber.

Lippard, Lucy (1966), *Pop Art*, London: Thames and Hudson.

Massey, Anne (1995), *The Independent Group: Modernism and Mass Culture in Britain, 1945–59*, Manchester: Manchester University Press.

Morrison, Richard (2003), *The Times*, 2 June, p. 3.

Nava, Mica (1999), 'Wider Horizons and Modern Desire', *New Formations* 37, 71–91.

Pells, Richard (1997), *Not Like Us: How Europeans Have Loved, Hated, and Transformed American Culture since World War Two*, New York: Basic Books.

Rudd, Natalie (2003), *PB*, London: Tate Publishing.

Sampson, Anthony (1962), *The Anatomy of Britain*, London: Hodder and Stoughton.

Seago, Alex (1995), *Burning the Box of Beautiful Things: The Development of a Postmodern Sensibility*, Oxford: Oxford University Press.

Sinfield, A. (1989), *Literature, Politics and Culture in Postwar Britain*, Oxford: Blackwell.

Walker, John (1998), *Cultural Offensive: America's Impact on British Art since 1945*, London: Pluto.

Whiteley, Nigel (1987), *Pop Design*, London: Design Council.

Further reading

Alloway, Lawrence (1997), 'Popular Culture and Pop Art', in Steven Madoff (ed.) *Pop Art: A Critical History*, Berkeley: University of California Press, pp. 167–74.

Christopher, David (1999), *British Culture: An Introduction*, London: Routledge.

Cooke, Lynn (1997), 'The Independent Group: British and American Pop Art, "Palimpcestuous" Legacy', in Steven Madoff (ed.), *Pop Art: A Critical History*, University of California Press, pp. 385–96.

Humphries, Patrick (2002), 'Picture Perfect', in *1000 Days That Shook the World (The Psychedelic Beatles Special Edition)*, *Mojo* special ed., March, 97.

Jones, Nick (1995), '1965: Well, What is Pop-Art?', in Hanif Kureishi and Jon Savage (eds), *The Faber Book of Pop*, London: Faber and Faber, pp. 239–40.

Livingstone, Marco (1990), *Pop Art*, London: Weidenfeld and Nicolson.

Marwick, Arthur (1991), *Culture in Britain since 1945*, Oxford: Blackwell.

Marwick, Arthur (1994), 'The Arts, Books, Media and Entertainments in Britain since 1945', in James Obelkevich and Peter Catterall (eds), *Understanding Post-war British Society*, London: Routledge.

Marwick, Arthur (1998), *The Sixties: Cultural Revolution in Britain, France, Italy and the United States, c.1958–c.1974*, Oxford: Oxford University Press.

Melly, George (1972), *Revolt into Style: The Pop Arts in Britain*, London: Penguin.

Roberts, John (1998), 'Pop Art, the Popular and British Art in the 1990s', in Duncan McCorquodale, Naomi Siderfin and Julian Stallabrass (eds), *Occupational Hazard: Critical Writing on Recent British Art*, London: Black Dog Publishing.

Spalding, Frances (1986), *British Art since 1900*, London: Thames and Hudson.

Walker, John (1987), *Crossovers: Art into Pop/Pop into Art*, London: Routledge/Comedia.

Wheale, Nigel (ed.) (1995), *Postmodern Arts: An Introductory Reader*, London: Routledge.

Globalisation, Americanisation and the 'New World Order'

Neil Campbell and George McKay with Jude Davies

Globalisation broadly describes the processes of gradually intercon-
necting world economies, politics and cultures into a global system
dominated by advanced capitalism. While acknowledging the transnational, even postnational, nature of contemporary global capitalism –
which may have within a single corporation businesses that originated
in the US, Europe, Japan, and south east Asia – the most recent forms of
globalisation frequently remain connected to the USA, whose political
economic and military power sustains, develops and promotes markets
across the planet. After the Cold War in particular America extended
its presence:

> Buoyed by the Reagan renaissance's military build-up, economic
> restructuring, and stress on America's special mission in the 'free
> world', the United States regained its confidence and eagerly
> embraced its role of the hegemonic power in a more complicated
> and dangerous world. (Antonio and Bonanno 2000: 45)

Under these conditions, economic and political hegemony combined
with the so-called *soft power* of US export cultures in a dominant, if
complex and contradictory, sweep across much of the world.
American-based corporations such as Coca-Cola, Nike, Philip Morris
and McDonald's developed their global markets through intense

295

advertising campaigns, asserting that 'selling American products means selling America' (Barber 1996: 60). This formulation of what Benjamin Barber terms 'McWorld' is a global network whose 'template is American' (ibid.: 17), that is, dominated by American methods, values, personnel and supported, as many would argue, by the US state's neo-liberal policies and its use of military, economic and cultural power (see Antonio and Bonanno 2000; Sardar and Davies 2002). Of course, many theories of globalisation would challenge the notion of Americanisation at its core, placing greater emphasis upon heterogeneity, local cultures, hybridity, interculturalism and transnationalism as consequences of global change, as well as presenting a characterisation of globalisation that is less dismal and imperially tainted. Here we can find a *globalisation from below*, dramatised most, perhaps, in the global rise of the anti-capitalist movement from the late 1990s on. This has effectively given us a counter-narrative of globalisation, including glimpses of international solidarity, decentralised networks of activists and movements, in spectacular gatherings and political gestures as well as in the longer-lasting structures of organisation necessary to make events like the 'global days of action' in London and Seattle in 1999, Prague in 2000 and Genoa in 2001 happen (see Notes from Nowhere 2003; Mertes 2004).

Globalisation can neither be reduced to Americanisation nor be separated from it. Therefore we conclude this book by exploring the extent to which America has become inseparable from the expansionary character of globalisation (see Appadurai 1996; Hall 1991). To do so, it is necessary to analyse the connections between different strands of Americanisation, in terms of cultural content, cultural forms and processes, and discourses of politics and economics. A vehemently supportive statement of what he termed 'Americanization-globalization' comes from the *New York Times* columnist Thomas L. Friedman's bestseller *Lexus and the Olive Tree* (2000), the very title of which suggests the tensions between global and local. Taking an optimistic view (or what Greg Palast calls 'a long, deep kiss to globalization' (Palast 2002: 141)), Friedman places the 'Washington consensus' at the heart of globalisation, extending the American 'template' via an examination of its neo-liberal or laissez-faire model of free markets, new technology and organisations as the 'nth' degree of leadership and guidance for the 'new world order'. By his use of brands like McDonald's, Michael Jordan and Microsoft in the book's arguments, Friedman stresses the Americanness of the expanding global market, but underwrites this, quite presciently, with the absolute need for US military might to secure

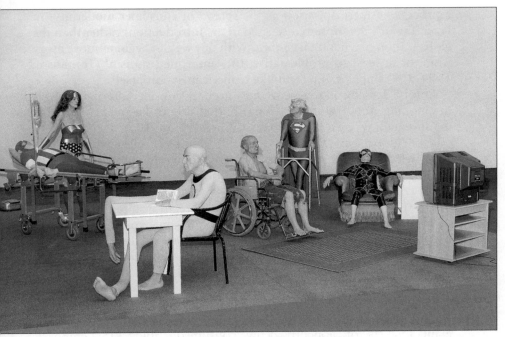

Figure 11 Gilles Barbier, *L'Hospice* (or *Nursing Home*).
Courtesy Galerie G.-P. & N. Vallois, Paris.

markets against potential 'disruptive' forces (see Antonio and Bonnano 2000). However, for others such a free-market ethos backed by state hyperpower represents the worst excesses of Americanisation as imperialism, seeing the USA as a 'rogue state' (Chomsky 2000; Blum 2000), as Ziauddin Sardar and Merryl Wyn Davies's potent, apocalyptic metaphor indicates:

> The tsunami of American consumerist culture assimilates everything, exerting immense, unstoppable pressure on the people of much of the world to change their lifestyles, to abandon all that gives meaning to their lives, to throw away not just their values but also their identity, stable relationships, attachment to history, buildings, places, families and received ways of doing and being. (Sardar and Davies 2003: 121)

The metaphor may be overly naturalistic, but it signals an important change of emphasis in that what is at stake here is less a content than a process – Americanisation as the spread of consumer modernity (in Peter Taylor's description discussed in the Introduction) rather than the globalisation of a national culture. With this we can begin to move away from, or at least to problematise, the 'embedded statism' (Tomlinson 1999: 104) implicit in a term like 'Americanisation' itself.

In John Tomlinson's view, we may need to 'consider alternative ways of thinking about globalized culture that do not keep us continually in the shadow cast by national cultures' (ibid.: 105). He prefers to talk of 'global capitalist monoculture' (ibid.: 81), even while swiftly acknowledging that many of the most powerful global 'capitalist firms . . . are regularly American ones' (ibid.: 83). Pulled by the appeal of the concept of 'deterritorialization' – 'which can help us understand broad transformations in the place–culture relationship in the context of global modernity' (ibid.: 106–7) – Tomlinson explores the idea of a constructed, perhaps postnational 'non-place'. However, one key instance of such a non-place experience for contemporary Britons which he offers is the 'oddly deterritorialized experience' of going to the cinema, which is 'clearly an *American* cinema, evident in the transatlantic voice-overs in the trailers and the slightly jarring terms in the signed announcements ("candy", "please deposit trash") to the giant buckets of popcorn being consumed' (ibid.: 118, emphasis original).

> And unsurprisingly, of the dozen or so movies on offer, the great majority will be Hollywood movies, since the multiplex is 'vertically aligned' with the American companies producing the films. What images of locality, what landscapes and what linguistic cadences will they find here as backdrops to the narratives? . . . Probably mainly ones from the US. Does this alienate them? Do they feel the victims of cultural imperialism? Or aren't these distant locations – the actual physical landscapes of America . . . – somehow, paradoxically, rather familiar? (ibid.: 119)

Such extreme poles of opinion, or ambivalencies, about Americanisation, although always present as we have seen throughout this collection, seem to have become more entrenched as America's global position, post-9/11, has shifted (or intensified) and people begin to recognise that the parameters of the globalisation debates may themselves have altered as a result. There are important policy issues here. Discussions of the declining role of the nation-state under globalisation may have to be heavily amended given the USA's influence over the

International Monetary Fund and World Trade Organisation, its overt 'war on terror' and highly visible involvement in other global events (see Sassen 1996; Sardar and Davies 2002: 72). In fact, Americanisation, at its most extreme expression, may indeed be articulated best by the right-wing think-tank The Project for the New American Century, whose members include Dick Cheney, Donald Rumsfeld, Paul Wolfowitz and Jeb Bush. Its 'Statement of Principles' (1997) declares clear connections between military and other economic and cultural goals so as to 'maintain American security and advantage American interests in the new century'. Their 'fundamental interests' espouse 'American global leadership' and working to 'shape a new century to American principles and interests ... before crises emerge and to meet threats before they become dire'. Such aims are further tied to four distinct principles: (1) to increase defence spending; (2) to strengthen allies and challenge 'regimes hostile to our interests and values'; (3) 'to promote political and economic freedom abroad' and (4) to 'accept responsibility for America's unique role in preserving and extending an international order friendly to our security, our prosperity, and our principles' (ibid.). This is perhaps the 'Washington consensus' defined by Friedman, given a new lease of life under what some term the 'Cheney–Bush junta', in which the priority is the *total* identification of American interests with global interests (see Vidal 2003, Moore 2002). According to Tom Mertes, recent Latin American mobilisations against the impact of neo-liberal economic policies have had a precise 'grasp of the immediate enemy', which would seem to offer confirmation of the US project, from below as it were:

> The architecture alone of most Third World embassies – those massive, reinforced blocks that loom more ominously than any national government buildings – not to mention the plain facts of the local USAF military base, is evidence enough ... of Yanqui power. ... [Globally,] US defence spending is more than that of the next twenty-five governments combined. It has bases in more than 59 countries. (Mertes 2004: 240–1)

It remains open to debate how much these economic, military, and political forms of Americanisation are interlinked with the spread of American cultural forms and contents. More precisely, perhaps, these connections work differently in different local, national and regional contexts. In the recent British example, the New Labour government headed by Tony Blair has emphasised cultural autonomy from the

299

USA, most notably through deliberate association with popular music under the dubious rubric of 'Cool Britannia', but also through various affiliations with 'European' culinary and café culture, while pursuing a political programme of 'modernisation' largely defined by reference to America. New Labour's electoral campaign of 1997 was deliberately and explicitly modelled on the example of Bill Clinton, while a raft of policy has copied US originals, starting with sweeping changes in the benefit system derived from the 'welfare to work' programme of Ronald Reagan and George Bush Sr, and culminating (so far) in the adoption of US principles for the funding of higher education. While this book was being completed, in February 2004, a series of further policy initiatives were announced: changes in the regulation of foreign workers to encourage cheap migrant labour that echoed White House policy on the Mexican border announced weeks earlier; the institution of a serious-crimes task force, described as 'Britain's FBI'; and the replacement of the Lord Chancellor by a Supreme Court. Clearly then America functions for the dominant forces in Blair's government as an ideal model of the modern nation-state, which can be emulated without copying its culture. Or more cynically, the ostentatious rejection of American culture camouflages an increasing political affiliation.

However, citizens may still experience political Americanisation in terms of cultural Americanisation, as is illustrated in a passing remark by the British Air Marshal Brian Burridge, making preparations for the US/UK invasion of Iraq in 2003:

> During the Cold War [my] job was like 'the second violin of the London Symphony Orchestra. You had a sheet of music with clear notation'. Now, in the Gulf, 'it's jazz, improvising'. (Norton-Taylor 2003)

Burridge describes his military job by the use of a music metaphor; the shift from European classical to American jazz music indicates the changing organisational strategy required in new warfare, from the rigid oppositional certainties of the Cold War to the apparently fluid circumstances of balancing 'shock and awe' with stealth tactics required in Iraq. But Burridge's comment does a number of other things, too: it clearly suggests some sort of a link between foreign policy, military action and national culture, and it betrays a downsizing of the British role in contemporary global politics. More complexly, perhaps, it may also signal a historical moment when the American domination of globalisation was seriously contested – by many nations around the world expressing their disapproval of the US/UK-led coalition's mission.

The American effect

One recent attempt to recomprehend and challenge some of these changing conditions and attitudes towards America was through an exhibition, 'The American Effect: Global Perspectives on the United States, 1990–2003', at the Whitney Museum of Modern Art, New York, (3 July–12 October 2003). Its premise, as curator Lawrence Rinder wrote, was that 'since the end of the Cold War, America has come to hold sway over a global empire' (Rinder 2003: 15) and the collection from thirty countries in Asia, Africa, Europe, Australia, South America and North America aimed to explore and comment upon precisely the 'American effect' as cultural, economic and political, and as an 'imaginative' and iconic presence permeating people's lives, both conscious and unconscious. In a renewed age of American empire since September 11th expressed through the 'war on terror', such an exhibition stood as an attempt to articulate fears about Americanisation and its various 'effects' on the lives of those near and far: 'As the global hegemon, America bears the weight of humanity's hopes, but it must also bear the brunt of resentment and, some of these artists suggest, assume responsibility for humanity's shattered dreams' (ibid.: 18). The exhibition was naturally, given the heightened sense of patriotism and global sensitivity, a provocative and controversial exhibit whose reception might gauge, to some extent, levels of awareness about Americanisation in the early twenty-first century. Coming after publications such as Mark Hertsgaard's *The Eagle's Shadow: Why America Fascinates and Infuriates the World* (2002), and UK work such as Granta's *What We Think of America* (2002) and Ziauddin Sardar and Merryl Wyn Davies's *Why Do People Hate America?* (2002), the exhibition represented a cultural moment when America invited (and controlled) similar questions about itself in the shape of a multi-media art show.

For some, the exhibition was an effort to critique American hyperpower and its encroaching influence on culture and politics on the global stage; for others such as Blake Gopnik, writing in the *Washington Post*, it was simply more proof of American 'navel-gazing' and egocentricity by a nation that 'only cares about foreign realities if they impinge back

301

home', and functioned as a kind of reassertion of dominance through the very fact that so many foreigners want to make art about America (Gopnik 2003). Steven Vincent, writing in the *National Review*, goes further, seeing the exhibition as a series of 'fatuous political statements . . . a somewhat mild exercise in America-bashing', but one which potentially gives a 'platform to artists' biases against the US . . . legitimiz[ing] the resentments that many in the world feel increasingly free to express against our nation and its people' (Vincent 2003).

However, the exhibition's liberal intention as stated in the catalogue was never to 'denigrate America', but to show its 'vitality . . . the unique strength that derives from an openness to difference', whilst simultaneously acting to 'remind us of our vulnerabilities and shock us into greater awareness of the realities of the world around us' (Rinder 2003: 21). The 'us' signals the approach of the book, aimed as it is at an American (New York) audience for whom the art is intended as a salutary lesson, a wake-up call to its current global position, a function demonstrated in one perceptive comment on the Whitney Museum website claiming the exhibition was 'both chilling and enlightening, forcing us to reconsider our own national history in an era when we are defining the histories of other nations' (http://whitney.org/exhibition/effect-comments.c.html). However, it is still apparent from other visitors' comments on the exhibition that many were indeed angered and deeply offended by what they took to be outright assaults on America: 'How dare the museum allow artists to put down our country'; 'The people who harbour animosity are jealous, evil, amoral, and dangerous. If America doesn't protect liberty around the world no one will'. In contrast, many emphasise the importance of 'learning' and 'dialogue', a need to be reeducated in how the world sees America, something that an insular hyperpower has often found difficult to do. One respondent writes: 'Humility is the way America must learn. To look into itself and improve the lot of its own people . . . Above all to learn from other cultures,' whilst another comments: 'My greatest hope is that people who view this exhibition will begin to understand the growing sense of feeling towards the US outside of its borders and start to act on it.' 'The USA should start looking at itself in the mirror,' one comment says, to get a new perspective on its sense of nationhood and location in the world. Both that 'mirror' image and those 'outside' perspectives indicate a desire to break down insularity and view America differently, multiply and critically. In the more enlightened comments here there is an echo of Benjamin Barber's statement at the end of his book *McWorld vs. Jihad* in which he writes that 'beyond the homogenous theme parks of commerce, we may rediscover spaces in which it is possible to live not only as consumers but as citizens' (Barber 1996: 300).

We might understand this more with the aid of the Russian critic Mikhail Bakhtin, who wrote of the importance of an 'excess of seeing' (Bakhtin 1995: 22–3) based on the recognition that 'I' can see what 'you' cannot and vice versa (your face, behind you, your back, etc.). He writes: 'I shall always see and know something that he, from his place outside and against me, cannot see himself . . . As we gaze at each other, two different worlds are reflected in the pupils of our eyes' (ibid.). Michael Holquist writes of this relational sense very succinctly: 'My excess is your lack, and vice versa. If we wish to overcome this lack, we try to see what is there *together*. We must share each other's excess in order to overcome our mutual lack' (Holquist 1995: xxvi). Thus simultaneously, in the acts of sharing our various 'excess[es] of seeing', we formulate a 'collective', negotiated, communal, sense of things that by its very nature denies the isolated vision or the 'single' point of view as the only right and true one:

> The excess of my seeing must 'fill in' the horizon of the other human being who is being contemplated, must render his horizon complete, without at the same time forfeiting his distinctiveness. I must empathize or project myself into this other human being. (ibid.: 25)

Extending this theory outwards from the individual to nations, one might see how studies of Americanisation, as in 'The American Effect' (and in *Issues in Americanisation and Culture* itself) are part of a dialogic process that can help us to understand the operations of power, to seek to negotiate a personal or regional space within its global networks, to understand what Paul Gilroy and others have referred to as 'outernationalism' as well as internationalism.

In one 'interdiction' within the show, a video, *How to Neuter the Mother Tongue* (2003) by the Builders' Association and motiroti, dramatises the clash of the global (American) with the local (Indian) culture by portraying call-centre workers in India being trained to 'sound' American, lose their native 'voice', take on American names and never reveal their locations. In another, *The Last Road Trip* (2000) by Dutchman Arno Coenen, America's roadside iconography and its associations with freedom, openness and youthful restlessness are revised and reconfigured to suggest an uncanny vision of glamour and horror where a restaurant sign reads 'Kill Anybody!!!' and the Monopoly board is rewritten with 'Car Rip-Off' and 'Franchise South Central' replacing the usual property squares. Often oblique and suggestive, something the critics did not like, the exhibition nonetheless jolts the audience through different and complex forms to see the multiple ways America figures in their lives – from rampant consumerism, waste, pornography, Wild West myths and dreams, comic books, Hollywood, and political intrusions and invasions. The latter is evident, if ambiguously, in Saira Wasim's Mughal-style paintings *History till 11 September* and *Friendship after 11 September 1* and 2, where George Bush is portrayed swathed in the flag with missiles, or embracing the Pakistani President Pervez Musharraf while surrounded by American icons like Ronald McDonald and the Statue of Liberty.

Perhaps the most represented and discussed exhibit was Gilles Barbier's *Nursing Home* (*L'Hospice*) installation (2002, see Figure 11) with a group of ageing superheroes – Captain America, the Hulk, Wonder Woman and Superman amongst others, all broken by time and infirmity, waiting for death. These inverted mythic signifiers of youthful power, iconic markers of a golden age of American empire and consensus, suggest a deeply ironic commentary on both the immense authority of these myths and of their increasingly 'tired' status in a changing world. The apparent, constructed 'innocence' of comic book heroes, loved by all, once fighting immortally against 'evil-doers' to keep the world (America) a safe place, is turned upside down here. For now they are grown old and decrepit, put out to pasture, condemned to watch themselves endlessly on video and television reruns whilst the world accelerates beyond them into a new age of global affairs. Positioned carefully in the installation so none of them interact or even look at each other, they appear bereft and isolated, atomised, semi-conscious and holding onto life like zombies. Catwoman slumps in front of the TV, Captain America is on a drip, Superman on a zimmer frame, and the Incredible Hulk shrivelled and wheelchair bound. Americanisation through 'innocent' fantasy, comic book heroes has been superseded by a new and different form of hyperpower exercised by real global corporations, governments and agencies who may feed on and recycle these older stories, but are busy rewriting narratives according to alternative rules and with very different outcomes.

What is the most significant result of exhibitions like this one is that they encourage and provoke new points of vision, a Bakhtinian 'excess of seeing' that can only help to stimulate debate and raise questions of perception and purpose. Edward Said's essay in the exhibition book,

'Global Crisis Over Iraq', comes closest to a recognition of this idea when he writes of how the 'obstinate dissenting traditions of the US – the unofficial counter-memory of an immigrant society – that flourish alongside or deep inside narrathemes are deliberately obscured' in the rush for a new consensus over America's actions in the world (Said 2003: 167). However, Said sees a 'forest of dissent' existing 'alongside or deep inside' President George W. Bush's America that potentially gives rise to '*another way of seeing* the U.S., as a troubled country with a contested reality' and, therefore, he continues, 'I think it is more accurate to apprehend the U.S. as a nation that is undergoing a serious clash of identities, similar to other contests in the rest of the world' (ibid.: 169 – emphasis added). In 2003, protests over the war in Iraq have taken place in the USA – as all around the world, another instance of a problematising globalisation – but against an increasingly hostile media 'narrowing . . . the already reduced ambit of national debate' (Sardar and Davies 2003: xi). For Said, America should not be seen as pure Bushville – or the 'executive's centralising military and political power' – since this 'ignores the internal dialectics that continue, and are far from settlement' (in Rinder 2003: 169). What Greg Palast has called the 'frightening Americanization of America' (Palast 2003: 318) might be applied to the government's renewed efforts post-9/11 to discourage these 'dialectics' (or 'dialogues' to invoke Bakhtin again) and to rebrand the USA as global policeman, a newly born 'hyperhero' for the twenty-first century. (The announcement by President Bush in January 2004 of an ambitious new space programme, including manned presences on both the moon and to Mars, is one further sign of the USA's newly raised rhetoric of global-and-beyond desire.) Said goes on to remind us of the complexity of history, which is always more than linear, and best viewed as 'a place of struggle over identity, self-definition, and projection into the future' (Said 2003: 171):

> Cultures, and especially the immigrant culture of the U.S., overlap with others; one of the perhaps unintended consequences of glob-alisation is the appearance of transnational communities of global interests – the human rights, women's and anti-war movements. The U.S. is not insulated from this, but we have to go behind the intimidatingly unified surface of the U.S. to see the disputes to which many of the world's other peoples are party. There is hope and encouragement in that. (ibid.: 171)

Inadvertently perhaps, as we have seen and as Said indicates here, globalisation's blurring of distinctions and increased information flows may help the formation of alternative ways of seeing that enable critiques of monologic power.

One of the dangers of recent shifts in America's global role and influence might be the continued diminution of what people imagine when they think about America, seeing only the projection ordained by the state and authorised through military, economic and cultural actions. Yet, as we noted in the introduction, Naomi Klein states, with clear references to Barber's work, that 'our task, never more pressing, is to point out that there are more than two worlds available, to expose all the invisible worlds between the economic fundamentalism of "McWorld" and the religious fundamentalism of "Jihad"' (Klein 2002). If Americanisation in some or all its various forms has become an overt strategy in the new American foreign policy, or what Gore Vidal calls its 'Empire' (Vidal 2003), then, as Klein says, it is absolutely imperative to analyse it and understand its 'effects' as central to comprehending that nation's status in global events. As Sardar and Davies put it, 'to create the ground for debate and engagement with America, the particularity of its nationalism, the national self-absorption in its myth and historic narrative, have to be subjected to analysis. Without analysis there is only the continuing mutual incomprehension' (Sardar and Davies 2003: xi). This 'engagement', as this collection has demonstrated, is about the detailed and diverse examination of Americanisation wherever it exists, as a complex, nuanced process, both negative and positive, spanning time and space, interacting with and diverging from definitions of globalisation and new imperialism. Sardar and Davies argue that the purpose of such analyses is to take us 'beyond hatred' by understanding America-in-the-world as fully as is possible, because, as they put it,

> the problem of America [of *Americanisation*, we might add] is everyone's problem. Finding an answer depends on making visible the nature, conditions and dimensions of the problem so that debates, new constituencies of dissent that bridge the divide between America and the rest of the world, can be built. (ibid.: xii)

Bibliography

Antonio, Roberto J. and Alessandro Bonanno (2000), 'A New Global Capitalism? From "Americanism and Fordism" to "Americanization-Globalization"', *American Studies*, 41:2/3, 33–78.

Appadurai, Arjun (1996), *Modernity at Large*, Minneapolis: Minnesota University Press.

Bakhtin, Mikhail (1995), *Art and Answerability*, Austin: University of Texas Press.

Barber, Benjamin (1996), *McWorld vs. Jihad: How Globalism and Tribalism are Reshaping the World*, New York: Ballantine.

Blum, William (2000), *Rogue State*, Monroe, ME: Common Courage.

Chomsky, Noam (2000), *Rogue States: The Rule of Force in World Affairs*, London: Pluto.

Friedman, Thomas L. (2000), *Lexus and the Olive Tree*, New York: Anchor.

Gopnik, Blake (2003), 'The Whitney, using a long lens for its U.S. close-up', *Washington Post*, 24 August p. N01.

Granta (2002), *What We Think of America*, London: Granta.

Hall, Stuart (1991), 'The Local and the Global: Globalization and Ethnicity', in Anthony D. King (ed.), *Culture, Globalization and the World System*, London: Macmillan, pp. 1–40.

Hertsgaard, Mark (2002), *The Eagle's Shadow: Why America Fascinates and Infuriates the World*, London: Bloomsbury.

Holquist, Michael (1995), 'Introduction', in Bakhtin 1995, pp. ix–xlix.

Klein, Naomi (2002), 'America is not a hamburger', *Guardian*, 14 March, p. 19.

Lasn, Kalle (2000), *Culture Jam: How To Reverse America's Suicidal Consumer Binge – and Why We Must*, New York: Quill.

Mertes, Tom (ed.) (2004), *A Movement of Movements: Is Another World Really Possible?*, London: Verso.

Moore, Michael (2002), *Stupid White Men*, London: Penguin.

Norton-Taylor, Richard (2003), 'Saddam aims to drag allies into a new Stalingrad, says British forces' chief', *Guardian*, 11 March.

Notes from Nowhere (eds) (2003), *We Are Everywhere: The Irresistible Rise of Global Anticapitalism*, London: Verso.

Palast, Greg [2002] (2003), *The Best Democracy Money Can Buy*, London: Robinson.

Project for the New American Century (1997), 'Statement of Principles', http://www.newamericancentury.org/statementofprinciples.htm

Rinder, Lawrence (ed.) (2003), *The American Effect: Global Perspectives on the United States, 1990–2003*, New York: Whitney Museum of American Art.

Said, Edward (2003), 'Global Crisis Over Iraq', in Rinder 2003, pp. 159–73.

Sardar, Ziauddin and Merryl Wyn Davies (2002), *Why Do People Hate America?*, London: Icon.

Sassen, Saskia (1996), *Losing Control? Sovereignty in the Age of Globalization*, New York: Columbia University Press.

Tomlinson, John (1999), *Globalization and Culture*, Cambridge: Polity.

Vidal, Gore [2002] (2003), *Dreaming War: Blood for Oil and the Cheney-Bush Junta*, London: Clairview.

Vincent, Steven (2003), 'Resisting the "American Effect"', *National Review*, 9 September.

Whitney Museum of American Art website: http://whitney.org

Notes on the Contributors

Andrew Blake is Professor of Cultural Studies, and the Head of the School of Cultural Studies, at University College Winchester. Recent publications include *The Land without Music: Music, Culture and Society in Twentieth Century Britain* (1997), *Living through Pop* (ed. 1999), *Salman Rushdie: A Beginner's Guide* (2001), *J. R. R. Tolkien: A Beginner's Guide* (2002), *The Irresistible Rise of Harry Potter* (2002), and 'To the Millennium: Music as Twentieth-Century Commodity', in Nicholas Cook and Anthony Pople (eds), *The Cambridge History of Twentieth-Century Music* (2004).

Neil Campbell is Reader in American Studies at the University of Derby. He is co-author of *American Cultural Studies* (1997), author of *The Cultures of the American New West* (2000), editor of *American Youth Cultures* (2004), and has written recent book chapters on Paul Bowles and transatlantic studies, Cormac McCarthy, Terrence Malick's *Badlands*, and John Sayles's *Lone Star*. He is currently writing a new book, *The Rhizomatic West: Western Iconography in a Transnational Global Age* for the University of Nebraska Press.

Jane Darcy is Senior Lecturer in English Literature at the University of Central Lancashire. She researches and teaches writing for children and has a particular interest in the fairy tale. Publications include an article on representations of nature in *The Wind in the Willows* and *The*

Secret Garden in the American journal of children's literature *The Lion and the Unicorn*, and a chapter on the Victorian children's writer Louisa Molesworth in a forthcoming book, *Popular Victorian Women Writers* (2004). From 2000–4 she was involved in the AMATAS project, offering workshops on Disney and the Fairy Tale.

Jude Davies is Principal Lecturer in American Studies and English at University College Winchester. His books are *Gender, Ethnicity and Sexuality in Contemporary American Film* (1998; jointly written with Carol Smith), and *Diana, a Cultural History: Gender, Race, Nation and the People's Princess* (2002).

Janet Floyd is Lecturer in American Studies at King's College, London. Her research interests lie in the writing of the domestic in America and the American West. She has co-edited *Domestic Space: Reading the Nineteenth-Century Interior* (1999) with Inga Bryden, and *The Recipe Reader: Narratives, Traditions, Debates* (2003) with Laurel Forster, and published a monograph on the writing of home in nineteenth-century emigrant autobiography, *Writing the Pioneer Woman* (2001). She is working at present on the writing of the late nineteenth-century mining West.

Paul Grainge is Lecturer in Film Studies at the University of Nottingham. He is the author of *Monochrome Memories: Nostalgia and Style in Retro America* (2002), the editor of *Memory and Popular Film* (2003), and co-editor of the forthcoming anthology *Film Histories*. He is currently working on a book entitled *Brand Hollywood: Selling Entertainment in a Global Media Age*.

Will Kaufman is Reader in English and American Studies at the University of Central Lancashire, and a founding director of the Maastricht Center for Transatlantic Studies. His monograph *The Comedian as Confidence Man* (1997) was followed by two co-edited collections, *Transatlantic Studies* (2000) and *New Perspectives in Transatlantic Studies* (2001). He is the series editor for the forthcoming ABC-Clio *Transatlantic Relations Encyclopedia Series*, and co-editor of the *Encyclopedia of British–American Relations* in that series.

Heidi Slettedahl Macpherson is Reader in North American Literature at the University of Central Lancashire. Her books include *Women's Movement: Escape as Transgression in North American Feminist Fiction* (2000), *Transatlantic Studies* (co-ed., 2000) and *New Perspectives in Transatlantic Studies* (co-ed., 2002). She is a director of the Maastricht Center for Transatlantic Studies and is currently at work on a monograph on women and the law in twentieth-century fiction.

George McKay is Professor of Cultural Studies at the University of Central Lancashire. His books are *Senseless Acts of Beauty: Cultures of Resistance since the Sixties* (1996), *Yankee Go Home (& Take Me with U): Americanisation and Popular Culture* (ed. 1997), *DiY Culture: Party & Protest in Nineties Britain* (ed. 1998), *Glastonbury: A Very English Fair* (2000), and the forthcoming *Circular Breathing: The Cultural Politics of Jazz in Britain* (Duke University Press). From 2000–4 he was Project Director for the AMATAS project. He is also co-editor of *Social Movement Studies: Journal of Social Cultural and Political Protest*.

Alasdair Pettinger is the editor of *Always Elsewhere* (1998), an anthology of travel writings of the Black Atlantic. He is currently working on a study of connections between Scotland and the antebellum South.

Simon Philo lectures in American Studies at the University of Derby. Recent publications include chapters and articles on punk and youth, popular music and war, *The Simpsons* at the BBC, and MTV and globalisation. He is currently researching the relationship between Jamaican popular music and US culture ('"A Small Axe": Reggae's Negotiations with America, 1962–76').

Alan Rice is Senior Lecturer in American Studies and Cultural Theory at the University of Central Lancashire. He has been the project manager of the AMATAS project from its inception in 2000. His work on Frederick Douglass's 1845 visit to Britain was published in a jointly edited volume (with Martin Crawford) *Liberating Sojourn: Frederick Douglass and Transatlantic Reform* (1999). He has edited a special volume on 'Issues of Blackness and Whiteness' for the *Saul Bellow Journal* (2000) and his first monograph, *Radical Narratives of the Black Atlantic*, was published in 2003. His most recent publication is an essay on Caryl Phillips and Jackie Kay and their relation to African Americans, in the collection *Blackening Europe* (ed. Heike Raphael, 2003), which includes a foreword by Paul Gilroy.

George Ritzer is Distinguished University Professor of Sociology at the University of Maryland. He has served as Chair of the American Sociological Association's sections on Theoretical Sociology and Organizations and Occupations. He is the author of *The McDonaldization of Society* (2000; translated into more than a dozen languages), *Enchanting a Disenchanted World: Revolutionizing the Means of Consumption* (1999), and *The Globalization of Nothing* (2004), as well as editor of the forthcoming *Encyclopedia of Social Theory* (two volumes).

Michael Ryan is a graduate student at the University of Maryland. He is a C. Wright Mills Fellow working towards a Ph.D. in Sociology. His interests include social theory, consumption, and globalization.

Victor Seidler is Professor of Sociology at Goldsmith's College, London. He has written extensively on masculinity, including *Unreasonable Men: Masculinity and Social Theory* (1993), and *Man Enough: Embodying Masculinities* (1997). More recently he has explored Jewishness in, for instance, *Shadows of the Shoah: Jewish Identity and Belonging* (2000).

Carol Smith lectures in American Studies and English at University College Winchester. She is co-author of *Gender, Ethnicity and Sexuality in Contemporary American Film* (EUP, 1998) and has published on ethnicity and representation in fiction, film, and visual culture.

Alasdair Spark is Head of American Studies at University College Winchester. His major research interests lie in the cultural meaning of conspiracy theory in the contemporary USA, particularly with regard to the popular appeal of their narrative. He is the author of several articles in this area and is currently working on a book on the same for Oneworld.

John K. Walton is Professor of Social History at the University of Central Lancashire. He moved to Preston in 1998 from a chair in

Modern Social History at Lancaster University. He writes mainly about tourism, resorts, sport and regional identities, especially in Britain and Spain. Books include *The English Seaside Resort: A Social History 1750–1914* (1983), *Lancashire: A Social History 1558–1939* (1987), *Fish and Chips and the British Working Class 1870–1940* (1992), and *The British Seaside: Holidays and Resorts in the Twentieth Century* (2000). He is currently working on *The Playful Crowd* (with Gary Cross, Columbia University Press) and extending his research interests into Argentina and Uruguay.

Russell White, formerly lecturer in American Studies at University College Winchester, is lecturer in Media and Cultural Studies at Southampton Institute of Higher Education. His article reflects his long-standing interest in the dissemination of contemporary African American popular culture.

Index